Armageddon And Okra

Australia's Air Operations In The Middle East A Century Apart

Lewis Frederickson

16pt

© Commonwealth of Australia 2020

This work is copyright. Apart from any use as permitted under the Copyright Act 1968, no part may be reproduced by any process without prior written permission. Enquiries should be made to the publisher.

All artwork illustrations of aircraft copyrighted to Juanita Franzi Aero Illustrations.

Disclaimer

The views expressed in this work are those of the author and do not necessarily reflect the official policy or position of the Department of Defence, the Royal Australian Air Force or the Government of Australia. The Commonwealth of Australia will not be legally responsible in contract, tort or otherwise, for any statements made in this document.

The publishing of this book has been funded and managed by the History and Heritage Branch, Royal Australian Air Force.

All enquiries should be made to the publishers.
Big Sky Publishing Pty Ltd
PO Box 303, Newport, NSW 2106, Australia
Phone: 1300 364 611
Email: info@bigskypublishing.com.au
Web: www.bigskypublishing.com.au

Series: Australian Air Campaign Series, 1

Cover design and typesetting by Think Productions, Melbourne

Front cover and title page: An F-A-18F over a city landscape in northern Iraq during Operation OKRA. Despite the urban setting, the austerity of the desert environment is striking, and many Australian crews were consistently reminded of just how foreign this part of the world was to them. (source: Department of Defence)

TABLE OF CONTENTS

SERIES FOREWORD	iii
TITLE FOREWORD	vi
ACKNOWLEDGEMENTS	ix
ACRONYMS	xv
PROLOGUE	xx
Part I: ARMAGEDDON	1
Part II: OPERATION OKRA	188
Appendix 1: TIMELINE OF EVENTS	405
Appendix 2: OPERATION OKRA STATISTICS	412
BIBLIOGRAPHY	415
BACK COVER MATERIAL	437
Index	439

For my USAF mates, Dave and Ray, with whom I served.

Private Frederick Charles Wright, a Photographer with No 1 Squadron Australian Flying Corps, fitting a camera on a B.E.2c (source: RAAF Museum).

SERIES FOREWORD

Armageddon and OKRA is the first in a new Australian Air Campaign Series of publications produced by Air Force's History and Heritage Branch. This series will consist of well-researched books on RAAF history that are not only underpinned by rigorous scholarship and solid evidence, but are also readable, well-illustrated, educative and enduring.

The intent of the Australian Air Campaign Series is to promote an understanding of Air Force history by examining the Air Force's development, performance, heritage, and contribution to the nation in war and peace. By using examples of air operations and exploring the use of the Air Force, including its development and impact during those operations, these publications contribute to the professional military education of Air Force members, and the education of those with an interest in Air Force history. The Air Campaign Series focuses on the elements of leadership, command, and tactics, drawing on lessons learned and personal experiences of the authors, as well as extensive research. A unique feature of this series is to draw attention to what can be learned from these historical campaigns and events.

It is anticipated that the Air Campaign Series will cover a number of focused studies of Air Force campaigns, including the elements of strategy and tactics, command and leadership, strategic and operational planning, the development of doctrine, administration, platforms or logistics, intelligence, peacekeeping, and humanitarian operations. The analysis conducted in these publications will provide a great source of information for current serving members, veterans, serious academic researchers, and casual readers with an interest in specific campaigns or topics. I am excited to start this series with *Armageddon and OKRA*, and equally excited to discover which campaign will be covered next.

Mel Hupfeld, AO, DSC
Air Marshal
Chief of Air Force
August 2020

Air Task Group Strike Element armament technicians work on the flight line, in the scorching mid-afternoon heat, at Australia's main air operating base in the Middle East Region. (source: Department of Defence).

TITLE FOREWORD

This, the first of the Australian Air Campaign Series, exemplifies the intent of this series of publications. In his study of the two individual air campaigns, the Australian Flying Corps operations during the Battle of Armageddon 1918 and Operation OKRA in 2014, Dr Lewis Frederickson draws together a narrative of the development of air power from the early beginnings of reconnaissance, surveillance and strike of World War I with the employment of the Australian Air Task Group over Iraq and Syria 100 years later.

Lewis first explores the operations of No 1 Squadron, Australian Flying Corps during the seminal Battle of Armageddon in September 1918 and the experiences of the unit's first wartime deployment. Equipped with the Bristol Fighter, regarded by Richard Williams as the finest combat aircraft of World War I, No 1 Squadron was flying one of the most advanced aircraft of the war and of the highest standard of military technology of its era. It was in these aircraft that No 1 Squadron conducted a series of devastating attacks on the Turkish Seventh Army as it was retreating through the Wadi Fara. Lewis goes into great detail in describing the intricacies of this significant event. The early use of air power in the Battle of Armageddon was an important step in Australia's involvement in future operations.

Similarly, Lewis extensively covers the Air Force deployment's central role in Operation OKRA, by the insertion of an Air Task Group into the Middle East Region in 2014 to combat the Islamic State of Iraq and the Levant (ISIL). The threat of terrorist action, the destruction of historically significant items, homes and lives as ISIL made its way through Iraq and Syria is captured through Lewis's own experiences, as well as the experiences of others who deployed to the area. These personal experiences, including those of personnel from No 1 Squadron, which was again thrust into theatre to combat a threat, have been captured by Lewis to portray the real environment of a modern air campaign.

With changing technologies and doctrine, from Bristol Fighters to F/A-18F Super Hornets, from small deployments to sizeable Air Task Groups, the common element of both campaigns is that of the utility of air power and its ability to affect the outcomes in joint campaigns. Lewis has captured this essentiality throughout the publication. It illustrates that over time, and over several generations, air power has continued to evolve and refine in order to generate enduring effects in any conflict.

This is a great topic to kick off the Australian Air Campaign Series for the History and Heritage Branch—Air Force.

John Meier
Air Commodore
Director General History and Heritage—Air Force
August 2020

ACKNOWLEDGEMENTS

When I was commissioned into the Royal Australian Air Force (RAAF) nearly thirty years ago I had little understanding that my service would be underwritten by a life-long passion for learning and teaching. However, I am pleased that it is so and I make no secret of my commitment to the RAAF, its values and to the people with whom I serve. I am indebted to the tens of dozens of officers and airmen who contributed to this work; equally to the hundreds of others who served on Operation OKRA that I did not have opportunity to chat with. Of course, in a small volume of this size and at the unclassified level, one can only hope to draw together the narrative of what has occurred in a period of three year's operations—firstly, in the air war over Palestine a century ago, and secondly, in the RAAF's most recent conflict in Iraq and Syria.

In November 2016, the newly appointed Director General History and Heritage—Air Force, Air Commodore John Meier, met with me at the Air Power Development Centre (APDC) in Canberra. There, he outlined his concept for a series of publications for the RAAF and asked if I would undertake the first volume.

His notion was sublime: well-researched books on RAAF history that are readable, well-illustrated, educative and enduring. We shook hands and agreed that I would finish the volume in the course of my wider duties as a professional military aviator, educator and scholar. What a treat! What a journey! Of course, one always underestimates the amount of work involved in such endeavours. Here I am three years later having 'culled' my work to a manageable 70 000 words. I also found that I had to shape the story of these men and women in a very different way to my recently completed PhD. I hope that I have done so to the satisfaction of you, the reader. Naturally, I also hope many people have the opportunity to see this work, but for those with whom I serve in the RAAF I want this volume to tell a factual story that will resonate.

There is always a problem in writing history with a set number of words and when we are still in the aftermath of the events described in Part II of this work. Such matters might be problematic. I served in Iraq during the 2007 surge, so I immediately acknowledge my views on events in this part of the world have been influenced. I am not separate from them. Notwithstanding this, as a writer and teacher, I have remained as dispassionate as I can be in recording these events. In any event, all of this is okay. This volume is but a start. Future researchers will look on this period in the history of the RAAF in greater detail when time offers context. They will discover nuances that I have missed. They will uncover individual stories not yet told, because my work cannot possibly name everyone who served. This is the way matters should be. The future Air Force and the people of Australia will pause and reflect on these events and their understanding will surpass this survey. And it should be this way, too. Organisations like the RAAF are constantly evolving, and individuals should grasp every opportunity to stop, review and reflect on their core business when the time permits.

I am deeply indebted to Air Commodore John Meier and for his enthusiasm to publish this work. John Meier's confidence in my ability to 'paint this picture' for the RAAF is an inspiration and privilege. As this goes, the book was thoroughly reviewed across the service, and I thank the History and Heritage Branch—Air Force for assisting in producing the final product. I am equally fortunate in the opportunity to have had access to AWM and RAAF records to put together the imagery contained throughout the work. When you look through this volume, please acknowledge the quality of the images, maps and level of detail surrounding them. While I am on this point, I must also make note of the splendid colour plates throughout the volume. Juanita Franzi's illustrations—commissioned by the RAAF for these works and depicting AFC and RAAF aircraft as they were—is simply first rate! I am grateful to my colleagues Steven Campbell-Wright, and Drs Tom Richardson and Rich Adams for also running a professional eye over my prose before it went to the publishers. All three are thorough gentlemen, and skilled masters in the business of putting the story down on paper. Thank you, too, to my mentors Group Captain Philip Edwards and Professor Sanu Kainikara; both gave significant encouragement for the spirit in which this work was undertaken.

Of course, in this inaugural work I am indebted to the record of the exploits of the earliest generation of officers and airmen of the AFC. These airmen established a pattern for Australian military aviation that remains as true as it was a century ago. They informed Part I of the work. As for Part II, I must highlight what a privilege it was to engage with a number of personnel who served on Operation OKRA between 2014 and 2017—some of them several times. In particular, I am most grateful for the recollections and insights of Stephen Chappell, Pete Mitchell, Mark Barry, Jeremy Feldhahn, Steve

Roberton, Melody Sadler-Barker, Lee-Anne Stanway, Sean Gardner, David 'Doc' Martin, Bryce Robinson, Leigh Collins and Andrew Earl. Some of these officers I have worked for or with in the past. Most of them are still serving, and I am deeply appreciative for the support that each showed for getting the story down. I am fortunate to have had access to the numerous interviews conducted with personnel involved in Operation OKRA. Without these recordings, I would not have been able to gain an appreciation for what the operational environment was like. There were dozens of interviews I did not get to, and hundreds of personnel I did not chat with about Operation OKRA. There simply wasn't time! I must acknowledge these officers and airmen, too.

Finally, though, I must acknowledge with love and gratitude the sacrifice made by my wonderful wife, Liz, and our youngsters in facilitating this narrative. In three years, there were countless (and I have lost count) Saturday and Sunday afternoons spent in front of a computer screen. These days were rightly dedicated to bike riding to the park, or games, or other outings. This work is equally for them and all the other families, separated by the exigencies of military service.

Wing Commander Lewis Frederickson PhD

Chief of Air Force Fellow
August 2020

ACRONYMS

AAR	Air-to-Air Refuelling
ABM	Air Battle Management
ACC	Air Component Commander
ACM	Air Chief Marshal
ACO	Air Combat Officer
ADAB	Al Dhafra Air Base
ADF	Australian Defence Force
ADFA	Australian Defence Force Academy
AEW&C	Airborne Early Warning and Control
AFC	Australian Flying Corps
AIF	Australian Imperial Force
AIRCDRE	Air Commodore
AMAB	Al Minhad Air Base
AME	Aero-Medical Evacuation
ANZUS	Australia, New Zealand & the United States
ARDU	Aircraft Research and Development Unit
ATG	Air Task Group
ATO	Air Task Order
BDE	Brigade
BIAP	Baghdad International Airport
BPC	Build Partner Capacity
CAOC	Combined Air Operations Centre
CAS	Close Air Support
CAP	Combat Air Patrol

CATG	Commander Air Task Group
CC	Combat Controller
CDF	Chief of the Defence Force
CENTCOM	Central Command
CFACC	Combined Force Air Component Commander
CFS	Central Flying School
CIS	Communications & Information Systems
CJFLCC	Combined Joint Force Land Component Command
CJOA	Combined Joint Operations Area
CJOPS	Commander Joint Operations
CJTF	Combined Joint Task Force
CJTFLCC	Combined Joint Task Force Land Component Command
CO	Commanding Officer
CSU	Combat Support Unit
C2	Command and control
DCA	Defensive Counter-Air
DCFACC	Deputy Combined Forces Air Component Commander
DIV	Division
DSO	Distinguished Service Order
EACS	Expeditionary Air Control Squadron
EAOU	Expeditionary Air Operations Unit
EBA	Effects Based Approach
EEF	Egyptian Expeditionary Force
ERV	Euphrates River Valley
FC	Fighter Controller

FCC	Fighter Combat Controller
FCI	Fighter Combat Instructor
FLT	Flight
ft	feet
GBU	Guided Bomb Unit
GLO	Ground Liaison Officer
GOC	General Officer Commanding
GPCAPT	Group Captain
HE	High explosive
HQJOC	Headquarters Joint Operations Command
ISF	Iraqi Security Forces
ISIL	Islamic State of Iraq and the Levant
ISIS	Islamic State of Iraq and Syria
ISR	Intelligence, Surveillance and Reconnaissance
JDAM	Joint Direct Attack Munitions
JIPTL	Joint Integrated Prioritised Target List
JOC	Joint Operations Command
JTAC	Joint Terminal Attack Controller
lb	pound
MANPADS	Man Portable Air Defence System
MC	Military Cross
MERV	Middle Euphrates River Valley
MER	Middle East Region
NATCOM	National Command
OC	Officer Commanding
OCA	Offensive Counter-Air
OEF	Operation ENDURINGFREEDOM

OPCOM	Operational Command
OPCON	Operational Control
OIF	Operation IRAQI FREEDOM
OIR	Operation INHERENT RESOLVE
PGM	Precision Guided Munitions
PRF	Pro-Regime Forces
RAF	Royal Air Force
RAAF	Royal Australian Air Force
RFC	Royal Flying Corps
RNAS	Royal Naval Air Service
ROE	Rules of Engagement
RPA	Remote Piloted Aircraft
RSO&I	Reception, Staging, Onwards-Clearance and Insertion
SAR	Search and Rescue
SDF	Syrian Democratic Forces
SOF	Special Operations Forces
SOTG	Special Operations Task Group
SPINS	Special Instructions
SQN	Squadron
SQNLDR	Squadron Leader
SRF	Syrian Regime Forces
TE	Task Element
TI	Target Interdiction
TU	Task Unit
UAE	United Arab Emirates
UAV	Unmanned Aerial Vehicle
UN	United Nations

UNESCO	United Nations Education Scientific and Cultural Organization
UNSW	University of New South Wales
US	United States
USA	United States Army
USAF	United States Air Force
USMC	United States Marine Corps
USN	United States Navy
VC	Victoria Cross
WG	Wing
WGCDR	Wing Commander
WMD	Weapons of Mass Destruction
WOE	Warrant Officer Engineering
WSO	Weapons Systems Officer

PROLOGUE

21 September 1918: Air Power over the Wadi Fara

So pristine were the azure early morning skies above the desert that the two Bristol Fighters seemed to float on the air as they went about their work. The buff and olive drab finish of the aeroplanes stood out starkly against the blue, and the big British roundels on their wings were very clear. The two aircraft rose and fell very slightly in a concertina effect as the pilot of the higher of the two aeroplanes maintained an overwatch position for the lower one. The Bristol was a big machine by the standards of the day; a biplane with a forty-foot wingspan, and a large 275 horsepower Rolls-Royce V12 powerplant. The crew comprised a pilot and observer, the aircraft was heavy and robust, and it was very well armed. It had a forward firing Vickers gun mounted in the engine nacelle, and the observer operated twin Lewis Guns mounted on a swivelling Scarff Ring from which he commanded a field of fire to the rear of the aircraft and above. When it was required the aircraft could be fitted with a dozen 20lb Cooper fragmentation bombs or two 112lb bombs. These were extremely effective anti-personal devices.

One advantage of the Bristol Fighter was that the fuselage was raised above the lower wing so that only the chord and shape of the aerofoil obstructed the downwards view. When engaged on reconnaissance duties, the Bristol also featured a radio from which the observer was able to send wireless signals to friendly forces on the ground. However, the set was so heavy that the aircraft could only carry a transmitter. Communications were therefore one way, and specially trained signallers were on station back at the squadron headquarters to receive updates from the aircraft as they operated over their objectives. With real time data at their disposal, squadron executives would then judiciously dispatch machines into the fray at the best possible time. Despite its size, the 'Brisfit'—as the airmen called their aircraft—was fast and manoeuvrable. It was a hardy platform and represented the highest standard of military technology of its era. So quickly had the capability of such machines been developed that only a decade earlier the concept of an aeroplane like the Bristol Fighter was a futuristic dream.

At 5000 feet, the Bristol Fighters were low enough for the crew to comfortably breathe and see the plain below, but high enough that the cooler air freed them from the punishing heat of the desert. It was still early though, and the wind cut into the crews as they worked in their open cockpits. At this altitude, the machines were also out of range of Turkish small arms fire. This was well; only the day before an aircraft from their very squadron had been forced down by rifle fire near Ramleh (today Ramla) in central Palestine with the crew wounded. The two downed aviators had burned their machine to prevent it falling into Turkish hands and were still struggling back to the British line even as the operation continued.

The air and ground crews of this Bristol Fighter squadron were tired. For the last several days they had been flying in support of General Allenby's ground offensive in an operation aimed to drive the Ottoman Turks out of Palestine. This was a massive effort and comprised over five divisions of British infantry and mounted rifles, including the famed Australian Light Horse. With supporting arms, Allenby's attackers numbered well over 120 000 men. Once the Ottomans had been ejected from Palestine, the British Army planned to drive northwards into Syria to capture Damascus and Aleppo, and free the Arab countryside from Turkish domination. That it would be replaced by a British Mandate for Palestine in 1918 mattered little. Great Britain was at war! All was fair; the British were arming and supporting thousands of irregular Arab tribesmen under such charismatic figures as 'Lawrence of Arabia' to field an overwhelming majority against their enemy. In September 1918, the efforts were succeeding beyond all expectations.

In operations north of the Red Sea, both Jerusalem and Jericho had been liberated, and the desert forces of the British Empire now manoeuvred on and above the Holy Lands of the Near East. On 19 September 1918, British might and technological prowess had hammered the Turks into headlong retreat. Ancient Samaria was captured, and then Nablus; then soon after the small oases of Balata and Khirbet Ferweh to the north were threatened. Away to the east of the Khirbet Ferweh, the biblical Plains of Megiddo stretched away to the distant River Jordan. The land was crisscrossed by deep ravines and wadis gouged out by perennial rains. The Turkish retreat across Megiddo soon turned into a rout. The battle of Armageddon had begun.

Flying in support of ground troops was hard work for the three squadrons of No 40 Wing of the Palestine Brigade, to which these two Brisfits belonged. The aircraft had an endurance of three hours, and it took an around the clock effort to ensure that several aircraft were in the air during the hours of daylight. While these machines flew, yet others were being maintained or made ready to fly—it took twenty aircraft to ensure that at least two, and generally four, were above the enemy. Neither aviator nor mechanic rested much under such a regimen. At the beginning of the battle, the flying crews had been greatly enthused about coming to grips with the weakened Turkish Army. The Palestine Brigade had spent the best part of the preceding year wresting control of the air from the German machines supporting the Ottoman Empire. Now, during the window of the coming battle, they flew freely in support of the British Army. Of the three squadrons in No 40 Wing, the Bristol Fighters were the element that posed the greatest threat to the enemy's ground troops. The other two squadrons, one each of Royal Aircraft Factory S.E.5a fighters and De Havilland D.H.9A bombers, were also formidable, but these aircraft were not 'dual rolled' like the Bristol Fighter.

What also distinguished the Bristol Fighter squadron was that the airmen manning and maintaining these machines were Australian. This set them apart, though in many respects it mattered little. The Australian aviators were elemental to a British Empire army of national contingents, using common tactics and procedures, and with a common headquarters controlling the activities of all the machines in the brigade. The crews of the Bristol Fighters quickly discovered that their uncontested superiority over the retreating columns of Turks created mayhem among their ranks. Over 19 and 20 September, hundreds—probably thousands—of Turks had been killed in their retreat along the congested roads out of Nablus. While the sun had been up, the Bristol Fighters had hammered them mercilessly in their retreat. Neither soldier nor animal escaped the machine gun fire or bombing along the choked roads; but worse was to come.

By 6.00am on 21 September, the sun had risen as the two Brisfits patrolled in an easterly direction along the deep and dry Wadi Fara. As the pale dawn light brightened, the scene that greeted the airmen was unforgettable. Along the road paralleling the wadi, and all the way back to Khirbet Ferweh, stretched hundreds of mules, motor transports, and thousands more retreating soldiers. The ground on either side of the creek line was precipitous and barren, unnegotiable for the wagons. There was no cover. The observer of the lower Bristol Fighter noted about '600 transports' along the gentle S-bend of the roadway as the aircraft tracked along its nine-mile length. It was packed. A signal was immediately sent back to the squadron headquarters before the two aircraft fell into a line astern formation to expend their ordnance into the trapped column. The butchery commenced.

The diary of No 1 Squadron Australian Flying Corps—the Bristol Fighter squadron—notes 600 machine gun rounds were expended in these first strafing attacks on 21 September. Thereafter, throughout the remainder of the day aircraft from all three squadrons of No 40 Wing maintained the offensive over the Turkish troops. The Bristol Fighter squadron alone expended 24 000 rounds of machine gun ammunition and dropped three tons of bombs into the enemy line that day. No quarter was given. In writing the *Official History*, Frederick Cutlack stated that in all the history of war there can be few more striking records of wholesale destruction. The aircraft were completely methodical as they went about their work. First, the ends of the wadi at the head and tail of the column were bombed, blocking any possible escape. After this had happened, No 40 Wing and several other squadrons of the Palestine Brigade went to work. Conservative estimates indicate there were 7000 troops of the Turkish Seventh Army ranged along the road beside the Wadi Fara. The noise of the diving aircraft, the machine gun fire and the exploding ordnance startled hundreds of horses off the track and over the precipitous cliffs above the creek line. They dragged both men and wagons with them. The rocky walls of the deep ravine amplified the high explosive dropped among the soldiers. The panic and slaughter beggared description. Nevertheless, the Officer Commanding No 40 Wing, another Australian, directed the operations continue throughout the day. He was Lieutenant Colonel Richard Williams and would go on to be the founding Chief of the Air Staff of the Royal Australian Air Force. As Williams noted, by the end of 21 September 1918, few unwounded or living Turks remained in the ravines of the Wadi Fara. The Turkish Seventh Army ceased to exist, and this was entirely the result of attack from the air. When the General Officer Commanding of the RAF in the Near East visited the site several days afterwards, the scene was so profoundly upsetting that he asked Williams to discourage the pilots and observers of No 40 Wing from going to see firsthand the results of their work.

The echoes of aircraft noise over the Wadi Fara resonate still. The operation was in so many ways a first: for air power, for technology, for the military ... for things to come. What the Palestine Brigade achieved in September 1918 was no fluke. It was a synchronised and orchestrated operation conducted by aviators from the farthest outposts of the British Empire in roles that transpose neatly onto the air power operations of today. That the bombing of the Seventh Army occurred only a century ago makes the event even more remarkable. The timeline is so short in the history of humanity. We, in a contemporary era, look to the Australian aviators who flew over South Vietnam in the same way that these now 'ancient' 1960s warriors looked to their forebears in the AFC. As we move to a fifth-generation air force—in the modern parlance—we might also realise that the age of air power is only five human generations old.

2014: Modern Air Power over the Middle East

In 2014 the Australian Government committed an RAAF Air Task Group to the Middle East Region for the express purpose of combating the extremist Islamic group, Islamic State of Iraq and the Levant (ISIL). Concurrently, special forces and conventional Australian trainers were dispatched to assist the Iraqi armed forces in building their capacity to internally combat the threat. The Australian commitment bolstered a coalition, led by the United States, formed in response to the danger posed by unchecked fundamentalist extremism in the region. A self-proclaimed state and caliphate, ISIL had its roots in the anti-Western Al-Qaeda insurgency that sprang up in Iraq after the US-led invasion of 2003. In every way though, ISIL's barbaric campaign of excess eclipsed the earlier Al-Qaeda movement, and the orgy of destruction perpetrated by the group was condemned by the entire world. Having come to prominence so quickly, ISIL proceeded to rampage throughout northern Iraq during 2014, and then along the Euphrates River valley down into the cradle of civilisation at the confluence of the Tigris and Euphrates Rivers. It then turned its attention west into Syria. Along the way, ISIL wantonly destroyed thousands of priceless items of historical and archaeological significance, and captured Iraq's second largest city, Mosul. Countless thousands have perished under the oppression imposed by the ISIL regime, and the egress of humanitarian refugees is felt the world over. As the movement steamrolled across the northern provinces of Iraq, it began to exert influence across Iraq's borders; and as it grew, so did it become an existential threat to the wider region.

The war in Iraq against ISIL is not yet complete; we can make no claims, nor yet draw any conclusions, from events as they unfold in that troubled land. History though, as always, provides superb context in the Middle East. What we might say is that the fight against ISIL is as just a war as any that Australia has ever embarked upon. What is definite is that the ferocity of ISIL represents an existential threat to humanity, to the ideals of civil society and to justice in Iraq and the wider Middle East. As this goes, it menaces the civilised world. However, this volume is not about ISIL. ISIL is (and will be) covered in tomes elsewhere in the coming years. ISIL and its activities in Iraq and Syria simply provide context. In Australia's response to the threat posed by ISIL, the ADF's commitment of a kinetically based ATG is a manifestation of so much of the long twentieth century history of the region.

This work is about contemporary Australian air power, its roots, and the independent utility offered by a balanced air force such as Australia's. At the core of this notion, six Australian squadrons would rotate in and out of the theatre as the RAAF contributed to the fight against ISIL. In particular, No 1 Squadron again found itself operating over the ancient landscapes of the cradle of civilisation, very near to where it flew a century ago. The juxtaposition of the squadron badge—the Cross of Jerusalem—depicted on the tails of the Australian F/A-18F Super Hornets operating in this region is striking when one contemplates the mission this modern force conducted. However, this is a superficial view. On deeper analysis, generations of technical development in air power stand the test of time well. The utility and lethality of modern military aircraft as an adjunct or lead element in an operation reveals air power to be integral to national power. Look even closer at what the contemporary ATG has done in the Middle East Region and the revelations are clear. The doctrine developed for the employment of Australian and Coalition air power today is sound—always a work in progress to be sure—but the roles are almost the same as those practiced by the first generation of Australian aviators over the Wadi Fara. One may reasonably conclude that just as air power exerted a dramatic influence upon the retreating Turks, so air power today exerts a compelling force upon extremists in the same part of the world.

The astute will again note that context is everything. In 2014, Australian airmen found themselves operating in a part of the world where their parent Service flew in its infancy. In fact, the deployment of the ATG is the largest such air commitment made by the Australian Government in nearly fifty years, and the decision has paid dividends. Air power is not a force unto itself. If we note anything of the offensive power afforded by the discipline it is that air power—as is any form of military power—is simply a means to an end.

What we might also note in the wider scheme of things is that one recent anniversary—one that attracted less attention than it should have—resonates deeply for the Australian commitment in the Middle East Region. The Sykes-Picot agreement of May 1916 divided the Ottoman world into areas of British and French influence.

'I should like to draw a line from the e in Acre to the last *k* in Kirkuk', proclaimed Mark Sykes when he viewed a map of the region with the intent of dividing it up after World War I. General Allenby knew of the agreement even as he armed the Arabs to fight Ottoman Turkey with promises of independence after a British victory. The British officer, T.E. Lawrence, operating with Bedouin irregulars, apparently did not know of the agreement and it haunted him until his death twenty years later—he felt he had betrayed the Arabs who helped him.

Many who contributed to this volume are professional military airmen. The harder nosed among us might say about such matters: 'So What?' In response, British and French decisions made in World War I left bitter legacies that last even today. Certainly, some of more erudite among the ISIL elite know this. When ISIL took Mosul in 2014, the group's leaders stated the line on the map was now erased. This may have been premature. Although ISIL has been ejected from Mosul, the future for the region is nothing if not confused and uncertain. Of itself, air power is not a solution to such matters. One highly intelligent young RAAF officer could not have articulated this more clearly when, interviewed in 2016, he mused: 'It never fails to surprise me that the side I was supporting against Saddam when I was here twelve years ago, I'm trying to kill today!'

Whatever our individual views, the military history of this region has helped shape the RAAF. Today, it does so again. The foundations of Australian air power lie in the Middle East. The practices that the aviators of Sir Richard Williams's generation tried and tested a century ago were once more honed, re-evaluated, practiced and refined as the RAAF again contributed elements of air power to operations in North Africa during World War II. And now, once more, two generations on, independent Australian air power has contributed in air combat operations against ISIL. This volume will walk the reader through the earliest days of Australian air power in the Middle East Region; but more significantly, it will draw this thread forwards in time to portray the complexity of the current ATG's daily operations over Iraq. Before we begin, one might conclude already that some things never change: air power roles—irrespective of Service—are both enduring and responsive to developments in technology.

An F/A-18F Super Hornet departs the main air operating base in the Middle East Region for the final time as it heads home to Australia after a successful operation (Source: Department of Defence)

Part I

ARMAGEDDON

No 1 Squadron AFC next to their Bristol Fighters, at Mejdel, Palestine, in mid-1918 (source: AWM B01472)

'Australian is no fair-weather partner in the Empire'
Senator Edward Millen, Minister for Defence, 31 July 1914

Australian Air Power in the Middle East 1915-1918

In July 1914, escalating violence between the declining Austro-Hungarian Empire and Balkans nationalism galvanised Europe to war within a month. On one side lay the Central Powers: Germany, Austro-Hungary, Bulgaria and the Ottoman Turks; on the other, the Allies: Imperial Russia, France and the Empire of Great Britain. The causes of the rapid escalation of the war remain hotly debated a century later. What is certain is that on the battlefields of Europe and the Middle East between 1914 and 1918 the resources of empires were drained. The devastation irrevocably altered the political, social and economic nature of the world, and even today World War I remains synonymous with futility and destruction. However, in this crucible was forged a new concept and a new capability—military aviation and air power. In Australia's circumstance, the contribution of a national contingent to the British Empire in 1914 established the essential pattern for the Australian way of war ever since. The new nation's participation in the conflict directly contributed to aviation developments which would result in the formation of the Royal Australian Air Force in 1921.

Pioneering military aviators were quick to realise the air domain offered an express and unique military advantage, quite beyond the domains of land and sea. The distinct characteristics of the air domain offered a perspective to military commanders that the other domains simply could not. All of the contemporary roles of air power were envisaged during the war, and many aspects of them were tried and tested. In doing so, it was found that air power was able to deliver specific and specialised effects. Air power proved able to penetrate adversary territory and realise strategic, operational and tactical outcomes largely unconstrained. This had never occurred before, and it developed rapidly in the space of a very short three years. In this period, aircraft developed from slow and flimsy contraptions in which the pilot sat open to the elements, to large, heavily armed and often multi-engined, enclosed platforms capable of flying long distances with significant payloads. The result was that by the end of World War I, air power had exerted influence in every theatre by virtue of the advantages that the characteristics of the air domain offered. And as pioneers, Australian aviators were at the forefront of the development. The context of how Australia came to be at war is important to its contributions to the development of air power.

Great Britain's declaration of war on Germany on 4 August 1914 brought an immediate and enthusiastic response throughout the British Empire, with the thirteen-year old Australian Federation ready and willing to commit to support the Mother Country. Even while the British Government was debating whether to participate in the conflict, the Australian Government was prematurely pledging a commitment of combat troops and offering to transfer control of the Royal Australian Navy—only a year old—to the British Admiralty. In fact, on 3 August 1914—a full day ahead of the British declaration of war—the Australian cabinet offered an expeditionary force of 20 000 men to anywhere, for any objective, under British command. There was little opposition to the war, and Australians everywhere anticipated with excitement the glory that war might bring to the young nation. Even so, Australia's entry into World War I was a legal obligation because of the nation's status as a Dominion in the British Empire. In 1914, Britain was the world's leading superpower, and within in the framework of its global presence, there was an identity offered by being a member of the 'British world'. At the essence of the identity were to be found the 'neo-Britons', migrants and British expatriates the world over who were attempting to forge nations and societies around the globe with similar core values. The Dominions of Australia, Canada and New Zealand were very much a part of this framework in 1914.

There was security afforded by Dominion status. These nations were recipients of economic, technological, security and defence benefits. Such matters were no more apparent than in the development and introduction of military technology. In this, there are curious parallels in the world of a century ago to what is now happening in the modern world. If the catchphrase a 'revolution in military affairs' resonates now, it is with good reason. Modern technological developments and the introduction of increasingly sophisticated weapons systems seem to be heralding a new era in warfare. While this may well be so, the circumstance was no different one hundred years ago. The advent of modern, quick-firing weaponry and munitions, and an arms race precipitated by the Dreadnought battleship, meant that the military organisations of 1914 were very different to their Napoleonic forebears. They were developing as exponentially as military organisations the world over are today, and they were doing so under the strain of the largest conflict the world had ever been through to that time. It is not surprising that the most significant technical developments occurring in 1914 were in the bourgeoning discipline of aviation. Such matters are vital to the understanding of air power—and in particular, Australian air power—during World War I. An overview of the men, machines and roles of the Australian aviators deployed to the Middle East during this conflict provides the perfect lens through which to view these developments.

Lesson #1

- Pioneering Australian military aviators were at the forefront of the development of air power.
- The Australian contribution of a force to a larger Empire force in 1914 has established the nation's way of waging war ever since.

Australian Air Power in the Beginning

In 1914, Australia was alone among the Dominions in establishing its own flying corps—the Australian Flying Corps. There were sound reasons behind the decision. Australia was a vast country, about the same size as the continental United States of America, albeit sparsely populated. Even by train it took days to travel the 550 miles between Australia's two largest cities, Melbourne and Sydney. At the time, flying was a novelty, with military and civil aviation interlinked and indistinguishable. Australia's pioneering aviation enthusiasts considered that aircraft—military or civil—might overcome the great 'tyranny of distance' across the expanses of the island nation. There were supporters at the highest levels of government. The Minister for Defence, George Foster Pearce, was a keen advocate for a military aviation capability. Under his guidance, the Senate Estimates Committee granted funding in 1912 to the establishment of the Australian Central Flying School, which was formed in 1913 at Point Cook, southwest of Melbourne, Victoria. The school's initial staff was modest and comprised two commissioned aviators: Lieutenants Henry Petre and Eric Harrison; and four air mechanics: Richard Chester, Ted Shortland, Cyril Heath and George Fonteneau. Five aircraft were procured from the British Government: two Royal Aircraft Factory B.E.2a aircraft, two Deperdussin Type As and a Bristol Boxkite. Flying commenced at Point Cook in March 1914.

Following the British approach to the establishment of the Royal Flying Corps (RFC) in 1912, the Australian Government amended the Army's establishment in July 1914, on the eve of the outbreak of the war, to form the AFC. The same month, four volunteers were called for to undertake the first flying training course, commencing on 17 August 1914 following the outbreak of World War I.

While the main theatre of World War I was in Europe, the first major operational activities conducted by Australian military aviators were in the Near East against Ottoman Turkey. The British Empire's interests in the region were several: to protect its trade route through the Suez Canal to India and the Far-East; to protect its Persian oil supply; and to strike through the Turkish belligerents into what Britain's First Sea Lord, Winston Churchill, had dubbed 'Europe's soft underbelly'. For its part, the Ottoman Empire opposed what it viewed as British incursions into its territories. This was particularly so in the region of Mesopotamia, the fertile lands that lay between the Tigris and Euphrates Rivers, now a part of the modern nation of Iraq, and stretching west across Jordan into Palestine. The defence of this region was vital to Turkish sovereignty, a fact well known to the Allied powers. Accordingly, in 1915, the British Army launched an offensive with Indian troops into Mesopotamia via the Persian Gulf, quickly capturing the coastal port of Basra. In part, this was also to secure the Anglo-Persian oil wells and to maintain a supply to meet the British war effort.

When British forces captured Basra, the British War Office requested Australia furnish aviators and mechanics to serve in a small unit supporting the Mesopotamian force. Dubbed the Mesopotamian HalfFlight, the AFC unit had eight pilots—initially four British and four Australian—in addition an RFC equipment officer, air mechanics and an eclectic mix of underpowered aircraft that included types such as the Caudron G.III, Royal Aircraft Factory B.E.2c, Martinsyde Scout, Maurice Farman Shorthorns and a single Longhorn. In particular, the Shorthorns and Longhorn were unusual aircraft types with a single bladed propeller shaped roughly to resemble a scythe. This aeroplane was not very fast, but very successful in the ground attack role, where it reportedly terrified sheep. The Half-Flight arrived in Basra in May 1915 just as the British enclave commenced forays northwest along the Tigris River into the Iraqi interior. The inordinately hot conditions were unsuitable for cavalry in the Iraqi delta region, and the Half-Flight's aircraft proved exceedingly useful as reconnaissance platforms in their stead. The heat, which was often in excess of fifty degrees Celsius, was equally punishing on the wooden aircraft, and even more for the ground crews who performed magnificently to keep their platforms flying. On operations, in addition to the assigned reconnaissance duties, the aircraft were used for bombing, strafing, artillery spotting/photography, and aerial resupply.

Group portrait of instructors and pupils of the Australian Central Flying School's first military flying training course taken with a B.E.2a aircraft in a hangar at Point Cook. Back row: Richard Williams; Thomas White. Front row: George Merz; Henry Petre (instructor); Eric Harrison (instructor); David Manwell. (source: AWM A04588)

The Ottoman Empire and its Reverberations

The Ottoman Empire, or Ottoman Turkey, was founded at the end of the thirteenth century in north-western Anatolia by Turkish tribal groups. At its height, the empire stretched west from Mesopotamia through Palestine and the Levant, also encompassing the northern and southern coastal nations of the eastern Mediterranean. These nations included Greece, Albania, the Trans-Jordan, Armenia and the approaches to Egypt. By the end of the nineteenth century, the Ottomans were in serious decline. Despite attempts to modernise, their empire was dubbed the 'sick man of Europe' and it continued to decay during the first decade of the twentieth century. In 1908, a group of progressive junior politicians, known as the 'Young Turks', attempted to institute modern constitutional reform. They made some headway, though the next decade remained a divisive and painful experience for the Turkish people as they endured the death throes of the Ottoman ruling elite. This period in Turkish history period is still darkened by the nation's involvement in World War I, and by the wanton destruction and sectarian violence that accompanied the fracturing of the empire along ethnic lines.

The Ottoman reforms of 1908 also comprised a comprehensive restructure and modernisation of its army. German munitions were procured, and large numbers of German soldiers served in an advisory capacity to Ottoman Turkey before and during World War I. The task of modernisation was difficult. The army was severely limited as traditional Ottoman forces depended on volunteers from the Muslim population of the empire. During the war millions of men from across the Turkish Empire enlisted into its army, making it a truly cosmopolitan force. Caucasian Turks served alongside Arab and ethnic Turks, Kurds and other nationalities, all with diverse ethnic and cultural backgrounds. However, the internal unrest of the fragmented Ottoman Empire resulted in an army of men with varying loyalties and military utility. Underwriting this, the Ottoman economy was almost entirely agrarian, relying on wool, cotton and other animal produce. Establishing arms foundries and factories proved difficult within this economy and was an ongoing problem for early twentieth century Turkey. With German tutelage the Turkish Army was remarkably successful in its modernisation program.

The Ottoman Empire had four Army-sized formations in 1914, comprising thirty-six infantry divisions. Each division had three infantry regiments and an artillery regiment. In 1915, the Turkish Army inflicted a major defeat on the Allies when it prevailed in the Gallipoli campaign. Mounting casualties necessitated the forming of the Fifth and Sixth Armies in 1915, followed by the Seventh and Eighth Armies in 1917. Up until this time, the Ottomans enjoyed relative parity with the Allies in the Near East and Palestine, though increasingly sophisticated British tactics and the use of technology during 1918—particularly air power—rapidly turned the tide of war against them. By the second half of 1918, the Turkish Army had been rendered ineffective. The Ottoman Empire collapsed and unconditionally surrendered to the Allies on 30 October 1918.

The quick dismemberment of Turkey's Ottoman Empire after the war still reverberates to this day in widespread regional instability and the need for continued Western involvement. The latest iteration of the many twentieth century conflicts in the region may be found in the war against the terror network of ISIS. Understanding the heritage of these countries is vital to any comprehension of the modern world.

On 23 September 1918 Captain Ross Smith flew No 1 Squadron's Handley Page O/400 to meet Lawrence at Um es Surab. Both air power and a T.E. Lawrence led Arab insurgency figured prominently in the downfall of the Ottoman Empire in 1918. Handley Page reaches rendezvous with Lawrence of Arabia (1918, oil on canvas, 50 x 61 cm, source: AWM ART14279)

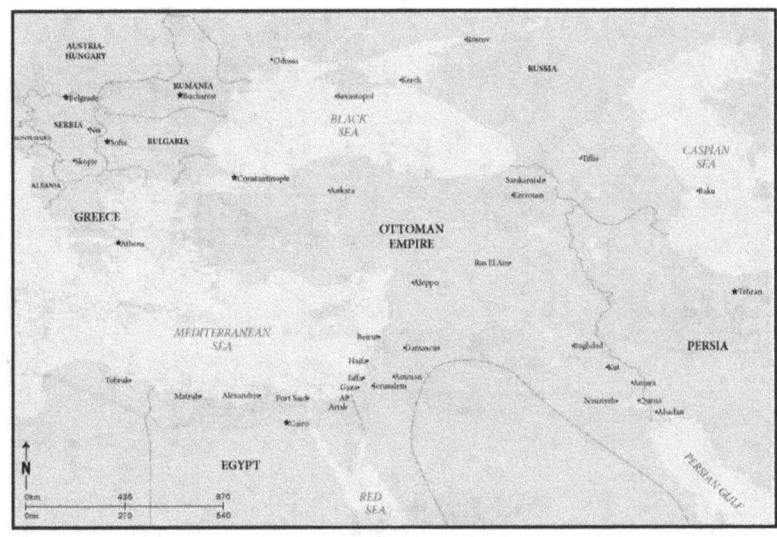

The wide expanse of the Ottoman Empire and Near East during World War I

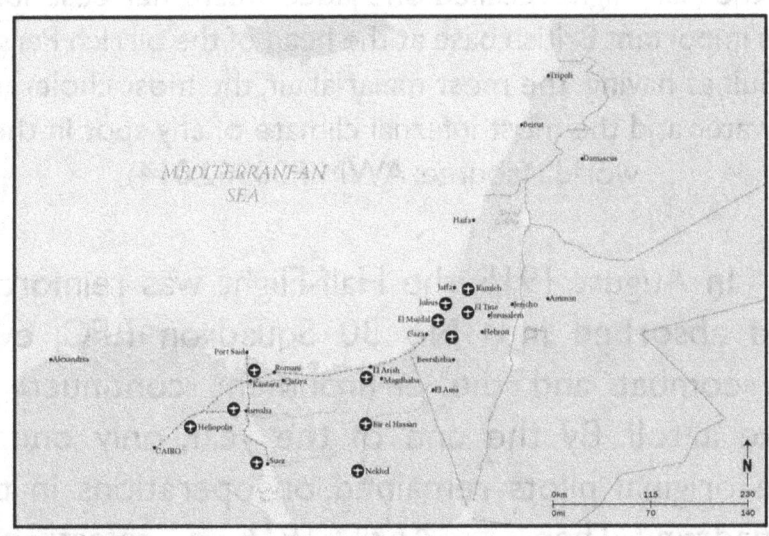

The airfields across Egypt, the Sinai and Palestine from which the AFC operated during World War I

An aerial view of Basra taken in 1918. In 1915 a member of the Half Flight recalled one jaded westerner describing this important British base at the head of the oil rich Persian Gulf as having 'the most malarial air, the most choleraic water and the most infernal climate of any spot in the world'. (source: AWM P00562.014)

In August 1915, the Half-Flight was reinforced and absorbed into No 30 Squadron RFC; even so, combat and the environment continued to take a toll. By the end of the year, only one of the original pilots remained on operations in the squadron. Then, in April 1916, a catastrophe occurred when an Indian Army division under Major General Sir Charles Townsend was surrounded and besieged at Kut Al Amara on the Tigris River, southeast of Baghdad. For weeks,

No 30 Squadron worked valiantly to support Townsend and prevent the fall of Kut. It dropped over thirteen tons of supplies and munitions to the besieged garrison, and even maintained facilities within the township to facilitate the supply missions which flew in every day. In effect, these sorties—manned from across the Empire—became the first air mobility resupply missions in history. All of this was to no avail. Townsend surrendered on 29 April 1916, and the No 30 Squadron ground crews at Kut were also placed into captivity. The privations endured by these men, many of whom died as prisoners of the Turks, would prove to be among the most extraordinary conditions ever endured by captured Australian servicemen during World War I.

The Turkish success at Kut, and the withdrawal of British forces from Gallipoli, gave the Ottomans ascendancy in the region during 1916. They would twice campaign across the Sinai Desert during the year in an attempt to capture the Suez Canal. In response, the War Office bolstered its defences along the approaches to the Suez Canal. In March 1916, these forces were unified to form the Egyptian Expeditionary Force (EEF) under the command of General Archibald Murray. Murray did not understand aircraft or air power, but thankfully his RFC commander did, and Murray did not prevent him from developing the air service's role in Egypt. Because of this, the RFC expanded its Middle East commitment with the formation of No 5 Wing under the command of Lieutenant Colonel (later Air Vice Marshal) William Geoffrey Salmond. No 5 Wing comprised Nos 14 and 17 Squadrons RFC, a training school and, in response to a War Office request, the soon to arrive No 1 Squadron AFC. Other AFC squadrons would later form for service on the Western Front. In mid-1916, No 5 Wing had several Martinsyde G100 'Elephant' bombers. However, its primary platform was the two-seat B.E.2c, as described by a contemporary:

> It was a development of the [earlier] B.E.2a, but a little larger, laterally controlled by ailerons, and with a 90 horsepower 8-cylinder, air cooled V-type engineered by the Royal Aircraft Factory ... The wings of this aircraft had a forward stagger and this with a dihedral on the upper wing gave it a substantial degree of inherent stability.

Members of the Half Flight with a B.E.2c used to resupply the garrison at Kut. (source: AWM A04144)

A flight of B.E.2c type aircraft as utilised by No 5 Wing in the Middle East. Inherently stable, the aircraft was unsuited to aerial combat particularly with the more advanced

German aircraft operating in the desert theatre. (source: AWM H12729/02)

Members of the Australian Flying Corps (AFC) in 1916 showing a variety of uniform types worn at the time. Included Are Lieutenant (Lt) Norman Steele; Lt A.T. Cole; Captain E. Roberts; Two Unidentified. (source: AWM P01034.013)

Mechanics from No 1 Squadron Australian Flying Corps (AFC) working on a Bristol F.2b aircraft, 1918. Observer Leslie William Sutherland was effusive in praise of the squadron's mechanics: These lads work night and day to keep their charges serviceable ... When their own machines are all in order they always lend a hand to the other lads who may be changing engines or fitting new wings. (source: AWM B02213)

Royal Flying Corps, Part 1. 1914: Care of Aeroplanes

General. The endurance and air worthiness of aeroplanes largely depend upon the care spent upon them. Aeroplanes should not be exposed to extremes of heat and cold. However well-seasoned the wood may be, if it is allowed to absorb moisture, it will invariably deteriorate. Sheds, therefore, should be kept dry, and, as far as possible, at an even temperature. An aeroplane can never be too clean. Rust, mud, dust and superfluous oil must be at once removed when it returns to the sheds. An aeroplane, once housed, must have its weight supported in such a manner that there is no strain on the flexible suspension of the wheels. In this connection it must be remembered that the supports should be placed in such a position that the main weight of the machine is directly over them. The best position is immediately under the points where the undercarriage struts meet the skids. Before an aeroplane proceeds on a flight, and after its return, all parts, such as control and aileron wires, fabric, etc., must be thoroughly examined, and the least of wear in any part must be at once corrected. It is important to watch the wear of the control wires at points where they pass over pulleys or through fair leads. For a thorough examination it is necessary to remove the grease first. All engines must be thoroughly tested before flying and after any repairs, or overhaul, have been affected. Once a week, a thorough examination must be made of all struts, internal bracing wires of fuselage with a view to checking any damage, or alignment. If an aeroplane makes a forced descent, and is left in the open, the aeroplane must be placed in as sheltered place as possible, such as a hollow, or under the lee of a hedge, facing the probable direction of the wind, and pegged down.

Fabric. The following points must be understood by all: Fabric is protected from the damp by doping it with 'emailite.' Oil deteriorates both fabric and proofing material and must at once be removed as far as possible. Portions of fabric, which are liable to get saturated with oil, will require more frequent doping than the remainder. It will also be necessary to examine the woodwork beneath the fabric. An aeroplane in regular use will require re-doping every six months. Holes in the fabric must be repaired at once. If the hole is small a strip of fabric can be stuck over the hole and doped. A large hole will require the patch sewn in.

Woods. Although proofing materials, such as 'emaillite' and 'cellon', are commonly thought of in connection with fabric, it must be remembered that they also afford an excellent protection to wood from damp.

Bracing wires. These must always be painted in the case of both main planes and fuselages. The colour of the paint should be light so as to show up any signs of rust. All external bracing wires must be either painted or greased. Turnbuckles must be protected from rust by a light film of grease ... and locked.

Tyres. Tyres are injured by oil and grease. If they come in contact with such substances, they must be at once cleaned. Pools of oil must not be allowed to remain on the floors of sheds.

Engines. Engines must be protected whenever possible, by means of canvas covers which should be specially made to fit. Electric cables must be fitted so that the insulating material will not be exposed to damage either by excessive heat or by chafing against some sharp edge of wood or metal. Long lengths of unsupported cables are should be avoided.

Propellers. Propellers must be protected in the same way, as exposure to damp renders them liable to warp. As soon as flying is finished propellers must be wiped over.

Logs. Rough logs kept in each flight in which all details of flights, overhauls, repairs, expenditure of fuel and oil, etc, are entered at the time the casualty occurs, are of assistance in making the fair logs an accurate history of the aeroplane and engine.

Care of Aeroplanes: A gathering of No 40 Wing aircraft in the harsh climatic conditions of Palestine in 1918 (source: History and Heritage Branch—Air Force).

Nascent Air Power Roles

The study of the genesis of Australian military aviation is important background information; not the least of which is that this period in Australian history has contributed to the national identity. Australia's association with Great Britain during World War I virtually assured the fledgling AFC access to the most innovative developments in air power. Both factors were particularly important in the Middle East where squadrons were employed in a variety of roles. In the Middle East, the nature of warfare was far more open than the type of operations being conducted on the Western Front. Because the desert war was fought over such a wide expanse of territory, the use of aircraft became all the more important to ensuring the success of the armies in the field. This meant that No 1 Squadron AFC would be employed in numerous roles including reconnaissance, scouting, artillery spotting and bombing operations. These roles developed rapidly during this pioneering period, either independently or in response to the environment. In the desert theatre by the middle of 1916, aircraft were operating closely with the mounted troops of Murray's command, including the Australian Light Horse. Initially, aircraft not only monitored Turkish activity but also conducted offensive operations to destroy the infrastructure that supported the Ottoman troops. Later, aircraft were used to prevent opposing aircraft from conducting similar functions. The resultant level of cooperation achieved between ground and air elements was a great leap forward for air power, and it was realised solely through the characteristics of the air domain: speed, reach, penetration and perspective.

Lesson # 2

- Air power is shaped by the unique characteristics of the air domain.
- While the roles are fundamental and enduring, the characteristics are dynamic and constantly changing according to the effects of the environment (particularly meteorological) and technical developments.

Air Reconnaissance

The British air arms had noted, even before the war, that aircraft would be extremely useful for conducting reconnaissance. Reconnaissance was once the sole purview of the cavalry; indeed, this arm was characterised by speed and reach in the land domain. However, the Field Service Regulations of 1912 and 1914 explicitly grouped aircraft and cavalry together to conduct the reconnaissance function.

Reconnaissance comprised two methods; the first, forward area patrolling; and the second, distant patrolling far over the adversary's rear area and lines of communication. Forward air patrolling—or 'tactical' reconnaissance—required detailed examination of trench works, gun positions, strength of wire and general defences. Distant patrolling, or 'strategical' reconnaissance, aimed at keeping a continuous record of railway activity, the state of the enemy's supplies, the size of his reserve camps, and all movements of troops behind the lines.

The Fragility of Air Power: Maintaining Aircraft in the Middle Eastern Climate

The Middle East has a punishing climatic environment. The region is hot and dry, although winters are mild with a little rain. To the north of the deserts of Western Iraq and Palestine are the great steppes. These have extremes of temperature and rain in winter and spring. Summers are long and hot and winters mild and wet along the Mediterranean coast. The coastal areas are humid but have a steady breeze to compensate. Lowland desert areas in the interior regions of the Arabian Peninsula, Iran, Iraq, and Egypt have extreme heat in the summer, with temperatures sometimes reaching sixty degrees

Celsius or higher. The extreme temperatures precipitate many updrafts of heated air and generally large dust storms—the 'Khamsin'—result. The Khamsin cross much of Palestine and dozens occur annually. Maintaining aircraft in such conditions remains a difficult endeavour. During World War I, the rudimentary tent, open-air living and maintenance facilities, and the doped fabric and wood construction of aircraft, were constantly affected by the extremes of the climate. The following extract from a 1914 War Office publication highlights just how fragile aircraft were.

The Fragility of Air Power: No 1 Squadron Hangars at Dier el Belah in the Middle East. The austerity of the conditions endured by ground crews maintaining aircraft in this part of the world is readily apparent (source: History and Heritage Branch—Air Force).

Section 95 of the Field Service Regulations was clear about the role of aircraft in reconnaissance, and it was with this document that the AFC and RFC went to war:

1. *One of the most valuable means of obtaining information at the disposal of a commander is the air service. The air service will not, however, replace the other means of acquiring information ... but will be used in conjunction with them, being employed in the work that can be undertaken by it to the greatest advantage, and used either to gain news of the enemy and his dispositions, or to confirm the accuracy or falseness of the information obtained from other sources.*
2. *Field units of the air service will, as a rule, work under the direct orders of general headquarters as army troops, but aircraft may be detached to army or other headquarters as required, the principle being observed that the air service shall be so distributed that the units may be placed in the best positions not only to gain information, but to cooperate with the other arms, and especially with the cavalry, in this all important service.*
3. *The commander or senior officer of the air service present should be in close touch with the operations section of the general staff,*

> *through which he should receive orders and to which he should act as adviser on all technical matters: e.g. as to the class of aircraft to be employed on each service, and as to how far weather conditions are favourable to flight, how many aircraft should be dispatched, etc.*

Within these short paragraphs, now over a century old, there was already a notion that air power was separate, though inherently joint; and that air power was best enabled through the tenet of centralised command and decentralised execution. In following this tenet, it was very quickly found that if aircraft could be further enhanced with innovative technology, then the potential to exploit the air domain would grow exponentially. This was particularly the case when cameras were first used to enhance reconnaissance products.

The RFC made the first extensive use of aerial photography during the British Army's preparations for the Battle of Neuve Chapelle in March 1915. The Royal Engineers also used a combination of photographs and ground survey techniques to produce trench maps. When Major General Sir Hugh Trenchard assumed command of the RFC in August 1915, he stipulated that photographic reconnaissance was to be elemental to the RFC's mission. Soon, aircraft on all sides were clamping large, high resolution cameras on the fuselage outside an observer's cockpit to photograph the ground terrain below the aircraft. The plate glass film frames were heavy and required half an hour to develop after the aircraft returned. Nevertheless, the photography revealed hitherto unrealised details of an enemy's defensive systems. Analysts could compile a photographic mosaic of opposing positions from which detailed cartographic products could be produced. Imagery analysts even used stereoscopic devices to enhance battlespace awareness. This was obtained via a dual-lensed camera that took two exposures simultaneously to provide a three-dimensional view of the ground.

By 1916, photographic reconnaissance was being used extensively by the RFC across every theatre of war. It was exceptionally dangerous work. Missions were conducted at anywhere from 5000 to 10 000 ft, often within range of ground fire. An accurate photo mosaic required close collaboration and focus between pilot and observer. The pilot had to continually look from map to ground to instrument panel in order to keep the aircraft on a precise course with consistent air speed and altitude. Managing the camera slung over the side of the aircraft was the full-time duty of the observer, who used a stopwatch to time the overlap of each image.

Flying prescriptive profiles like this made photo-reconnaissance aircraft easy prey for enemy scouting aircraft.

Aerial view of the aerodrome and camp of No 1 Squadron, Australian Flying Corps. The quality of such imagery, in this case taken by the Australians themselves, had great operational utility. (source: AWM A00630)

Lesson # 3

• Air power is inherently joint.
• Air power is most effectively utilised through the tenet of centralised command and decentralised execution.

Imagery Analysis

Lieutenant Adrian Cole of the AFC in a Martinsyde G100 'Elephant' aircraft equipped for aerial photography with an observation camera. (source: AWM P01034.038)

The RFC established sections specifically to compile photographic imagery, with staff maintaining cameras, magazines of unexposed glass plates, and dark rooms to develop prints from these plates. Analysts were trained to spot signs giving away enemy positions, improvements to trenches or concentrations of troops and equipment for an offensive. Nevertheless, early photo development equipment was crude, and the correct mixture of chemicals, exposures and drying times was very much a trial and error process. Subtle atmospheric anomalies were also challenging, as the camera lens would record atmospheric haze that was transparent to aircrews. This was particularly prevalent in the harsh desert climate. However, like air power, aerial photography initiated a technological revolution that quickly realised major improvements in camera stability, shutter speed and lens quality.

Scouting and Air Combat

As aerial reconnaissance became more effective during the first year of World War I, both sides realised the necessity of preventing their opponent's aircraft from conducting this key role. Larger calibre anti-aircraft weapons were developed, though initially these were inefficient and ineffective. It was not long before pilots and observers over the Western Front attempted to shoot at other aircraft using rifles and even pistols. This proved equally ineffective. It was of course the machine gun, the embodiment of technical development during the war, that so profoundly affected the nature of air power. However, machine guns were large and heavy, and only a few were small and light enough to be practicable for use on aircraft. Another problem was that firing sideways seriously decreased accuracy, while firing forward through the aircraft's propeller arc was equally problematic.

In April 1915, the Frenchman Roland Garros fitted steel wedges to the propeller blades of his Morane-Saulnier N aircraft to deflect bullets fired forward through the propeller arc that would previously have struck the blades. The Dutch aircraft designer, Anthony Fokker, took this solution further when he developed the 'interrupter gear', a timing mechanism that synchronised the machine gun with the moving propeller blades. Mounting a machine gun over the engine, Fokker's system used a cam that worked a push rod from the aircraft engine connected to a wire attached to the gun hammer. Over the time the propeller blade passed in front of the gun, the wire engaged the hammer and stopped the gun from firing. The result was revolutionary: when a pilot in an aircraft fitted with a forward-firing machine gun and the interrupter mechanism flew directly towards an enemy aircraft, he could shoot the enemy down without risk to himself or his aircraft.

The notion of destroying enemy aerial reconnaissance efforts, while still conducting unhindered reconnaissance for friendly forces, became the focus of airmen on both sides. Scouting aircraft—as these platforms were called—provided a form of armed reconnaissance that drew on the nomenclature of the cavalry. The resources of numerous companies such as Sopwith, Bristol and De Havilland—names to become famous in aviation history—were devoted to the design of dedicated scouting aircraft. An armed scouting aircraft, while still able to observe enemy movements and positions, was also in a position to attack enemy ground troops or prevent enemy aircraft from conducting observation work of his own. It was an innovative concept for military aviation and marked the point at which aircraft operations became offensive in nature. The notion of scouting crosses the boundaries of several modern air power roles, with modern fighter/attack platforms able to trace their heritage to this early form of air power.

It does not take much imagination to envisage how aircraft design then developed from scouting to pure air combat. When Fokker coupled his interrupter gear with an aircraft that he had also designed, the fighter aircraft was conceived. The pairing of these designs was war changing; it led to a period of German air dominance in late 1915 and early 1916 over the Western Front known as the 'Fokker Scourge'. Quite simply, British and French aircraft had no interrupter gear of their own, with only a rudimentary blade-mounted bullet deflector method available for forward firing, which limited their ability to combat the enemy. Fokker's E-type—often referred to simply as the 'Eindekker', meaning 'one deck' or monoplane in German—was a design that wasn't necessarily fast nor manoeuvrable. It had a top speed of approximately 78 knots (144 km/h), but it made up for the shortfall with the lethal integrated weapons system and the tactical acumen of its early protagonists. German pilots soon developed a whole new set of air combat tactics, many of which are still used to this day. Led by pioneers like Max Immelmann and Oswald Boelcke, the Fokkers attacked from a higher altitude, diving down out of the sun, firing long concentrated bursts of machine gun fire, and then diving past their target until they were out of range. For a short period, the Fokker Eindekker reigned supreme. The aircraft was even deployed to the Middle East in support of Ottoman forces in 1916, and there it was also ascendant over the opposing B.E.2 platforms.

Unable to combat the Fokker Eindekkers, British engineers designed an entire series of 'pusher' aircraft in which the engine nacelle was mounted behind the crew thereby leaving an uninterrupted field of fire for forward-firing machine guns. Until Allied aircraft developed their own interrupter gear in late 1916, pusher aircraft served a necessary purpose in combatting the Fokker Eindekker. Even so, the pusher aircraft remain a technical cul-de-sac in aviation history. After more capable British and French aircraft came to be fitted with forward-firing guns, the Eindekker was driven from the skies. Thereafter, the war in the air became an arms race in which more sophisticated and higher performing machines on both sides were developed in response to the enemy.

In the interim, in combat the B.E.2 was essentially helpless. Based on pre-war considerations, the design required the pilot to sit in the rear seat to maintain the centre of gravity. The observer occupied the front seat and could fire a gun effectively only in a rearward direction, and then only in a limited arc over the hapless pilot's head. To do this, he had a single Lewis gun for which several sockets were provided on either side of and behind his cockpit. In combat he was obliged to move the 30 lb weapon from mounting to mounting, an undertaking that was nigh on impossible even for the normally sedate B.E.2. Apart from these difficulties, the B.E.2's inherent stability also proved to be a disadvantage, depriving the aircraft of manoeuvrability. This was even more problematic when the aircraft was loaded; over besieged Kut during the campaign in Mesopotamia the air drops comprised 50 lb bags on each lower wing root, and two 25 lb bags between the undercarriage struts. Fortunately, the aircraft flew these sorties without any airborne contact with the enemy. This was not the case in Egypt. The AFC's arrival in the Middle East in mid-1916 coincided with the arrival of armed German aircraft, which was to cause much consternation among Allied aviators for the following year.

Fokker E-type Eindekker (source: AIRCDRE Mark Lax PhD)

An Australian Observer Describes a Desert photo-reconnaissance Mission

We have two types of camera—vertical and aspect. Vertical are far from satisfactory, because they are so liable to jam when the negative boxes are being changed. That reminds me of an interesting incident. One of our pilots, Lieutenant Taplin ... came up against this jamming business. He was flying a B.E.12a single seater. As usual, the vertical camera was fixed outside the fuselage, on his right. He and his companions were flying at 12 000 feet and 1000 yards apart, when his camera jammed. Flying his machine with his knees—that is, he gripped the stick between his knees—he dismantled the camera to adjust it. A Hun [German] ... chose this very inconvenient time to attack him. 'Taps' turned to engage but his forward firing Vickers gun jammed.

Meanwhile, the German dived to come up under his tail. Taplin's gun responded to treatment, and he turned his aircraft on the Hun's tail, put a burst of thirty [rounds] into him, and down went the German in a dive. Taps completed his roadside repairs to the camera; picked up his place in the formation and carried on. By the way, that particular photographic formation [of five aircraft] carried out 39 patrols and exposed 1616 plates, which exposed a complete map, accurate to the smallest detail, of 624 square miles of Turkish territory.

Captain Leslie Sutherland MC DCM 1936

Captain Leslie Sutherland MC DCM. (Source: Sutherland Collection, via History and Heritage Branch—Air Force)

'Fokker Fodder' the Royal Aircraft Factory B.E.2

The Royal Aircraft Factory *Bleriot Experimental 2* (B.E.2) was a British tractor, two-seat biplane and was one of only a few aircraft to remain in continuous service with the RFC and RAF over the course of World War I. Designed and tested by the famous aircraft engineer Geoffrey de Havilland, eight versions totalling 3500 aircraft were manufactured, with the type serving long after reaching obsolescence. The B.E.2's early pre-war performance was impressive, and it was immediately earmarked for reconnaissance duties with the British Army. During trials in August 1912, the B.E.2 scored impressively over the Army training grounds on the Wiltshire Plains. It broke the British altitude record, climbing to 10 560 feet. After further development, the unarmed B.E.2a was introduced in 1913 and was the first British aircraft to arrive in France during the conflict. The B.E.2b was introduced in 1914, soon followed by the B.E.2c. Often called the 'Quirk', the B.E.2c was armed with a Lewis gun and was inherently stable—this made it a most useful reconnaissance platform. The aircraft served extensively over the Western Front in 1915 and was deployed to the Middle East the same year. There it took part in the ill-fated Mesopotamian campaign and was used extensively the following year by the RFC and AFC over Palestine. Completely outclassed by more modern German designs, the B.E.2 was phased out of frontline service in Palestine during the second half of 1917. Despite its shortfalls, the B.E.2 served the British well, and is remembered for its utility.

> During 1916 the [B.E.2] was a sort of maid of all work, a general-purpose hack, which could be used for reconnaissance, artillery observation, photography, spy dropping or any other job that turned up.
>
> Captain Cecil Lewis MC, No 56 Squadron

Royal Aircraft Factory B.E.2

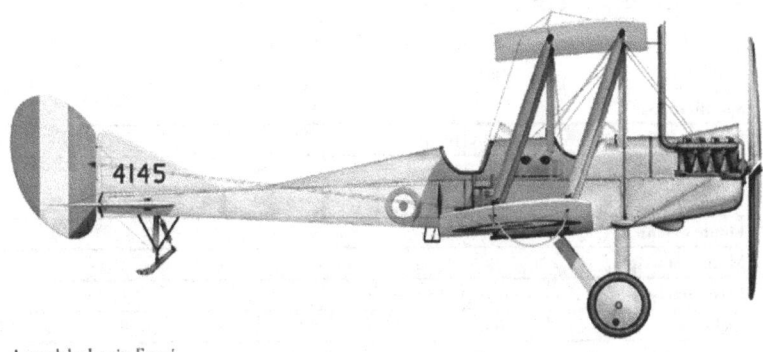

Artwork by Juanita Franzi

Specifications

Wingspan:	36 ft 10 in
Length:	27 ft
Empty weight:	1370 lb
Max weight:	2142 lb
Powerplant:	90 hp RAF1a air cooled engine
Armament:	Single Lewis machine gun fitted in observer's cockpit, and up to 200 lb of bombs
Maximum speed:	63 kts (116 km/h)
Ceiling:	10 000 ft (reduced to approximately 6000 ft in desert conditions)
Crew:	Two

Fokker E-type Eindekker M.14V E-III

Artwork by Juanita Franzi

Specifications	
Wingspan:	32 ft 8 in (10 m)
Length:	23 ft 6 in (7.16 m)
Height:	7 ft 10 in (2.29 m)
Empty weight:	878 lb (398.2 kg)
Maximum weight:	1342 lb (608.7 kg)
Maximum speed:	76 knots (140.8 km/h)
Endurance:	1.5 hours
Service ceiling:	13 500 ft (4118 m)
Primary powerplant:	One 100 hp Oberursel 9-cylinder air-cooled rotary engine
Crew:	One
Armament:	One forward-firing 7.92mm machine gun
Production:	594 (all variants)

The Fokker Eindekker

The Fokker Eindekker (literally single wing) comprised a series of German monoplanes that came from the workshops of Dutch aircraft designer Anthony Fokker. The most famous of the series was the Fokker E.III which was an unremarkable and conventional design other than the fact that it was that first aircraft of the war fitted with a synchronised machine gun that could be fired through the spinning arc of the air screw. This gave the platform a decided advantage over all Allied platforms at the same stage of the war. In the hands of early pioneers of air combat aviators such as Max Immelmann, the Eindecker precipitated a period of air combat which came to be known as the 'Fokker scourge' in late 1915 and early 1916 during which time the inferior British and French aircraft designs were swept away. After the Battle of the Somme in France in 1916, Britain and France developed interrupter gear for Allied aircraft and from this time the Fokker E.III was rendered obsolete.

Aerial Observation: Artillery Spotting

The RFC pioneered artillery spotting during World War I, and despite exponential developments in aircraft technology, it remained a dangerous business throughout the conflict. Artillery spotting required an airframe with a crew of two. It was a complex task for the aircrew to organise. The pilot had to operate the aircraft, positioning it in the best airspace to enable the observer to conduct his duties. This required the aircraft to be flown on a steady path, resulting in spotting aircraft being incredibly vulnerable to anti-aircraft fire and enemy fighters.

This was compounded by crews not being allowed to carry parachutes until late in 1918. Because they typically flew at an altitude similar to the apex of an artillery shell's flight, it was also not unusual for the pilot or observer to actually see the shell as it stopped at the top of its climb before arcing downward. It was not unknown for aircraft to be hit by those shells. Early in the war, both on the Western Front and over the Middle East, aircraft would fly over enemy positions at a predetermined altitude and drop a signal flare or smoke bomb when directly over the target. Ground spotters, who used binoculars to keep watch on the aircraft, would calculate range to the target using the known altitude of the aircraft and its 'look angle' above the horizon. Trigonometry improved general ranging of artillery, though the aircraft had to remain under continual observation by the ground spotters. Atmospheric glare or haze—particularly in the desert—sometimes prevented the crew from observing the target or obstructed the ground spotters from seeing the aircraft. Direct communication via wireless telegraph from the aircraft to the ground eventually overcame this difficulty.

Artillery spotting and reconnaissance squadrons were generally allocated to a corps, and individual aircraft worked in conjunction with a single artillery battery. It required precise planning between the battery and the crew involved. Once airborne, the observer navigated to the area of operations to identify the target. Orders for opening fire were then issued. The observer was then able to adjust fire via wireless telegraphy using Morse code as he observed the fall of shot. By modern standards, the wireless equipment was so heavy that aircraft could not carry both a transmitter and receiver, so aircraft only flew with a transmitter. Despite these travails, aerial spotting increased the effect of artillery accuracy exponentially.

At the beginning of each mission, the aircraft had to locate their assigned battery by way of large canvass letters that were laid out upon the ground near each battery to form the letters of a code. Once the position of the battery was established and a target was identified, the observer would transmit a firing order to the battery using the 'clock code' system. When the observer saw the battery's first round fall in relation to the target, using this clock code method a second round could be directed with deadly accuracy. By the end of the war, wireless technology was integral to aerial reconnaissance and the targeting process. This weapons system wrought havoc on the battlefields on a scale that could not have been envisaged before the conflict.

Weapons of War
Maxim MG08/15 Light Machine Gun

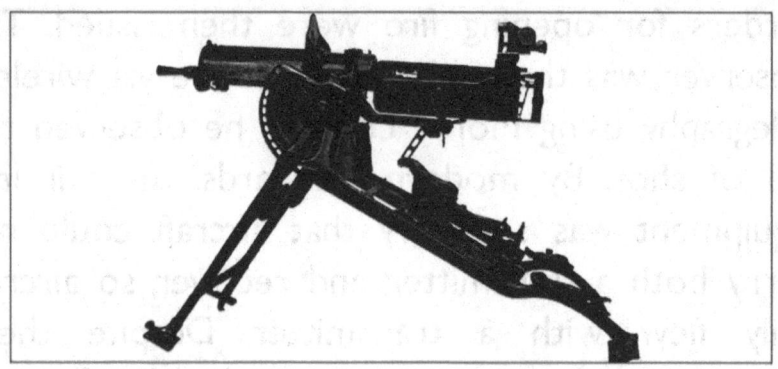

Nicknamed the 'Devil's Paintbrush' for the manner in which it cut down advancing infantry on the Western Front, the German *Maschinengewehr 08* (or MG08)—numbered for 1908, its year of adoption—was the German Army's standard machine gun of the war and was an almost direct copy of the original 1884 Maxim gun. The weapon was a water-cooled, belt-fed heavy weapon initially mounted on a sled, though this was later changed to bipod and tripod configurations. The Germans quickly grasped the potential importance of the MG08 on the battlefield and created separate machine gun companies to support infantry battalions. In 1915, the MG 08/15 was adapted for aircraft use. After modification, the LMG 08/15 weighed 26 lb compared to the original MG 08 weight of 57

1b. One very visible modification was the change to the cocking handle and introduction of cooling vents instead of the water-cooled system. Another practical modification was the introduction of a rear mounted safety interlocks, useful considering that ground crew had to stand in the line of fire during engine start up. All MG08 and MG 08/15 were manufactured at the Spandau Arsenal and, because of the Arsenal imprint on the fusee cover, quickly became known as Spandau to the Allies. The word Spandau is synonymous with the concept of machine gun development to this day. This image of the weapon depicts a ground-based system. When used in a flying machine the barrel jacket was perforated and air cooled. (source: AHU Library)

Specifications	
Calibre:	7.92 mm x 57
Muzzle velocity:	2821 ft/sec.
Rate of fire:	400-500 rounds/min; synchroniser and engine speed dependent
Length (overall):	46 in.
Barrel length:	28.35 in.
Weight:	26 lb.

The Lewis Gun

Captain Ross Macpherson Smith, (later Sir Ross Macpherson Smith, KBE, MC, DFC, AFC) left, and his observer, Lieutenant Ernest Andrew Mustard, DFC, of No 1 Squadron behind his twin air-cooled Lewis guns on a Scarff Ring, in their Bristol Fighter B.1229. (source: AWM A00658)

Designed by US Army Colonel Isaac Newton in 1911, the Lewis gun was at first adopted by the British Army. Produced at the Birmingham Small Arms (BSA) factory in Birmingham, the Lewis was cheaper and more economical to produce than a Vickers gun, and soon gained popularity with British, Belgian and Italian armies as an infantry weapon. The BSA factory alone made 145 397 of these weapons during World War I. Weighing only 12.7 kg (28 lb) which was around half the weight of other machine guns of the period, the Lewis became immediately popular amongst troops. It could be carried by a single soldier and was easy to load with its drum magazine. Later, the Lewis Gun also became one of the most important aircraft machine guns of World War I. The magazine for an aircraft mounted Lewis gun held a ninety-seven round drum magazine that required careful storage as it had an open underside which left it vulnerable to dirt and dust. The Lewis gun was a gas-operated weapon which meant that it could not be synchronised to fire through a spinning propeller. It was able to be fitted on the top wing of some aircraft designs later in the war so that it could be fired outside the propeller's arc. Increasingly sophisticated modifications then enabled this mount to be swung down into the cockpit so that the magazine could be changed without the pilot having to face the exciting prospect of standing up while the aircraft was in flight. In 1916, when more advanced aircraft designs moved the pilot to the front cockpit location, Warrant Officer Frederick Scarff of the Royal Naval Air Service came up with ring and barbette assembly for the rear seat. Officially called the *No 3, Mark II Barbette*, the Scarff Ring enabled single or twin Lewis guns to be mounted, rotated and elevated whilst supporting the weight of the weapons.

Specifications			
Weight:	28 lb	Rate of Fire:	550 rounds/min
Length:	39 in	Muzzle velocity:	2400 ft/sec
Cartridge:	0.303 British	Feed system:	97 round drum magazine
Action:	Gas operated		

Bombing

Until the beginning of World War I, the RFC concentrated on reconnaissance and army co-operation duties. Pre-war aircraft were simply not built or powered to undertake any other function. When it arrived in France, the RFC then began experimenting with tactical bombing on a very small scale. There were no effective bomb cradles, release or sighting mechanisms, so individual RFC crews dropped hand-held bombs or grenades onto German columns and positions. Even so, the RFC's principal mission was still reconnaissance in support of the Army, and reliable bombs with safe and effective racks for carrying them did not become available for some time. As the utility of aircraft and air power became evident during 1915, important doctrinal developments were captured from operations conducted in Europe and the Middle East and resulted in the seminal *Notes on Bombing Attacks* of December 1915. This short document highlighted the developing offensive nature air power, with corresponding technical developments soon following.

An airman of No 1 Squadron, Australian Flying Corps, examining and fitting fuses to the bombs to be used in a bombing expedition before being loaded onto the Martinsyde G. 100 Elephant aircraft in the foreground and the Bristol F.2b Fighter aircraft in the background. (source: AWM B01588)

During 1916, the Royal Laboratory developed the 112 lb Mk 1 bomb and supplemented this with the smaller Hales 20 lb fragmentation bomb. By the end of the year, Britain had developed a larger 230 lb bomb, as well as the ubiquitous 25 lb Cooper bomb (replacing the Hales weapon) which could be fitted to a wide range of aircraft, including fighters. As the war progressed, various other bombs were introduced—including 250 and 520 lb types, and even a 1650 lb behemoth—all of which were carried by large multi-engined platforms. Because single-engined aircraft predominantly operated in the Middle East, the bombs most commonly used in that theatre were the 20/25 and 112 lb types. The smaller bombs were generally designed to fragment on exploding, proving to be fearful anti-personnel devices. The larger bombs had an ability to penetrate before exploding, and these bombs were capable of destroying buildings and hangars. As the 20/25 lb bombs were introduced into service, the Royal Aircraft Factory designed a four-bomb rack for the smaller bombs as a standard fitting under each wing. During 1916 a 'Skeleton' type cradle carrier was introduced in three standard sizes for the 112, 250 and 520 lb weapons. The bomb release mechanisms were mechanical: a Bowden wire fitted with a toggle which led around the outside of the aircraft to within easy reach of the pilot. The perennial problem remained in the sighting mechanism for aerial bombs.

The accurate delivery of ordnance dropped from aircraft was (and remains) a difficult task that requires an understanding of pure and applied mathematics—particularly trigonometry and ballistics. The problem required an engineering solution and several iterations of optical/mechanical bombsights were developed during 1915 and 1916 before the War Office settled on the CFS bomb sight. This was a metal framed contraption mounted on the outside of the fuselage, with both a height and time scale, and a levelling device to indicate the aircraft was flying straight and level; even a slight bank would result in ordnance missing the target. It was a complicated device and did not factor in wind drift. Numerous other factors could hinder the delivery of a bomb on to its target before the aircraft had even arrived overhead. These included the weather, which often obscured the ground, and which could even preclude an aircraft from flying. Once a crew was airborne, they then often faced the danger of having to fight their way to a target through ground fire. After the middle of 1916 in Palestine there was also the threat of enemy machines. If an aircraft arrived over the target, the crew then had to overcome the mathematical problem of delivering their ordnance. The ever-present wind was always a factor, though this was mitigated somewhat with the development of the high-altitude drift sight in 1918 with a periscope mirror-device fitted to view the target. This sight was still a mechanical system and required a pilot and observer who were trying to operate an aircraft—often under fire—to work out precise calculations of speed, time and distance for a triangulated bomb release solution to a moving trigonometrical problem. If this sounded difficult and complicated, it is because it was. Smaller, single-engined machines were not fitted with bomb sights, and in these aircraft, ordnance was delivered by learning from 'experience':

> *For example, it was found that bombing down-wind on a D.H.4 at a target such as a munitions factory, if one released the bombs as the centre of the target disappeared under the leading edge of the bottom plane in line with the port inside bay strut, this coincided with the moment when the target appeared on the intersection of the wires of your mirror sight.*

Clock Codes and Artillery Spotting

In an artillery observation shoot, observation and the fall of shot was signalled to the battery using the 'Clock Code' analogy; that being, the target was at the centre of the clock face with due north at 12 o'clock. From the target, concentric circles labelled alphabetically, were scribed outwards to a range of 500 yards. The zones were labelled:

OK: fall of shot on target
Z: 25 yards out

B: 100 yards out
D: 300 yards out
F: 500 yards out
Y: 10 yards out
A: 50 yards out
C: 200 yards out
E: 400 yards out

The fall of the rounds was noted with reference to the smallest diameter circle in which the round fell, followed then by the clock hour to which the shot was nearest. For example, using this method, a round falling 50 yards to the east of a target would be signalled from the aircraft to battery as **A3**.

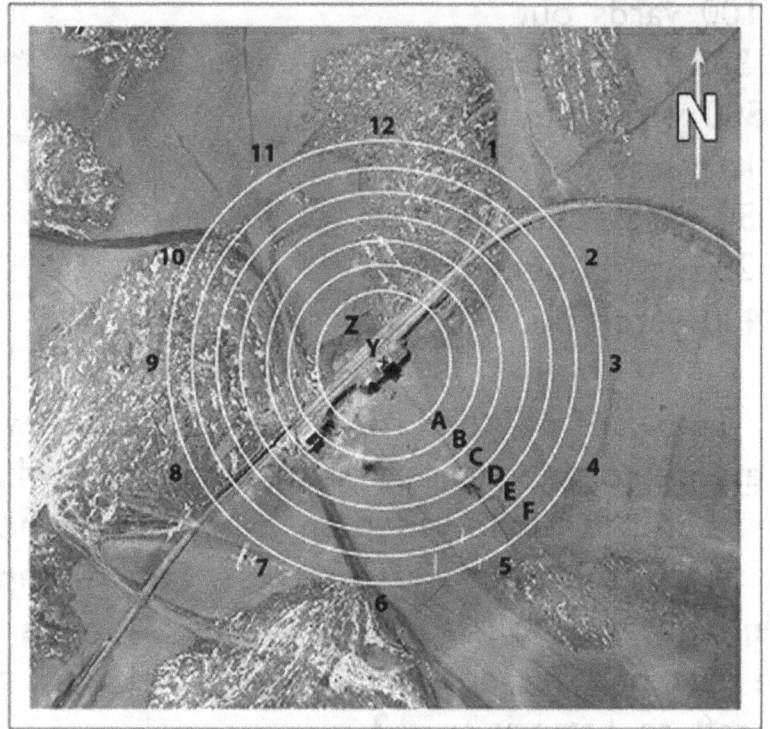

(Source: FSGT Daryll Fell)

The Dangers of Artillery Spotting

British doctrine indicated that spotting aircraft should watch *especially for movements of immediate reserves, massing of troops for counterattack, minenwerfers, machine-guns and strong points holding up the advance, and targets of such nature.* Hostile batteries were to be dealt with by [friendly] artillery machines. Often, judgements over whether the information obtained, or the effect realised, was of enough importance that it justified the risks taken by the crews, and this became a difficult decision for the responsible commanders. The doctrine was explicit with regard to the dangers faced by aircrews:

> *Commanders and staffs when giving orders for reconnaissance [missions] must fully consider the risks run by pilots and observers in carrying them out. At an altitude of 1500 feet or less an aeroplane is almost certain to be hit by rifle and machine-gun fire from the ground, unless the enemy is fully occupied in fighting. Conditions will arise in which these dangers should and must be run, but it must be borne in mind that the loss of one or two pilots or observers who know the ground impairs the value and efficiency of squadrons for a considerable time, and is only justified by obtaining information of really first-class importance.*

Accuracy in delivering ordnance: a perennial problem

The Official Historian of the Royal Air Force during the World War I, Henry Albert Jones, himself a former observer and recipient of the Military Cross, clearly captures the difficulties associated with bomb-sighting in Vol II of his history:

If an observer in an aeroplane, flying on a straight course, releases a bomb and watches its downward path, he will see it always vertically under him. On the other hand, an observer on the ground watching the missile will see it fall in a curved path. The explanation, of course, is that the bomb maintains the forward speed which it shared with the aeroplane when it was attached to its carrier. The air resistance which the bomb has to overcome causes it to trail a little behind the vertical of the aeroplane observer and affects, very rightly, the time of its fall, but the small corrections for air resistance, allowed for in the construction of bomb-sights, need not be considered here. There is, then, along any given course, one place in the air, and one only, from which a bomb may be released from an aeroplane with the certainty that it will hit its objective, and that place is not immediately above the target. In still air the problem would be simple of solution. The speed of the aeroplane over the ground would be the same as its speed through the air, the pilot would know his height and the rate of fall of his bomb, and so have the necessary data to construct a triangle to tell him what he wants to know, that is, the angle, in advance of the vertical, at which he must release his bomb to hit the target. It would be a simple matter to make an instrument which could be adjusted before he went into the air to give the bomb-dropping angle for any pre-determined height. But the air is never still. The speed of the aeroplane over the ground is greater or less than its speed through the air according as it is helped or retarded by the movements of the wind. A bombsight to be practicable must enable the airman to find his ground speed, at any moment, and allow of a consequent simple adjustment to give the bomb-dropping angle.

A member of one of the Australian Light Horse Brigades in Palestine, displaying three different sized aerial bombs, as used by the RFC and the AFC against the Turkish and German forces in the Middle East. The bombs are identified from largest to smallest: RFC 230 lb bomb; Royal Laboratory 100 or 120 lb bomb and a Hales 20 lb bomb. (source: AWM P03423.004)

The Airco D.H.4 and later De Havilland D.H.9 (which would serve in Palestine in 1918) were larger two-seat, single-engined aircraft designed for level-bombing. Both were fitted with a drift bombsight and generally flew in level formation to deliver ordnance at altitudes of at least several thousand feet. While these techniques in bombing during the war were rudimentary, they became increasingly effective by the conflict's end. When it came to aircraft directly engaging enemy ground forces at low level, there was a great deal more fluidity in the tactics and type of aircraft employed. Because of the type of aircraft and ordnance available at the beginning of 1917, the RFC did not conduct dedicated close air support missions; that is, attacking adversary ground formations which were in direct contact with friendly forces or elements. However, as bomb racks and the 20/25 lb bombs were developed and fitted to most British machines, aircraft became increasingly employed in close air support. This occurred in both Europe and the Near East. By the last year of the war, technology and tactics had improved to the point where the air service was charged with conducting three missions: maintaining control of the air for friendly forces; the ever-present requirement for strategic and tactical reconnaissance; and bombing and strafing enemy troops and emplacements.

Getting it Right

The development of these roles, while vital, was not the only factor that contributed to the wide-ranging success and evolution of air power during World War I. Equally important developments can be found in the broader organisational structure of the British and Empire air services. Commanders and airmen at all levels of these respective hierarchies quickly realised that in order for air power to most effective, it had to be applied in a balanced manner. In particular, what the British understood, and their opponents did not, was that to realise the effects of air power was not a simple process. To merely possess a number of superior platforms would not necessarily result in achieving control of the air. A successful air service required mastery of many complex and challenging facets.

The most straightforward aspect to address was the matter of organisation. From the earliest days of the war, the British War Office had well-defined establishment charts that provided lines along which flying squadrons and their subordinate elements were organised. This structure constantly evolved to meet the developing needs of the RFC. The organisation addressed considerations as to how flying units fitted into the wider structure of the armed services—they were inherently joint—and how squadrons were fully capable of providing independent support to an Army or Naval element. A century on, such concepts are captured in the notion of airmindedness—the appreciation of the unique characteristics and methods of the employment of air power, either independently or in support of a wider force. In this philosophy, both the RFC and AFC had a purposeful structure and defined goals.

Secondly, the British and Empire air services expanded rapidly after the outbreak of the war, necessitating a significant influx of suitably qualified personnel. Their training did not immediately occur as efficiently as it could have done, and during the first two years of the conflict the demand for aircrew meant that training was often rudimentary at best. Among ground crews, both Services required expert tradesmen who would be in a position to service and maintain the intricate flying machines. For their part, the War Office eventually realised that aircrew required efficient, effective and standardised training in order to operate to the safe limits of their aircraft's capabilities, while at the same time realising the greatest possible kinetic effects against any adversary. In contemporary parlance, such practices form an enduring pursuit for professional mastery: the sum of an individual's and organisation's depth and breadth of knowledge and understanding of a profession combined with the ability to apply it through the lens of personal experience and intellect. By 1918 the RFC and AFC—particularly in Palestine—had achieved professional mastery. The squadrons of the Palestine Brigade were manned and led by highly trained and experienced aviators, tradesmen and administrators who had an expert understanding of their own function and of the goals of the organisation.

Thirdly was the matter of command, leadership and training. While each of these were closely related to organisation, it was among the intangibles of command and leadership that the air services in Palestine found success. The precise definition of command has changed little in the century since 1914. It includes the authority and responsibility for effectively using available resources, and for planning the employment of organising, directing, coordinating and controlling military forces for the accomplishment of the assigned mission. The British air services in Palestine had a particularly astute commander in Geoffrey Salmond. Salmond recognised that conditions in the Near East were ideal for flying training. What was equally important was that the wider RFC was beginning to emphasise sound, standardised training to instil a quality in its aircrew superior to that of their opposition. Salmond coupled these two concepts together.

In mid-1916, Salmond directly petitioned the War Office to establish a flying training wing of three squadrons in Egypt with the aim of having up to 100 student pilots on strength at any one time. The scheme had the full backing of the commander of the RFC, Major General Sir Hugh Trenchard. Salmond's request was approved, and after the arrival of both men and machines during July—August 1916, the flying training school began producing not only enough quality pilots for the Palestine theatre, but also an additional overflow for the Western Front. By the end of the year, Salmond had expanded his training establishment to include another squadron—the 'School of Aeronautics'—which aimed to facilitate the training of mechanics, fitters, riggers and armourers in the intricacies of the machines that they were operating. During 1917, classes in aerial gunnery, tactical bombing and artillery spotting were added to the school's syllabus, greatly enhancing the training of non-pilot aircrew who served in the Palestine theatre.

Salmond's organisational vision was a motivating factor among his operational squadrons at a time when German aircraft dominated the air. He had identified and articulated a plan, and then put in place a structured system in order that the flying service might wrestle complete control of the air for EEF. This was a well-defined and completely tangible goal, and while Salmond's air force fell under Sir Archibald Murray's ostensible command, he had complete autonomy in facilitating the operational support provided by his squadrons. In turn, he passed this autonomy on to his squadrons in their individual endeavours.

Salmond's vision and purpose strengthened the morale of the RFC and AFC in the Near East. His visionary command, his insistence for first rate performance, and the provision of the latest machines for his crews were reinforced by his demand for like standards among his subordinate aviation commanders. Salmond's efforts saw to the health, welfare, moral and discipline of the air component in the EEF, and as much as any technical edge, this contributed to the eventual defeat of the Ottoman Turks.

By 1917 the role of the RFC and AFC in Palestine had expanded to cover the breadth and depth of British efforts across all levels of operations in the theatre. The strategic success of the air service in controlling the air over the Turks and Germans was central to Allenby's eventual success across the biblical plains. The Palestine Brigade provided the EEF with intelligence of enemy positions, freedom to manoeuvre forces undetected, and the depth to attack and rout the retreating Turkish forces to the point of annihilation. The evolution of local air superiority in Palestine, properly coordinated with the ground offensive, was the deciding factor for victory in that theatre. The foundation for this success could be traced to 1916 and coincided with the arrival of No 1 Squadron AFC.

Lesson # 4

- The notion of balance in the application of air power is one of the discipline's enduring features.
- Merely possessing platforms without an appreciation of the complexity of requirements needed to effectively operate the platforms will surely degrade the capability to a point where it will fail.
- The elements central to a successful air force were equally as applicable during World War I as they are today.

Videmus Agamus: We See, Let Us Act

No 1 Squadron AFC Arrives

In his biography, *These are Facts*, Sir Richard Williams would write that No 1 Squadron was assembled at Point Cook very quickly during early 1916 in readiness for overseas service. It would duly deploy from Melbourne on 16 March 1916 without aircraft or technical equipment of any kind. The squadron had been formed in accordance with RFC establishment guidelines, providing for a Headquarters element and three Flights–A, B and C Flights—with a constrained establishment of twenty-eight officers (including nineteen aircrew officers) and 186 'other ranks'. Among the latter, volunteers with specialised trade training in wood and metalworking, sail and pattern making, and mechanical engineering were highly sought after to work on the wood and fabric-covered aircraft. All 'other ranks' had to additionally enlist in the Australian Imperial Force and fulfil the requirements associated with wartime service. Even after meeting these conditions, most of the volunteers had very limited exposure to actual aircraft before deploying. The commissioned aircrew were slightly different. Quite a few of the pilots were permanent officers in the aviation specialisation;

all of the observers were on secondment from different specialisations to the new Service. By 1917, such was the cooperation between the Australian Light Horse and No 1 Squadron that many mounted officers transferred to the AFC for training as observers. In the interim, with no specific observer training in Australia, all non-pilot aircrew and the less experienced pilots would continue on to England for training when the squadron docked in Egypt in April 1916 as the secondary flying school in Egypt was unable to assist in the Australians' training until later that year. Consequently, upon arrival, even the more experienced Australian pilots were attached to No 14 Squadron or No 17 Squadron for in-theatre familiarisation (and because the British RFC hierarchy did not trust the quality of their training).

The squadron's arrival in Egypt coincided with a seasonal change in the Middle East. From May to August the heat of the Sinai desert ranges from one extreme to the next. With the heat comes the dusty Khamsin, turning the atmosphere into a haze of fine floating sand particles born along by a hot southerly wind. Murray's EEF, now established in its defences along the eastern side of the Suez Canal, suffered in the inexorable climate. This was particularly so for Murray's Mounted Division which comprised light horsemen and yeomanry from Australia, New Zealand and Great Britain. The troops and their mounts, engaged on deep reconnaissance patrols east of the Suez, endured terrible conditions with the heat and lack of water. Augmenting their function meant that the RFC and AFC would be very active.

HMAT Orsova pulls away from the wharf in Melbourne as women wave farewell. Many of those on board were members of No 1 Squadron bound for the Middle East.
(source: AWM P05140.007)

No 1 Squadron passes Romani Camp while crossing the northern Sinai to Mustabig aerodrome by train, 1916. (source: AWM P00588.007)

Cutlack's *Official History* indicates that when No 1 Squadron AFC arrived in Egypt, its ground crews were also apportioned among the RFC's No 14 Squadron and No 17 Squadron in eastern Egypt to gain experience. Each man understudied a corresponding experienced tradesman in the British squadrons over the summer period, with the result that after six weeks most of the men were trained. Salmond, now a brigadier commanding all air assets in the Middle East, was impressed with the Australians' progress. By August, he had become quite particular that all crews be 'worked-up' at his flying training establishment after their arrival from England.

The doyen of Australian balladeers, Banjo Patterson, serving as a remounting officer for the Australian Light Horse in Egypt, wrote of this daily activity:

> *Everything is being hurried up. The big English flying school near our camp has been ordered to turn out as many pilots as quickly as possible and there is an average of eighteen planes in the air all day long, just over our heads. The din is indescribable, but the horses never look up, or otherwise take the slightest notice of the planes. The life of a pilot, computed in flying hours, is pitifully short; many of them are killed while learning. My wife is working as voluntary aid at a hospital in Ismailia, and she and her associates are constantly making shrouds for these boys that have perhaps made one little mistake in their first solo flight and have paid for it with their lives.*

As the mechanics and crews of No 1 Squadron gained their competencies during the height of summer, the unit's individual flights were dispatched to outposts east of the Suez Canal in support of the ground offensive. There, in close cooperation with the British squadrons and mounted troops and infantry, the individual flights from No 1 Squadron ranged ahead of the Army, the B.E.2s patrolling, reconnoitring and occasionally bombing the Turks. At the height of the appalling heat in July and August, the EEF engaged and defeated the Ottomans at Romani, inland to the east of the Suez. There, any Turkish designs on capturing the canal were halted.

The first aircraft issued to the squadron six weeks after its arrival were the B.E.2c type, which were greatly inferior to the German Pfalz monoplane and Rumpler aircraft which had recently arrived to support the Turkish ground forces in the Sinai Peninsula. The B.E.2c's inherent stability was both a blessing and a curse; it was ideal for observation but rendered the aircraft's defensive manoeuvrability against the German single-seaters virtually impossible. British and Australian aviators were soon engaged in a long and arduous struggle against the well-equipped German Air Service. Their aviation tasks were many and varied. They carried out aerial photographic and reconnaissance missions, spotted for naval and artillery bombardments, mounted bombing strikes and of course engaged in air—to—air combat, often in desperate encounters against the superior aircraft of the enemy.

The German adversaries provide a useful contrast. *Flieger Abteilung 300* (literally 'Flying Department', equating to squadron) arrived in

Palestine in April 1916. An element of the German 'Pascha' commitment to the Turkish war efforts, FA300 had made a difficult journey to its operating airfields at Beersheba and El Arish. Given German interests, the squadron's spotting, bombing and air-to-air roles were difficult and diverse. Germany well knew the strategic importance of the British lifeline through the Suez Canal to India and the Antipodes. Germany's support to the Ottoman Empire, which eventually comprised nearly 25 000 troops over the duration of the war, was provided to reduce pressure on the Western Front by disrupting the supply of goods to British industry. FA300 was the first of six German squadrons that would eventually serve in Palestine. Its initial equipment comprised two Pfalz E.II monoplanes—which were very similar in appearance and performance to the Fokker E-type Eindekker—and six Rumpler C.I two-seat dual purpose biplanes.

The Rumpler was a particularly capable aircraft. It was powered by a 160 horsepower Mercedes in-line engine that had an enlarged radiator for the desert conditions. It could fly at 95 knots and was well-armed with a forward-firing synchronised machine gun for the pilot and a similar swivel-mounted weapon for the observer. The Rumpler also had under-wing racks that could carry up to 100 kg of bombs.

With a service ceiling of 16 000 feet and a four-hour endurance, the Rumpler's performance exceeded that of any British aircraft type in Egypt or Palestine. The advantages of the Pfalz's synchronised gun also made it an equally dangerous adversary.

FA300 aircraft made their presence felt almost immediately. When the Khamsin dissipated in May, the Germans commenced extensive reconnaissance missions over British lines. By June 1916, they were conducting bombing missions against EEF forces, with one raid against the 1st Australian Light Horse lines at Romani on 1 June being particularly effective with one officer, seven men and thirty-six horses killed. On 20 July, the Turks then made a concerted effort to capture Romani. The subsequent weeks of battle up until 8 August proved to be a period of significant operations for the air services on both sides.

The Demographic of Military Flying Squadrons

Australian popular history derives much from the Anzac myth that stems from its experiences in World War 1. As it goes, Australian soldiers performed so well because of the environment of their homeland. Australia was an egalitarian and frontier society in which it took initiative, resourcefulness, independent judgement and moral and physical courage to survive. These qualities transferred straight into the ranks of the armed forces and continue to inform the values of each arm of the Australian Defence Force today.

Such heritage is meaningful, though not completely true. While these qualities were, and continue to be, valued among airmen, they say nothing of the specialist and technical natures of the discipline of air power. To this end, aviation units stand apart from the other units that made up the AIF, and this demographic remains in the modern professional force. To start with, flying squadrons were uniquely established. Several hundred strong, only a minimal number of men were engaged in flying duties or combat, and almost all of these were commissioned officers. Concurrently, the majority of the 'other ranks' performed highly specialised and technical support functions in the comparative safety—though this was not always the case—of an aerodrome workshop. In contrast, an infantry battalion comprised about 1000 officers and men, with all ranks exposed to danger albeit the greater portion of close combat being conducted by the 'other ranks'. Even a cursory glance of Cutlack's *Official History* distinguishes the AFC from the other branches of the Services. Many of the aviators were well-educated, established professionals, or were in training to become so. Professional vocations such as teacher, engineer and doctor, or university student predominate among Cutlack's biographical footnotes; and this highlights the academic rigour associated with learning to aviate even in the earliest years of military aviation. Equally, and particularly in the Middle East, a great many aviation recruits were former light horsemen; this points to certain similarities in spatial orientation and physical coordination that existed between aviators and mounted men. Even here, the Anzac myth falls short. Many of the former light horse troopers who found themselves as aviators in No 1 Squadron were listed, for example, as graziers, pastoralists, motor drivers or engineers; and this went against the notion that aircrew ranks were filled by skilled or educated professionals. Among the supporting ranks, most were almost certainly experienced, specialist tradesmen. This meant that airmen were generally older than the rest of the AIF, and more likely to be married. Technical trades would likely have comprised builders, shipwrights, sail makers, fitters, turners, blacksmiths, armourers, mechanics, cabinet makers, woodcraftsmen, jewellers and watchmakers. Many of these professions continue to make invaluable contributions to society in the twenty-first century, requiring specialist training and particular focus in order to master their associated skill requirements.

The Development of RFC Pilot Training

AFC Flying Badge (source: AWM REL27060)

What is remarkable about the aviators who piloted the earliest military aircraft is that they were older than the advent of powered flight. At the beginning of the war aircraft were still quite primitive. A pilot generally sat in a wicker seat atop the fuel tank and, in earlier types, was exposed to the elements. The aircraft fuselages were made of thin longerons of hardwood, with a framed wing of spars and ribs covered with doped linen. Unreliable and often underpowered engines provided thrust, and a rudimentary set of controls attached by a 'cable and pulley' system provided the means for the pilot to 'steer' the aircraft, connected to a vertical stabiliser with a rudder to control yaw; a horizontal stabiliser with elevator for pitch; and ailerons on the wings for roll.

While the technology associated with the earliest flying machines developed exponentially as a result of World War I, the skills required to pilot these aircraft remained difficult and unique. They remain so today! A pilot required the physical balance and dexterity to manoeuvre a machine in three axes, while concurrently exercising the mental acumen to consider speed, distance, time and fuel consumption. Combat aviation, irrespective of the role, also required higher levels of spatial orientation—pilots were required to judge distances, determine the adversary's aspect, and conduct trigonometrical and vector projections mentally. On top of this, every type of aircraft had its own unique performance characteristics which the pilot—and observer if a two-seater aircraft—had to know well and operate within.

At the beginning of the conflict both the RFC and AFC had their own Central Flying Schools. However, neither Service had the capacity to train pilots in sufficient numbers to meet the demands of their rapidly expanding organisations. Accordingly, new training units were opened in the United Kingdom, Canada and Egypt to train pilots and, later, observers. Because of the rapid expansion of the Services, there were few training or instructional standards, and the quality of tuition a trainee pilot received during the first two years of the war varied widely. Some of the aircraft used were unsuitable—they had only one set of controls and none had any effective method of communication between the instructor or student pilots. Accidents were common, with casualties at flying training units throughout the war outnumbering losses in combat.

During 1916, the RFC began regulating flying training standards. The AFC's status as an operational element in Imperial service ensured that the Australian air service also adopted the same standards. Prospective pilots and observers were posted to a school of aeronautics—a ground school—for a period of up to six weeks. There, in addition to military drill and regimentation, they undertook a series of aviation-related subjects that included flight theory, aircraft and engine construction, armament engineering, aerial gunnery, meteorology and basic navigation. Even so, it took until well into the war before these subjects were regulated across schools to a common standard. After ground school, prospective aircrew were posted to undertake flying training. The introduction of dual-controlled training aircraft into basic and advanced flying training schools in 1917—using the Gosport communication system—proved a watershed moment in British aircrew education. Under this system, a student pilot sat in the front cockpit of an aircraft which was equipped with a full set of controls, while the instructor sat behind, communicating a 'patter' of instructions through a device called the 'Gosport Tube'.

The Gosport system clearly articulated what and how an instructor had to teach a student pilot in order that the trainee gain a flying qualification. This was further refined and codified in October 1917 with the publishing of *General Methods of Teaching Scout Pilots*; in essence, the first flying training manual in history. *The General Methods* publication was underwritten by specialist flying training instructor courses conducted for the experienced aviators, posted to training schools, to pass on their knowledge. Through this system, students were encouraged to explore the performance envelope of their aircraft—under instruction—and to safely operate it to its limits. By the final year of the war, the refined *General Methods* publication stated that in order to qualify, a trainee must meet the following minimum standards:

To Qualify:

1. Undergone instruction at a School of Military Aeronautics.
2. 20 hours solo in the air.
3. Flown a service aeroplane satisfactorily.
4. Carried out a cross-country flight of at least 60 miles successfully—during which he must have landed at two outside landing places under supervision of a R.F.C. officer.
5. Climbed to 8 000 ft and remained there for at least 15 mins after which he will land with his engine stopped, the aeroplane first touching the ground within a circular mark of 50 ft in diameter.
6. Made two landings in the dark, assisted by flares (only applicable to B.E.2 and F.E.2 pilots; pilots of other machines may do this at discretion of Wing Commanders and Commandant C.F.S.).[1]
7. Passed Gas Course.

B. To wear a flying badge [wings] on posting overseas:

1. Passed tests applicable in 'A' above.

---

[1] Night landings were required for B.E.2 pilots because this machine was used for anti-Zeppelin work, while the F.E.2 was used in night bombing.

2. *Have had dual control instruction + solo air experience amounting in all to 35 hours: of which no less than 5 hrs must be made upon a service type.*
3. *Carried out 15 'tail down' landings on service type. He will then be known as a service pilot and will wear wings. If a service pilot is required for overseas on a type other than that on which he is qualified as such, he must do a further five hours solo and 15 'tail down' landings on new type.*

A class of RFC students being given instruction on the rotary engine at the School of Military Aeronautics (source: RAF Museum)

Salmond's No 5 Wing now comprised only No 1 Squadron, AFC and No 14 Squadron, RFC;

No 17 Squadron, RFC having deployed to Macedonia in early July. These two squadrons could muster about twenty serviceable aircraft at any one time. Added to No 5 Wing's number were about ten seaplanes serving in the Royal Naval Air Service (RNAS). With this number of aircraft, the RFC, AFC and RNAS ostensibly outnumbered the German FA300 by more than a ratio of three to one. However, the eclectic mix of B.E.2, Martinsyde, single-seat Bristol Scouts and De Havilland DH1 pusher aircraft allocated to the British and Australian squadrons were no match for the German Pfalz and Rumpler machines.

Group portrait of observers of No 1 Squadron, AFC. Back row, left to right: Lieutenant (Lt) Howard Bowden Fletcher DFC; Lt Hudson Fysh DFC; Lt Charles James Vyner; Lt Harold Alexander Letch MC; Lt Ernest Andrew Mustard

DFC; Lt Leslie William Sutherland DCM MM. Front row: Lt Frederic Cecil Hawley; Lt Walter Alistair Kirk; Lt Richard Andrew Camm; Lt Garfield Finlay; Lt Edward Balfour Somerset Beaton, Charlie the dog. (source: AWM B02076)

Bombing and reconnaissance missions by both sides were an almost daily affair across the expanse of the northern Sinai Peninsula. Anti-aircraft fire was also significant. On 29 July a B.E.2c of No 14 Squadron was hit by anti-aircraft fire on the enemy side of the Turkish lines while operating at 6000 ft. The British airmen brought their aircraft down safely enough, and then burned it to prevent it from falling into enemy hands. Unable to carry the aircraft's machine guns, they threw them into the sea. Given the wide expanse of the area of operations, the two aviators then proceeded to walk back through enemy lines to safety where they arrived two days later.

Each combatant attacked their opposing airfields during this period, with extensive strafing and bombing missions also conducted by both sides. Elements of No 1 Squadron, including Captain Richard Williams, came under intense shellfire when Romani airfield was attacked on 4 August. Several air-to-air encounters also took place. A No 14 Squadron machine was shot down by the Germans, though no AFC aircraft suffered this fate. On several further occasions, the higher performance German aircraft drove their British counterparts off, inflicting gunshot and shrapnel wounds on several British and Australian aircrews. However, at other times the numerical superiority of No 1 Squadron AFC and No 14 Squadron RFC was able to halt German aerial forays over Allied positions.

At face value, such activity seemed to yield inconclusive results. This was not the full story. By the end of August, FA300 could only muster one or two serviceable aircraft at a time, and its fuel supplies were almost exhausted. The German logistics lines were so strained that supplies of replacement aircraft and spare crews could not keep up with demand. On the other hand, while Salmond's force was equally rundown, the establishment of a higher air component headquarters—even if only in name in late 1916—was a step forward in the command and control arrangements for the RFC in Egypt. When the lessons of Romani were tabulated by the British, the tactical and operational liaison processes were further refined between air and ground elements so that by the end of the year, integrated air power was intrinsic to the wider EEF. Equally, the presence of a nearby flying school was beginning to yield results; a steady production of aircrew and proficiently trained technical specialists were able to bolster No 5 Wing's ranks to satisfy demand. The only matter that required serious redress was the issue of obtaining quality aircraft, with Salmond addressing this as best he could. It would not be fully resolved for another year but, thankfully for No 5 Wing, air operations over the Sinai for the remainder of 1916 were reduced as the both sides regrouped. Even so, there was a significant amount of photographic work conducted during the second half of 1916. The Australian *Official History* does highlight No 1 Squadron's bombing activities in October and November, including No 1 Squadron's raid on FA300 at Beersheba on 11 November which delivered significant damage to the German unit and killed dozens of men. However, the final months of 1916 remained a relatively quiet period for the air services of both sides in Palestine.

Perhaps the most significant event that occurred during late 1916 was the first occasion in which an Australian airman forced down an adversary in air-to-air combat. Flying a Martinsyde G100 Elephant fitted with a wing-mounted Lewis gun firing over the propeller arc, Lieutenant Stanley Muir was engaged in a bombing operation near Beersheba on 22 December. His formation was attacked by a German two-seater Aviatik and a Fokker Eindekker during their transit home, and air-to-air combat ensued. While the Aviatik was more capable than the Rumpler, it was driven off by the combined fire power of several other Martinsydes. Muir got into a turning fight with the smaller Eindekker, several of which FA300 had procured now that they were considered obsolete for use on the Western Front. It was here that the Martinsyde's solid construction and forward-firing weapon came to the fore. Muir scored several hits on the light German aircraft, and it was seen to force land in the desert below. This was perhaps a portent. On the same day, after a decisive defeat at Magdhaba, Turkish forces withdrew completely from the Sinai Peninsula, and Salmond's squadrons moved into new lodgings recently occupied by their German adversaries. For No 1 Squadron, this involved relocation to El Arish on the northern Sinai coastline.

While Turkish forays across the Sinai were unsuccessful, and the casualties slight—in comparison to the carnage on the Somme and at Verdun—by late 1916 the Ottoman Empire was reeling. Internally, nomadic Bedouin Arabs from the region that today comprises parts of Saudi Arabia, Jordan and Syria had revolted against their Ottoman rulers. Britain saw the opportunity and quickly supplied them arms and military advisers—most notable among these was

Colonel T.E. Lawrence, also referred to as 'Lawrence of Arabia'—to aid in the insurrection. The results were promising, and the Turkish Army was soon bogged down in an ugly counterinsurgency. British officials in Egypt continually encouraged the main Arab protagonist, the Hashemite Sherif Hussein of Mecca, to press home his advantage against the Turks. His son Feisal, aided by Lawrence, launched guerrilla attacks along the Hijaz railway into Palestine itself.

Meanwhile, in Mesopotamia a new commander, General Sir Stanley Frederick Maude, assembled a new force of 150 000 men, now equipped with more modern weapons. Basra, still in British hands, was transformed into a modern port. A railway and metal road were constructed, and river transportation on the Tigris was dramatically expanded. In Egypt too, Murray now had the resources to go on the offensive, and the EEF's mission evolved from Britain's defence of Egypt and the Suez to an invasion of Ottoman-occupied Palestine. British and Dominion troops would link into the Arab insurrection to defeat the Ottoman Turks. Immediately, the sandstorms and searing temperature of the Sinai Desert had to be crossed. This would be the utmost test of endurance as well as of engineering for the British and Dominion men involved. Access to water dictated what could be achieved. Tens of thousands of pack animals, camels and drivers were required to supply the army. A water pipe and a railway were extended to Rafa on the border of Egypt and Palestine.

With these developments, in early 1917 Britain seemed on the verge of knocking Turkey out of the war. Salmond's No 5 Wing was charged with bombing and reconnaissance duties during the first months of 1917 to cover the Turkish forces, while the EEF prepared to attack Palestine. No 5 Wing's activity was conducted so well that, despite the superiority of the aircraft of FA300, the Germans were forced to withdraw from Beersheba and to relocate to Ramleh during late February. On 11 March, Maude's forces captured Baghdad. Two weeks later, Murray's troops drove into Palestine and attacked Gaza with infantry and cavalry. The attack failed primarily because Murray withdrew when victory was within his grasp. Murray did not report this, but instead sent a misleading communiqué to the War Office which hinted at greater successes than what the EEF had achieved. Because of this misleading report, London ordered another attempt to capture the coastal town, though Murray procrastinated for several weeks. When he eventually attacked again in what would be the Second Battle of Gaza

(17—19 April 1917), a frontal assault with inadequate artillery support proved a disaster.

Observers: The developing importance of non-pilot officer aircrew

AFC Observer Badge (source: AWM REL/12793)

During World War I, as the size, complexity and capability of aircraft rapidly increased, so too did the variety of newly emerging air power roles that could be carried out. The potential of aircraft in warfare seemed to grow exponentially over the four years of war and encompassed roles including reconnaissance and scouting, artillery spotting, air combat, strafing and bombing, air lift, and anti-shipping operations. The full potential of aircraft performing these roles could only be realised by training a large number of non-pilot aircrew specialists.

Observers played a significant role in the application of air power from the earliest days of the conflict. By the standards of today observer training was quite rudimentary during the first year of the war, often performed 'on the job'. It was not until June 1915 that the War Office had the RFC Flying Training Manual updated to standardise the elementary duties required of observers in a flying squadron:

> *Observation from aeroplanes can be carried out by the pilot single-handed, but as undivided attention is necessary for observing, it is usually advantageous to carry a passenger who is free to devote his whole attention to this task. The observer requires air-experience and special training. He should have good eyesight and possess sufficient military knowledge to enable him to recognise units of all arms in their various formations, and to be able to discern the most probable places in which to search for them. He should be able to read the Morse Code.*

In the same month, the RFC defined the qualifications required of observers more succinctly:

> *a. Know the Lewis gun thoroughly*
> *b. Use the RFC camera successfully*
> *c. Can send and receive by wireless at six words/minute.*
> *d. Knows the method of artillery/aeroplane cooperation thoroughly.*

e. Has conducted two reconnaissances or ranged batteries successfully twice.

No 1 Squadron AFC and No 14 Squadron had supported the attacks continuously over the several weeks, bombing and reconnoitring Turkish positions. During this time, several aircraft were lost to ground fire while others were forced down in the desert due to mechanical difficulties. A particularly eventful day was 19 March, when a No 14 Squadron Martinsyde was shot down by ground fire. A No 1 Squadron B.E.2c, crewed by pilot Lieutenant Reg Ballieu and observer Lieutenant Ross Smith, landed nearby to pick up their downed colleague. The British airman, Lieutenant Kirby, burned himself setting his aircraft on fire to prevent its capture and was helped onto the wing by Smith, while Baillieu engaged the advancing Turks with the aircraft's Lewis gun. All three made it back to the No 1 Squadron airfield safely. For this, both Australian aviators were awarded the Military Cross. Later the same day the action resulting in the only Victoria Cross (VC) awarded to an Australian aviator during the war occurred when a wounded Lieutenant Frank McNamara rescued Captain Douglas Rutherford after he was forced down behind enemy lines.

The next day, No 1 Squadron AFC lost a Martinsyde aircraft to ground fire with its twenty-one year old pilot, Lieutenant Norman Steele of Melbourne, dying of the wounds he had sustained when the aircraft was shot down. On 21 March, Lieutenant Adrian Cole was forced down by anti-aircraft fire while on a reconnaissance mission. He was rescued by Captain Richard Williams who was flying as his escort. Then, on 27 March, Rutherford's luck ran out. His B.E.2c was intercepted by a German two-seater near Gaza and forced down. Both he and his observer, Lieutenant William Hyam, were wounded and subsequently captured. Hyam died of his wounds on 30 March 1916. On the day Rutherford was captured, No 1 Squadron mechanic Joe Bull wrote in his diary:

> The RFC [14 and 17 SQNs] have been most unfortunate, having lost seven machines in the last three days. They have only three serviceable machines left. Our 15 machines [No 1 Squadron] have been bombing and assisting artillery all day. The enemy airmen are German and have the very latest aircraft which we have not got. The 'Heads' do not seem to think that they are needed on this front; however, we have quantity and have the best end of the stick every time.

Joe Bull's views are relevant on several levels. His notion of quantity and the rate of effort of the Empire air elements indicate that Salmond's organisational efforts were reaching all levels of his command. Bull was also correct in indicating that the British forces were numerically superior. This would remain the case in Palestine for the remainder of the war and, by the end of 1917, the quality of British machines equalled that of the German types. Finally, Bull's indication of the Germans having the 'latest aircraft' highlighted that by the beginning of summer 1917, FA300 was beginning to receive small numbers of new aircraft—Halberstadts were arriving in Mesopotamia and Albatros fighters in Palestine. Both types far exceeded the capabilities of Salmond's aircraft in mid-1917, each armed with two Spandau machine guns. The Albatros D.III in particular was a first-rate aircraft at the time.

The superiority of German aircraft in Palestine in 1916

The members of FA300 were incensed with No 1 Squadron's raid on their airfield on 11 November 1916, and immediately planned a retaliatory raid. The response was significant enough that its psychological effects were noted in Cutlack's Australian *Official History* of the campaign. The raid, which took place on 13 November, involved an FA300 Rumpler fitted with a larger fuel tank, twelve 4.5 kg bombs, and a camera. The aircraft left Beersheba at 6.30am in the morning and flew to FA300's airfield at El Arish to refuel. Departing El Arish at 7.30am it flew across the northern Sinai climbing to 10 000 ft (3000 m). The crew crossed the Suez Canal near Ismailia at 10.30am and turned south towards Cairo. When they reached the Cairo suburb of Heliopolis, they set course for the Cairo central railway station and, there, released their bombs. The Rumpler was then flown to the pyramids of Giza where it circled to take images of the famous landmarks before flying off. After another refuelling stop at El Arish, the aircraft recovered to Beersheba at 4pm. This magnificent feat of flying covered more than 500 miles over enemy territory. A British report indicated that while sixteen people were killed in the bombing, the damage was slight. The psychological impact was sufficient that the British aircraft were withdrawn from the frontline to defend the city against the potential of future German attacks.

An image of the Pyramids of Giza taken from a German aircraft during a raid on Cairo, 13 November 1916 (source: AWM P00588.014)

Lieutenant Frank McNamara VC

An artist's depiction of the feat for which Frank McNamara received the Victoria Cross. He and Rutherford make their getaway leaving their pursuers behind, while smoke rises in the background from McNamara's wrecked Martinsyde. (The incident for which Lieutenant F H. McNamara was awarded the VC, by Septimus Power, oil on canvas, 1924 (source: AWM ART08007)

On 20 March 1917, a No 1 Squadron Martinsyde aircraft flown by Lieutenant Frank McNamara was engaged in attacking the Turkish railway lines near Gaza, along with his colleague, fellow No 1 Squadron pilot Captain Douglas Rutherford, flying a B.E.2c. After dropping his ordnance, Rutherford's aircraft was hit and could not develop sufficient power to climb away. Rutherford was forced to land under the observation of the Turkish ground forces. Following close behind, McNamara pressed home the attack, despite being wounded in the left leg when a piece of shrapnel from one of Rutherford's bombs tore into his aircraft. Although faint from the loss of blood, McNamara observed Rutherford to be alive on the ground, with Turkish cavalry approaching his machine. Undaunted, McNamara landed his aircraft beside Rutherford as the Turks continued to approach and picked his fellow aviator up. By this point, McNamara did not have enough strength left in his leg to control the Martinsyde during take-off, and the aircraft crashed as it gathered speed.

With his propeller broken, McNamara's aircraft was now unserviceable. After climbing out and then setting the Martinsyde alight, McNamara and Rutherford proceeded back to Rutherford's damaged B.E.2c. With Rutherford swinging the propeller, McNamara took the aircraft's controls while under Turkish fire. McNamara managed to get the B.E.2c airborne and proceeded to fly the aircraft seventy miles (110 kilometres) back to friendly territory before landing and promptly passing out. For his audacious acts of bravery, McNamara was awarded the only Victoria Cross awarded to an Australian airman during World War I.

Lieutenant Reg Baillieu MC, No 1 Squadron AFC (source: AWM P00588.011)

By the end of May 1917, Murray was replaced, having failed to take Gaza. He had been viewed within his command as something of a 'ditherer', and his locating of his headquarters (HQ) in Cairo, hundreds of miles from the fighting, did little to endear him to his men. Concurrently, No 1 Squadron's Commanding Officer, Major Foster Rutledge, was posted to England on training duties, with one of the squadron's flight commanders, Richard Williams, assuming command on promotion to major. Williams' view of Murray was typically succinct:

> We had never seen [Murray]. The only time we were aware of his presence when we had to provide a patrol over his special train. I must say that I thought this was a foolish idea. It not only wasted many engine hours, but we thought it would draw attention to the train ... Allenby stopped all that.

General Sir Edmund Allenby arrived on 27 June to command the EEF, and he immediately began to strengthen his forces. He built an army comprising two corps of infantry (the British XX and XXI Corps), a mounted corps (under Australian Lieutenant General Sir Harry Chauvel), and Salmond's air service. His plan was to conduct a new type of war in the Middle East based on lessons stemming from the Somme on the Western Front. A new combined arms doctrine comprising synchronised arms, including aircraft, would form the basis of this new approach. It was a sound decision. Allenby had recent operational experience on the Western Front, and he was a great advocate of technology, particularly air power. It took some weeks during August and September to build his forces, after which he tasked the EEF to take Gaza as a prelude to capturing Jerusalem by the end of 1917. The Official Historian of Australian operations in the Middle East during the war, Henry Gullet, indicated that Allenby's transformation of the force was immediate. 'What had hitherto been a rather casual military adventure with no definite goal,' he wrote, 'was suddenly converted into a stern, clear-cut campaign with nothing short of the complete destruction of the Turkish force in Palestine and the capture of Jerusalem as its immediate objective.' Williams wrote that Allenby was a bit of a whirlwind. The first thing he did was to move his HQ to the front where the fighting was taking place. He visited every unit in his command, including No 1 Squadron, and Williams noted that he was a big man who had the appearance of a commander who inspired confidence at once.

Lieutenant Frank McNamara, No 1 Squadron AFC, convalescing after the action for which he was awarded the Victoria Cross over Gaza. (source: AWM P01034.080)

This change in command was timely. Salmond's No 5 Wing had continued operations throughout May and June, and FA300—now augmented by several more Albatros D.III fighters—held the upper hand when they engaged British and Australian aircraft. For their part, No 1 Squadron AFC and No 14 Squadron had the use of the B.E.12 fighter-bomber. This was essentially a single-seat version of the B.E.2c; the Albatros was nearly thirty knots faster, better armed and more manoeuvrable. No 14 Squadron had also received a few de Havilland 2 (D.H.2) 'pusher' fighters, which were considered obsolete on the Western Front. Both the B.E.12 and

D.H.2 were completely outclassed by the German aircraft. Even the robust Martinsyde Elephant was not immune to the German supremacy. On 6 April 1917, No 1 Squadron pilot Alan Murray-Jones was forced down while escorting a bombing raid in his Martinsyde by Oberleutnant Gerhard Felmy and his observer, Oberleutnant Richard Falke. Murray-Jones had fought off five German machines while the bombers got away. He managed to land in friendly territory, though his aircraft was then bombed and strafed by the Germans and badly damaged. It was subsequently recovered by Australian ground crews. Joe Bull was Murray-Jones' rigger and wrote on 8 April:

> *I am working on Captain Jones' Martinsyde in which he was driven down by five Huns. She is very badly hit and in so many places that she will have to be practically rebuilt. The pilot never even got a scratch.*

Murray-Jones was soon flying again. In several subsequent bombing operations, he descended to below 500 feet to deliver his ordnance. Then, on 16 May, Murray-Jones was again intercepted by Oberleutnant Felmy who this time was flying an Albatros. In a completely one-sided contest, the Australian was wounded and forced down. Murray-Jones was evacuated to hospital in Cairo where, while convalescing, he was awarded the

MC for his work throughout the preceding month.

In June 1917, RFC and AFC aircraft were intercepted several more times by Albatros fighters. A No 14 Squadron Martinsyde was lost, and its pilot captured. This was followed by an Australian B.E.12 also shot down. Its pilot was an AFC officer who had been born in the United Kingdom, Lieutenant Jack Stanley Brassell. Brassell had flown with No 14 Squadron for several months before posting to No 1 Squadron on 15 May 1917. On 25 June, Brassell was severely wounded in the head in an uneven exchange with Leutnant Franz Schleiff flying a Rumpler two-seater—Schleiff was a German ace with twenty-one aerial victories. Despite his wounds, Brassell landed his aircraft safely behind Turkish lines, but died shortly afterwards. FA300 struck again on 8 July when another Martinsyde broke up in combat with a German two-seater, with the Martinsyde's pilot, Captain Charles Brooks, RFC, killed when his wings collapsed. During the same operation, Oberleutnant Felmy added another B.E.12 to his tally when he shot down Lieutenant Claude Vautin. On 13 July, two more No 1 Squadron B.E.2s were lost to Albatros fighters with one crew killed.

Williams had had enough of these losses. He petitioned Salmond quietly and forthrightly:

'Pointing out', he later wrote, 'that unless we received aircraft with which we could meet the Hun on much more favourable terms, the morale of the squadron must crack.' Williams was well aware of the necessity for these No 5 Wing operations. Nevertheless, Williams's probity and the way in which he appealed to Salmond withstands the most rigorous of inspections. Williams sought not to stop No 1 Squadron from flying; he was most concerned that it continued to fulfil its obligations. In order to do so effectively, Williams knew that his squadron needed the latest equipment. In this, his display of moral courage stands the test of time.

Lesson # 5

- Integrity and the moral courage to respectfully communicate with one's chain of command-irrespective of rank—are timeless values.
- Keeping air power at a level that offers an effective and credible capability edge over adversaries requires an air service to consistently invest in quality technology and training.

Oberleutnant Gerhardt Felmy poses with Lieutenant C.H. Vautin of No 1 Squadron AFC. Vautin had been taken prisoner, having crash-landed on 8 July 1917. Two days later Felmy dropped this photo over Vautin's home aerodrome to prove the Australian was all right. A member of No 1 Squadron then flew over Felmy's aerodrome to drop Vautin's clothes, kit, and some letters from home. (source: AWM P02097.002)

Allenby had listened to the officers within the EEF's air component, and he petitioned the War Office for more modern aircraft. These duly began to arrive, and the air service expanded. Williams wrote that, in particular, the arrival of the Bristol Fighter into theatre had a profound effect on RFC morale and an equally deleterious effect on the German psyche. In fact, despite British losses, the German aviators had never been keen to attack RFC or AFC machines that were escorted by fighter or scouting aircraft. The lack of a robust German logistics infrastructure ensured that FA300 was constantly husbanding its resources and equipment. With the arrival of aircraft of equal performance, the Germans were now on the back foot.

On 8 October 1917, a Bristol Fighter was engaged by an Albatros D.III. The German aircraft was forced down and captured. The event highlighted several matters. First, it heralded the end of German air superiority in the theatre; second, it was a display of the cosmopolitan nature of the British Empire air force. A Canadian pilot, Lieutenant Robert Steele, with English observer, Lieutenant R. Sutherland, flying an aircraft in No 111 Squadron RFC shot down a German aircraft, with its pilot then captured by a member of the Australian Light Horse. The light horsemen subsequently handed the aircraft and pilot, Oberleutnant Gustav Dittmar, over to No 1 Squadron AFC. From there, Williams personally flew the German airman to Wing Headquarters in an R.E.8 two-seater aircraft.

A Worthy Foe: Oberleutnant Gerhard Felmy of FA300

During his tenure as CO No 1 Squadron AFC, Sir Richard Williams recorded that the most formidable aviator opposing his squadron was the young German pilot, Gerhard Felmy. Felmy had *'enterprise'*, Williams would record; though he tempered this with the notion that German endeavours were limited to operations on their own side of the lines, and then in machines that were, at the time, vastly superior to British aircraft. Even so, among the British and Australian airmen, Felmy was considered *Public Enemy No 1*. A newly arrived Australian observer and decorated light horseman, Leslie Sutherland, wrote that Felmy was colloquially considered:

> *...a crackerjack pilot and a splendid shot. The Albatros that he flew was nearly twice as fast as the B.E.2c, and as manoeuvrable as any aircraft then in production. In our innermost thoughts we new chums hoped he would have an early death—a very early death. He did not.*

In any event, Felmy was viewed with equal parts of courtesy and disdain among the British and Australian crews—a worthy opponent and chivalrous knight of the air. When he brought down Australian Lieutenant Claude Vautin on 8 July 1917, Felmy courteously had a letter dropped over the AFC pilot's home aerodrome indicating that Vautin was alive and well, requesting that some of the Australian officer's kit could be delivered by return flight. Felmy included in the air drop an image of himself with Vautin and gave news of the fate of several other British and Australian airmen that had been brought down by FA300. He mentioned Murray-Jones in particular as a courageous man, and on the strength of this, Williams allowed Murray-Jones to fly Vautin's kit to the German airfield. Such was the spirit of chivalry—at least superficially—between the opposing squadrons that Murray-Jones duly made the flight without incident and without an enemy shot fired at him.

Flying in the Middle East, Felmy was not as well-known as the German protagonists on the Western Front. Given the environment, his tally did not approach the dozens of 'kills' that other German fighter pilots scored in the European theatre, though it appears that his personality and panache were on a par with his colleagues. He was known to and well regarded by the first generation of Australian military aviators, and his biography is worthy of note. In particular, Felmy's time as a professional military aviator and later career as a police officer span perhaps the most difficult decades of modern Germany's existence. Born in Berlin in 1891, Gerhard Felmy commenced his compulsory military service on 22 March 1909 when he joined the 'von der Marwitz' (8th Pomeranian) No 61 Infantry Regiment of the Prussian Army. He was promoted to leutnant on 22 August 1910. His period of service concluded on 2 August 1914, the same day that Britain formerly delivered an ultimatum to Germany to leave neutral Belgium or face war with the British Empire.

Felmy departed the infantry and immediately entered a civilian flying school in the German city of Nieder Neundorf, where he spent the next five months learning to fly. He voluntarily re-entered military service on 1 March 1915 and was posted to FA300 in September 1916. The squadron was commanded by his older brother, Hauptman Helmuth Felmy. The elder Felmy would continue to serve as a military aviator in Hitler's Luftwaffe in World War II as a General Officer, and in 1946 was imprisoned for war crimes committed during the war.

Gerhard Felmy had an eventful nine months with FA300, flying every single-and two-seater type of aircraft allocated to the squadron until he was permanently assigned one of FA300's precious Albatros fighters because of his flying skills. In August 1917, Felmy was forced to return to Germany to recuperate from a particularly severe bout of malaria. It was noted that with his departure, FA300's luck ran out too. This period coincided with the arrival of equal, if not superior, British aircraft. By October 1917, with the impending Third Battle of Gaza, the German ascendency in the skies over the Palestine was forever lost. Gerhard Felmy briefly returned to Palestine to command FA300 in January 1918 but was again repatriated to Germany in April with recurring malaria. He finished the war still convalescing. Felmy recorded several victories (sources vary—certainly less than five) during his service in Palestine, and several more probable kills. He was awarded the Iron Cross First and Second Class on 31 May 1917, and later received the Knight's Cross of the Royal House Order of Hohenzollern with swords. He retired from military service on 17 April 1919, joining the German police force and serving the majority of the next twenty-five years in the German state of Mecklenburg. He was promoted Lieutenant General of Police in 1945 just before the war in Europe finished.

After his second war, Gerhard Felmy retired to the city of Frankfurt where he lived until passing away on 8 December 1955.

Group portrait of German aviators of FA300 in various forms of tropical and other uniform, some pre-colonial. The photograph was dropped on the No 1 Squadron AFC aerodrome as a compliment by Oberleutnant Gerhardt Felmy who communicated with members of the AFC in late July 1917 following the capture of Lieutenant C.H. Vautin AFC. (source: AWM P02097.001)

Albatros D.III (Oef) series 153

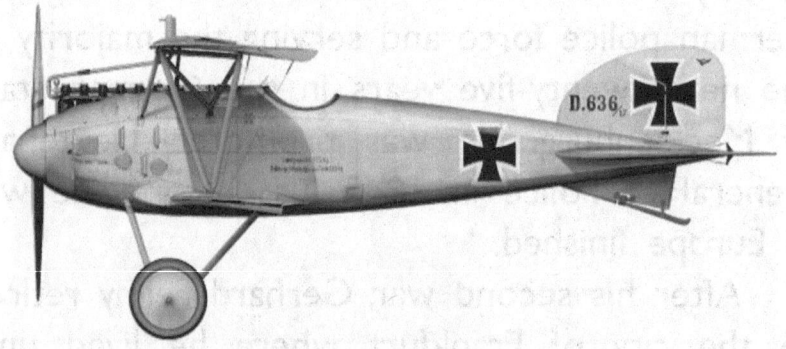

Artwork by Juanita Franzi

Specifications	
Wingspan: (upper wing)	29 ft 6 in (9 m)
Length:	24 ft 1 in (7.35 m)
Height:	9 ft 2 in (2.8 m)
Max weight:	2176 lb (987 kg)
Empty weight:	1565 lb (710 kg)
Max speed:	102 kts (188 km/h)
Crew:	One
Armament:	Two Maschinengewehr 08 (MG 08) 7.92mm synchronised machine guns
Primary powerplant:	One Mercedes D.IIIa 175 hp. 6-cylinder water-cooled, in-line piston engine
Production:	286

The Albatros D.III

The Albatros D.III was third in a series of new fighter aircraft entering the German Air Service over the period from late 1916 to early 1917. A sesquiplane biplane (the lower wings were shorter than the upper) the designers overcame early deficiencies in the aircraft by incorporating a 'V' strut between the wings. The new aircraft immediately proved to be one of the most manoeuvrable and capable fighters in the world at the time. Power was provided by a Mercedes D.IIIa series engine which was progressively uprated from 170 horsepower to 175 during production. The aircraft was armed with twin 7.92mm Spandau LMG 08/15 machine guns synchronised to fire through the spinning propeller blades. A semi-monocoque construction, in the right hands during 1917 the Albatros was a world class aircraft that was virtually unbeatable.

While Williams's Australians had also hoped for Bristol Fighters—and they would duly receive them in 1918—for the moment No 1 Squadron only received several R.E.8s to supplement their B.E.2s. The R.E.8 was a large aircraft used extensively for light bombing, reconnaissance and spotting on the Western Front. Although it had an ungainly appearance, it was well-armed with a synchronised Vickers gun and a Scarff Ring mounted Lewis gun for the observer. It was not fast—though it was quicker than the B.E.2—but this was made up for with its robust construction and endurance. The R.E.8 was well-suited to strategical reconnaissance, and when it was escorted by the Bristol Fighter, the two aircraft made a formidable combination. These aircraft signalled the advent of increasing RFC ascendency in Palestine, and a growing EEF confidence in the capabilities of air power.

A German Air Force DIII Albatros Scout aircraft, D636/17, flown by Oberleutnant Gustav Adolf Dittmar of Fliegerabteilung 300 squadron. The aircraft had been shot down, practically intact, into AIF Light Horse lines near

Beersheba by a Bristol fighter aircraft flown by Lieutenant R Steele a Canadian pilot with No 111 Squadron, Royal Flying Corps. No 1 Squadron, Australian Flying Corps, members recovered the machine and moved it to their airfield where repairs, including a bullet holed radiator, were carried out returning it to flying condition. The aircraft is at the aerodrome at Sheikh Nuran. (source: AWM A04141)

During the Third Battle of Gaza, Allenby intended to fight a war of manoeuvre that had been denied through the extensive trench warfare on the Western Front. The approaches into the Bible lands from the southwest had wide and relatively flat expanses of territory for an army to operate on, and this was superbly suited for the use of new mechanical weapons such as armoured cars, mechanised artillery, tanks and aircraft. This technology was the key to cracking the extensive twenty-seven miles (forty-three kilometres) of Turkish trench systems that stretched from Gaza on the coast inland to Beersheba. Beersheba was, in fact, central to the plan. The freshwater wells in the small township were a vital operational consideration in the harsh desert climate, and their capture would provide a vital staging post for further advance.

In the lead up to the attack on Gaza, over 300 hours of artillery observation flights were flown in October, while 894 negatives were exposed, and 21 126 prints developed. These formed a comprehensive battlespace picture from which Allenby's staff could prosecute combat against the Turks. Both Official Histories of the air services (Jones' Volume V of *The War in the Air* and Cutlack's Volume VIII of the *Australian Official History*) make it clear that the AFC and RFC were heavily engaged in bombing Turkish targets and in reconnaissance and artillery spotting duties leading up to and during the Third Battle of Gaza. Both official histories also point to the lack of German air opposition. There were seven encounters with German aircraft in the four days from 28 to 31 October 1917 and, in every case, the German pilots retreated. This was despite the German air service being reinforced with several more squadrons during October 1917—FA300 was joined by FA301, FA302, FA303 and FA304b, and the Turkish No 14 Squadron. With these squadrons, there were about forty German aircraft in Palestine by the Third Battle of Gaza. The RFC had approximately double this number. Like the British and Australians, the German units operated a variety of types, many of which—again like the RFC—were no longer suitable for operational use on the Western Front. Among the German aircraft now were the AEG C.IV, which had a steel-framed construction suited to desert operations; the Albatros D.III single-seat fighter; supplementing the ubiquitous Rumpler C.I—used mainly for reconnaissance. Eight new Rumplers C. IVs were later delivered to Palestine in the spring of 1918.

On 27 October 1917 the Palestine Brigade was established. It comprised:

5 (Corps) Wing

No 14 Squadron (sixteen B.E.2e) at Deir el Balah

No 113 Squadron (eight B.E.2e and five R.E.8) at Weli Sheikh Nuran

40 (Army) Wing

No 111 Squadron (six Bristol F.2b, five Vickers Bullet, three D.H.2, two Bristol M.1 and one Bristol Scout) at Deir el Balah

No 1 Squadron AFC (seven B.E.2c/2e, five R.E.8, five B.E.12a and one Martinsyde) at Weli Sheikh Nuran.

A temporary bombing unit, called 'X' Squadron out of No 14 Squadron to work with Lawrence, arrived at Weli Sheikh Nuran on 30 October. The Brigade also had a Kite Balloon Company and an Aircraft Park. Generally, a Corps Wing squadron was engaged in direct army co-operation duties, such as artillery observation, reconnaissance, and contact patrols; while Army Wing squadrons (No 111 Squadron and No 1 Squadron AFC) were used for air combat and strategic reconnaissance over the entire front. For their part, No 14 Squadron was allocated to the XXI Corps Front, and No 113 Squadron to XX Corps and the Desert Mounted Corps. The Army Wing aircraft flew escort missions and No 1 Squadron also conducted bombing beyond the forward edge of troops, aerial photography and long-range reconnaissance. The system worked well. For example, on 31 October, five Turkish gun batteries were spotted from the air and were put out of action by British artillery assisted by air observation.

On the same day that the Palestine Brigade was formed on 5 October 1917, Allenby commenced operations against the Turkish defensive line. He bombarded the coastal town of Gaza with artillery and naval gunfire; this was a ruse that convinced the Turks that the attack would come against Gaza as twice before. Concurrently, he ordered his Desert Mounted and XX Corps to attack Beersheba. Both formations advanced strongly against the township over the ensuing several days; the Australian Light Horse and New Zealand Mounted Rifles manoeuvred to the northeast of the town to outflank and confuse the Turkish defenders. Then, on 31 October, the 4th Australian Light Horse Regiment, on the direction of Australian Major General Harry Chauvel, took Beersheba in a daring charge across the open plains to the east of the town. Cutlack wrote that the Turks were thrown out of Beersheba in great disorder, leaving 2000 prisoners and thirteen guns; over 500 of their dead were buried on the field of battle. With Beersheba taken, Gaza was now open to attack from the south-east and south-west. RFC and RNAS spotting immediately assisted the preparatory artillery bombardments against the Turkish defences. The Palestine Brigade's headquarters then ordered coordinated attacks across the range of Turkish positions and German flying units.

An Aerial mosaic compilation taken of the Turkish held town of Beersheba. (Source: Sutherland Collection, via History and Heritage Branch—Air Force)

Williams himself bombed Gaza in a B.E.12 on 1 November as the EEF advanced on the township. By 6 November, it was nearly surrounded, and the beleaguered Turks were under constant shellfire and air attack. Their every movement was observed and reported by RFC aircraft to Allenby's staff, and British divisions advanced to cut their adversaries off. Where the Turks had withdrawn from Beersheba to the north and north-east, there too they were harassed by Chauvel's mounted columns and under constant air attack. Late on 6 November, the Turkish defences at Gaza cracked, and the defenders commenced an uncoordinated retreat across the plains towards Jerusalem. The Palestine Brigade attacked the Turks at Mejdel as they retreated along the coast. Over thirty aircraft were involved—including from No 1 Squadron—and the raid prevented the Turks from organising any sort of coordinated defence. What is significant in this air activity is that only once from late October through to the end of the first week of November did the Germans manage to intercept British or Australian aircraft—that occurred late on 6 November and then without any Allied loss. While the retreating Turks were under attack from elements of the air brigade, other elements of Allied air power were raiding the German airfields to stop them from getting airborne to intercept the bombers.

During the second week in November, the RFC and AFC divided their attention between raids against the retreating Turks and the German airfields. During these raids, hangars, support facilities and aircraft on the ground were destroyed, significantly degrading the German ability to mount any form of air defence. Then, as the EEF ground forces advanced, the Germans were forced to retreat from several airfields with further losses in men and aircraft. By the middle of the month, under this relentless attack, the *Flieger Abteilung* were almost ineffective and the Turks were in headlong retreat. Allenby made good use of his infantry and large mounted force in the pursuit across the Judean hills towards Jerusalem. On 16 November, the New Zealand Mounted Rifles captured the Jaffa Gate, the historic entry to a holy city from the Mediterranean coast. By the end of the month, the Turks had withdrawn from Jerusalem, leaving it open to occupation by the EEF.

Many of Allenby's soldiers were deeply conscious that they were fighting on sacred soil—some viewed themselves as modern-day crusaders—but Allenby was acutely aware of Islamic and Jewish sensitivities. Accordingly, when he entered Jerusalem on 11 December 1917, he did so with respect—on foot and with his hat off. Allenby's masters were equally aware of the delicate nature of the political landscape in which the EEF was serving, and the British Government publicly declared that the Jewish peoples of the region would be given autonomy in their traditional homeland at some point after the war. Whether or not this declaration was made of altruism or with British interests in mind—or both—the fact remains that along with the Sykes-Picot agreement, the British announcement has profoundly shaped the Middle East Region in the hundred years since.

Given its contributions to the Gaza campaign, the role of the RFC in the EEF was now expanded to encompass the full spectrum of the war in the Middle East, from the tactical to strategic levels. Salmond, having earlier departed for Europe, now returned to the EEF and was promoted Major General to command all air operations in the theatre. Every nascent role that his aircrews could envisage of air power would be utilised to establish air superiority for the advancing EEF. He furnished the squadrons of No 40 Wing with new and superior platforms: No 111 Squadron received the Royal Aircraft Factory Scouting Experimental 5 (S.E.5a) and, much to its relief, No 1 Squadron AFC was refitted with the superlative Bristol Fighter while keeping several of its existing aircraft for photographic and general duties. Williams wrote that for the first time after seventeen months in the field, his squadron had aircraft with which it could deal with the enemy in the air. Air power would enable the EEF to prepare and conduct its campaign against the Turks across the plains of Armageddon. It would also give Allenby's forces an absolute perspective of the battlespace; the speed and reach to strike the Turks where and when they least expected it; the flexibility to re-role aircraft and operate under a centralised command structure but with decentralised execution; and the precision and payload to engage and defeat the retreating Ottoman forces to the point of annihilation. This was the genesis of modern air power. Similar activity was occurring in Europe, but it was to be in Palestine where air power would for the first time prove to be the decisive factor for victory in war.

Lesson # 6

- Military power and National Power (of which political diplomacy comprises an element) are interdependent.
- Applying military power arbitrarily without thought for social, cultural or political circumstance will surely result in long-term failure.
- Equally, political or diplomatic assurances given without the balancing effects of the other elements of National Power (including military power) are also likely to have long term deleterious consequences.

The lasting consequences of the Balfour Declaration

The Balfour Declaration was a public pledge by Britain in 1917 declaring its aim to establish 'a national home for the Jewish people' in Palestine. The declaration was given in an open letter from Britain's then-foreign secretary, Arthur Balfour, to Lionel Walter Rothschild, a doyen in the British Jewish community. Balfour proposed that Palestine be administered under a British mandate until it and the other newly emerging states in the region could become independent. The case of Palestine was unique. Unlike other states in the post-Ottoman mandates, the British Mandate for Palestine was to establish a Jewish homeland, where Jews comprised only one tenth of the population at the time. The question of why the Balfour Declaration was issued has been a subject of debate for a century. Some historians argue that many in the British Government at the time were Zionists themselves. Others suggest the contrary that the declaration was anti-Semitic—giving Palestine to the Jews would solve the 'Jewish problem'. Like most matters, the truth is probably somewhere between the extremes. Four factors most likely influenced British decision making:

1. Control over Palestine was a strategic Imperial interest to keep Egypt and the Suez Canal within Britain's sphere of influence.
2. Britain sought to rally support among Jews in the United States and Russia, hoping they could encourage their governments to stay in the war until victory.
3. There were strong connections between the Zionist community in Britain and the British Government.
4. Jews were being persecuted and the British Government was sympathetic to their suffering.

Understandably, the Arabic peoples of the region showed much animosity towards the decisions dictated by the Balfour Declaration, and resisted any attempt to create a Jewish state. Their efforts were to no avail, and Israel came into being as a nation when Britain relinquished its mandate in 1948. Jewish peoples from the world over flooded into their traditional 'homeland', while hundreds of thousands of Arabic residents were displaced. In the ensuing seventy years, simmering and often explosive tensions have never been resolved. While violence in Palestine today cannot be attributed to the Balfour Declaration, the British Mandate did create the preconditions for a minority to gain ascendancy in Palestine. There are strong arguments for independent Jewish and Palestinian states in the region, and equally for coexistence; unfortunately, Israeli-Palestinian violence continues to vex the international community.

Sir Richard Williams: Father of the Royal Australian Air Force

Major Richard Williams DSO Commanding Officer No 1 Squadron, AFC (source: AWM A04556)

A number of AFC officers gained experience as commanders of squadrons during the war and went on in later years to reach the highest positions in the RAAF. Sir Richard Williams is pre-eminent among them. Williams was born in 1890 in Moonta, South Australia, and received his schooling in the State's public education system. For several years he worked locally as a telegraphist's messenger, and then as a bank clerk. In 1911, Williams commissioned into the South Australian Infantry Regiment as a militia officer, the equivalent of the contemporary Army Reserves. He was soon offered a commission in the Permanent Military Forces and posted to Melbourne where he had opportunity to observe the nascent military air service.

Williams was fascinated with what he saw and submitted an application to train as a pilot. He was duly selected and appointed one of the original four students on the Central Flying School's first flying course in August 1914. He undertook an advanced flying course the following year. When the Half-Flight deployed to Mesopotamia, Williams fully expected to be among its number, but he was held in Australia to assist in raising the squadrons required to deploy with the AFC. He deployed with No 1 Squadron in 1916.

Williams was an original flight commander with the squadron and later became its commanding officer. He gained extensive experience of air operations in Sinai and Palestine, and after being promoted to lieutenant colonel in 1918, he was appointed officer commanding of the RAF's No 40 Wing. In addition to No 1 Squadron, Williams was now responsible for three operational squadrons of the RAF. He continued to lead his wing during the final battles of World War I, finishing the war in Palestine. Williams was twice mentioned in dispatches and awarded the Distinguished Service Order for acts of gallantry and leadership on operations. In 1919, he proceeded to London where he was engaged by the Air Ministry to discuss the requirements for an independent post-war air service in Australia. While on this secondment, Williams was awarded the OBE for his wartime service. On his return to Australia, he was posted to Victoria Barracks in Melbourne where he served as the air adviser to the joint Army-Navy Board.

Williams was an absolute advocate for an independent air service, and his ambitions were realised in the early 1920s. When the RAAF was formed in 1921, Williams was appointed to its senior position and for the next eighteen years played a crucial role in the development of this Service. This was a tenuous period in the RAAF's existence, and Williams worked tirelessly to maintain the independence of the RAAF. He overcame deep and internecine Service rivalries that threatened to disband the RAAF during the

1920s, and he remained committed to the air force's early development. The RAAF was fortunate that it had an officer of Williams's character in this role. He was a slender man; a teetotaller and he possessed a piercing gaze. His intellect was of the highest order, and he had an innate ability to focus on the task at hand, with a legendary attention to detail. Williams' views on air power were insightful and progressive. During the 1920s and 1930s, Williams's professional commitment was to the establishment, preservation and development of the RAAF.

Air Marshal Sir Richard Williams is rightly remembered as the 'Father of the Royal Australian Air Force'.

Bristol F2B Fighter

A coloured Paget Plate taken by celebrated war artist Frank Hurley depicting an observer, pilot, and Bristol Fighter F.2b aircraft of No 1 Squadron, AFC in 1918. The pilot (left) is Lieutenant Leonard Malcolm Sumner Potts and observer Lieutenant James Hamilton Traill. (source: AWM B01650)

Of the many aircraft designs from the genius of English aeronautical engineer, Frank Sowter Barnwell, the Bristol Fighter became the most successful. The aircraft originated in 1916 as the Bristol R.2A, designed to replace the RFC's B.E.2 series of reconnaissance platforms. However, when the R.2A airframe was coupled with the new 190 hp Rolls-Royce Falcon engine, Bristol came up with a world-class design. Fitted with a forward firing Vickers gun and rear mounted Lewis gun, the Bristol F.2a Fighter first flew in September 1916 and deliveries began in December of the same year. The first operational squadron to reequip with the Bristol Fighter was the RFC's No 48 Squadron, which deployed to France with eighteen of the aircraft in early 1917. The squadron commenced operations in March 1917 and operated their aircraft as they did other conventional two-seaters. The aircraft flew in a steady formation with the primary defensive armament being the observer's gun. Losses were heavy. However, when No 48 Squadron developed tactics to fly the Bristol Fighter in the same manner as a single-seat aircraft, the platform became an immediate success. Not content with its performance, Barnwell sought to improve the design and came up with the definitive Bristol F.2b, which had twin Lewis guns, a larger tail plane and a strengthened centre section.

It was the F.2b version that went on to serve with distinction, not just during World War I, but afterwards in the outposts of the Empire where it was used in air policing and equipping many of the fledgling Dominion services. The utility of the Bristol Fighter—or 'Brisfit' as it was often called—made it capable of performing a variety of roles including reconnaissance, bombing, scouting, transport, air-to-air fighting, and artillery spotting. All of these functions would be recognised in the contemporary air force as among the core air power roles. In early 1918, the F.2b's reputation meant that enemy aircraft would not attack more than two Bristol Fighters unless they had a significant numerical superiority. The aircraft saw service in several theatres during the war, including the Western Front, Italy and Palestine. It was in Palestine that No 1 Squadron, AFC used the aircraft so successfully; this included using them to transport Colonel T.E. Lawrence—the famed 'Lawrence of Arabia—between Allenby's headquarters and Feisal's guerrilla forces. Production of the F.2b ceased in 1919 with over 5000 examples produced.

Artwork by Juanita Franzi

Bristol F.2b Fighter Specifications	
Wingspan:	39' 3" (11.96 m)
Length:	25' 9" (7.85 m)
Max weight: 2,800 lbs	(1070 kg)
Max speed:	113 mph (182 km/h)
Endurance:	3 hours
Service ceiling:	18 000 ft
Primary powerplant:	Rolls-Royce Falcon I (190 hp), II (220 hp) and III (280 hp)
Production:	Aug 1916 to Aug 1919 (No ordered: 5250)

1918: The Realisation of Air Power

At the end of 1917, Allenby's lines were stabilised in Palestine along a front that ran from Jaffa on the coast to Jerusalem. Winter rains precluded any sort of large-scale operations in the region, and the EEF took the opportunity to consolidate its gains. Allenby's land forces were expanded and equipped with the latest weaponry available. Contemporary operational and tactical doctrine and training methods were then introduced from the Western Front. All arms conducted extensive Mission Rehearsal Exercises (MREs) to coordinate and prepare the various arms elements for the coming 1918 offensives. Soldier or airman, while the skillsets were different, the training processes were similar; standardised, realistic and consistent reinforcement would ostensibly result in any man from any part of the British Empire being able to effectively conduct his function in any like unit across Allenby's entire force. In this lay a crucial key to the eventual success of the EEF. With his force thus prepared, Allenby's ultimate objective remained unchanged: the complete destruction of Turkish forces in Palestine and Syria. He planned for operations after the heat of Palestine's mid-year summer but before the winter rains commenced at the beginning of November. Operations during 1917 had split the Ottoman forces into two Armies of five and six divisions to the north and north-east of Jerusalem. The force on the right lay in Allenby's direct advance into Syria. It had to be reduced. To do so, Allenby had two prerequisites. Firstly, he had to link with the large band of Arab irregulars under Feisal and Lawrence on the other side of the Jordan River. Together, the British and Arab armies would prove an irrepressible force. Secondly, and immediately, Allenby needed maps of the area, and this is where Salmond's Palestine Brigade came to the fore. He immediately set his reconnaissance elements to work. In No 40 Wing, the task fell to No 1 Squadron AFC.

The Australian *Official History* indicates that Williams's squadron was allocated a strip of the Turkish defences and beyond to photograph; a landmass that comprised 624 square miles (over a 1000 kilometres) of territory. While No 1 Squadron's residual B.E.12s and Martinsydes would conduct the work, they would be covered by the newly acquired Bristol Fighters and the S.E.5s of No 111 Squadron. The work commenced on 15 January 1918 with two photographic aircraft scheduled to operate line-abreast at 12 000 feet and flying on a level course while their photographic plates were exposed. The process proved highly successful and ensured that there was an overlap between the exposures of both cameras. For two weeks, No 1 Squadron aircraft photographed the Palestinian countryside, sweeping the landscape to the north-east towards Nablus and all the way east to the Jordan River. The work was not without its travails. It was during this period that Lieutenant Len Taplin's encounter with an Albatros fighter occurred. On 17 January 1918, Lieutenant Taplin was forced to clear a jammed camera while on a photographic mission in a B.E.12a over Nablus. Holding the control stick between his knees while he did so, Taplin was focussing on the task at hand and did not see an Albatros approach and attack him from behind. On hearing the gunfire, Taplin turned to engage but his Vickers gun jammed immediately. While he cleared the weapon, the Albatros dived to get beneath him, and Taplin followed. When his gun was cleared, he managed to fire about twenty rounds into the Albatros which he observed to fall away in a vertical dive. On another occasion, five German aircraft attempted to intercept a No 1 Squadron reconnaissance aircraft near Jenin, north of Nablus, but were driven off by two escorting Bristol Fighters. These two events were the only German attempts to interfere with British or Australian aircraft during the entire operation, and they highlight the dwindling and fragile state of the German air service in Palestine by early 1918. By the end of January, No 40 Wing had taken over 1600 photographs of the landscape, and these were duly compiled and converted into maps by survey specialists. The General Officer Commanding of the Palestine Brigade, Brigadier—later to be Air Vice-Marshal—Amyas Eden 'Biffy' Borton, would state of the work that:

> *the photographs are a very fine achievement, and probably mark the highest point which has yet been achieved in map making photography.*

In describing the maps, the British *Official History* notes the difficult nature of the territory ahead of the EEF's front lines. It was much changed from the sandy plains of the Sinai, and now comprised a semi-arid landscape of plains and rolling rocky hills on which grew a variety of grasses and tree species indigenous to the Middle East: native oaks, carob, date palms, almond, pear, hawthorn, cypress and the exotic Atlantic cedar. Interspersed among these hills lay dry river and creek beds—wadis—which were steep-sided and treacherous, gouged out by the ferocity of perennial rains. Across the landscape could be found the townships and villages that the soldiers of the EEF now recognised from the pages of the bible—Jericho to the east and Nazareth further to the north—but closer than these sites lay Nablus, Jenin and the ancient ruins of Megiddo. The lands seemed unchanged since the days of Christ, and the value of the photographic reconnaissance was vital to the EEF's operations.

The maps and disposition of Ottoman forces were of immediate value. During the three months of February to April 1918, Allenby used the information on several minor operations to the east and north of the British lines aimed at isolating the Turkish forces, and to assist Lawrence and Arab operations on the other side of the Jordan. Salmond's air services kept up a constant overwatch while this occurred, and his squadrons attacked the German airfields at Nablus, Jenin and El Affule to neutralise and degrade any effort to oppose the EEF's operations. It is important to realise the complexity and complementary nature of the work carried out in Allenby's massive command during these and subsequent operations. Not the least important of this work was the level of integration achieved by the various elements involved. This was particularly so among the air forces, in which No 1 Squadron AFC had become a leading unit and highlights the immediate and inherently joint nature of air power. Despite the preparedness of the EEF, Allenby had several setbacks during his first forays across the Jordan. But his forces finally prevailed for two reasons. Firstly, the British training, technical (including logistical) and doctrinal approach to preparing for and fighting battles were superior to those of the Ottoman Army. Combined arms operations including infantry, armour, artillery and aviation were conducted with precision and flexibility; when it came to air operations, both factors were—and remain—among the defining characteristics of air power. Combined arms operations were dynamic and difficult to mount any sort of fixed defence against. The concept of defending a fixed line points to the second element of British superiority. Allenby was not tied to the notion of holding territory in the manner that his Ottoman and German opponents were. The Ottomans were well aware that they were defending the last vestiges of an empire, and undoubtedly found it difficult to relinquish any amount of territory—this would lead to catastrophic consequences.

As these events unfolded, the Royal Air Force (RAF) was formed by Imperial decree on 1 April 1918 through the amalgamation of the RFC and RNAS into one service. Inauguration of the RAF did not affect the function of the AFC, though it doubtless prompted many Australian airmen to envisage an independently established RAAF. As Williams's autobiography highlights, he believed the formation of the RAF of a separate service was necessary, especially in the face of the internecine rivalry of the Army and Navy and their attempts to gain access to scarce aviation resources. When the RAAF was established barely three years later, Williams might well have remembered the fratricidal rivalry which was, in part, a seed for the establishment of the RAF; likewise, the RAAF emerged from similar unconstructive inter-service competition in Australia. In any case, Williams would be well prepared. The utility of the air service—indispensable in a modern force—had already been firmly established.

Types of aerial cameras used by the Australian and Royal flying Corps in the Middle East during World War I. Many thousands of square kilometres were photographed by No 1 Squadron AFC, and ultimately these photographs gave rise to the first detailed maps of much of the Middle East. (source: AWM P01184.002)

Seven unidentified members of No 1 Squadron, Australian Flying Corps at work in the engine shop at Ramleh. (source: AWM B02077)

In January and June 1918 Allenby's HQ issued Notes on the Interpretation of Aeroplane Photographs taken on the Palestine Front, from which the British Army Survey Corps was able to produce a comprehensive series of maps and charts of the Palestinian countryside. In the immediate, the images and mapping provided the EEF a detailed overview of Ottoman defences in the region. Of equal importance, the work comprised the first detailed charting of this area of the Middle East. Here, five unidentified members of the Photographic Section of the Australian Flying Corps engaged in trimming and drying prints, Ramleh, Palestine 1918. (source: AWM B02072)

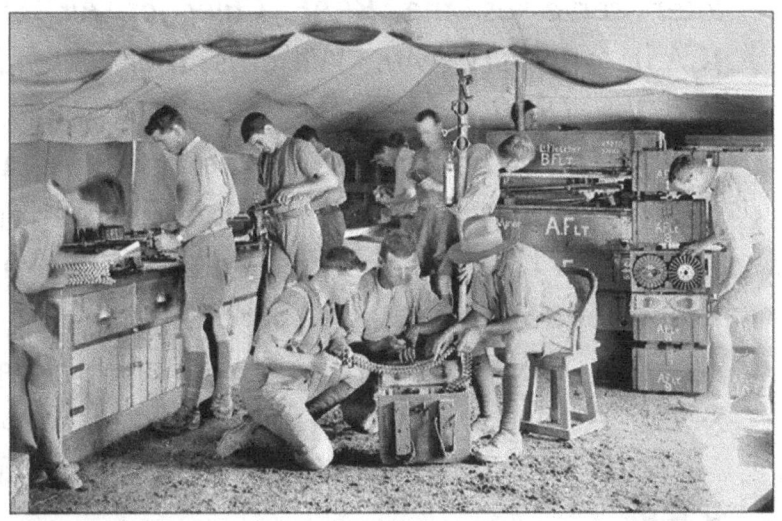

No 1 Squadron armourers concentrate on their work, Palestine c1917. Every bullet was checked to minimise the possibility of stoppages in combat. (source: AWM B02066)

The overwhelming size of Allenby's force is significant in considering the operations that were about to commence. In mid-1918 Allenby's army now comprised more than three corps manned by men from every part of the Empire.

Air power would be integral to the land forces, though the Palestine Brigade—the fighting element of Salmond's air force—fell under a separate chain of command.

Headquarters Palestine Brigade: Brigadier A.E. Borton DSO – Bir Salem

No 5 Wing: Lieutenant Colonel Charles Burnett DSO – Ramleh

(Burnett was an English officer who would later serve as the RAAF Chief of Air Staff (CAS), a rivalry with Williams that extended into the 1940s)

No 14 Squadron: sixteen R.E.8s and three Nieuport fighters – Junction Station

No 113 Squadron: sixteen R.E.8s and five Nieuport fighters – Sarona

No 142 Squadron (less one Flight): seven Armstrong Whitworth FK8 – Sarona

No 142 Squadron (Jerusalem Flight): five R.E.8s

No 40 Wing: Lieutenant Colonel Richard Williams DSO – Ramleh

No 1 Squadron AFC: eighteen Bristol Fighters and a single Handley Page Heavy Bomber Ramleh

No 111 Squadron: fifteen S.E.5s – Ramleh

No 144 Squadron: thirteen D.H.9 bombers – Junction Station

No 145 Squadron (1 Flight): six S.E.5s

Importantly for the Australians, the officer promoted to command No 40 Wing was the now Lieutenant Colonel Richard Williams. Williams, just twenty-seven years old, recorded that:

> I am sure that my appointment to the command of the Wing was the direct result not only of my length of service on that front but also of the excellence of the work of No 1 Squadron over the preceding 12 months. Flight commanders, air crews, NCOs and men, technical and otherwise, were excellent. I could not have had better.

Williams might well have been writing of Salmond's entire air force in Palestine. The Palestine Brigade could muster more than 105 modern, well-armed and capable operational aircraft. These were operated and maintained by aviators, technicians and administrative/logistics staff who were highly trained to common standards of excellence.

The German Air Service, affected by the growing quality and confidence of the British and Australian aircraft and personnel, could not hope to match their foes. The only method by which the Ottoman and German forces could obtain any overview of the battlespace was through the use of aerial reconnaissance. However, by mid-1918 the RAF and AFC constantly patrolled the frontline, and this effectively precluded German aircraft from any type of foray over the front while the EEF concentrated its forces for the coming campaign. Williams noted that 'German aircraft put their noses down and dived for home every time they saw a British aircraft'. When the Germans did not see their foes first, the consequences were invariably disastrous for them. The Australian contribution during this period of flying operations was not insignificant.

On 7 May 1918, two No 1 Squadron Bristol Fighters shot a German two-seater down while they reconnoitred over the German aerodrome at Jenin. On the way home, they engaged and shot down two more Albatros scouts. Two days later, the D.H.9s of No 144 Squadron RAF, escorted by No 1 Squadron Bristol Fighters, bombed Jenin airfield, burned its hangars and damaged or destroyed most of the aircraft parked there. On 22 May 1918, a pair of No 1 Squadron Bristol Fighters, led by Lieutenant Ross Smith, engaged two Albatros fighters over Nablus, with both shot down by the Australian observers before the Germans could fire a single shot.

Aside from air combat, the Australian airmen involved in this sortie are noteworthy. The four Australian crew, including Smith and Lieutenants Kirk (Smith's observer), Kenny (pilot) and Weir (observer) were all formerly 'other ranks' in the

Light Horse—they were the realisation of the potential and calibre of the airmen forming the AFC.

A few days later, four more Albatroses were encountered near Nablus by two No 1 Squadron Bristol Fighters. Two of them were immediately shot down. A third was forced down after a running fight with one of the Australians, and its pilot was forced to flee on foot when the Bristol Fighter strafed the downed machine. The fourth Albatros fled. On 29 May 1918, Lieutenant Stooke, another former mounted man, with Lieutenant Weir as observer, shot a Rumpler two-seater down in flames.

By the time Williams assumed command of No 40 Wing, German air power was ineffectual and the EEF enjoyed air supremacy in the Palestine theatre. British and Australian aircraft had played a crucial role in foiling German reconnaissance aircraft during the summer months, and because of this, the Ottomans were completely unaware of Allenby's preparations for the coming offensive.

Lesson # 7

- The achievement of excellence—professional and technical

> mastery—is not simply an act; it requires habitual practice.
> - The development of confidence comes as the result of achieving excellence.

With the Palestine Brigade's rising ascendency there was a commensurate increase of confidence among the British and Australian airmen. This was reflected in their encounters with German aircraft, though also in the continually developing and extensive nature of the reconnaissance effort conducted. No 1 Squadron received an accolade when Ross Smith was seconded to transport Lawrence around the Jordan valley to discuss with Arab leaders how best to coordinate their irregular forces with the EEF. No 40 Wing flew in support of the wider Bedouin operations, and Lawrence and Feisal's forces benefitted from aircraft support. Lawrence was enamoured with the Australian aviators.

When their work around the Jordan River was completed, No 40 Wing was redirected to focus on the regions to the north in preparation for the final offensive. This work was particularly suited to No 1 Squadron, which now conducted only strategic reconnaissance, escort and offensive duties. No 1 Squadron's function was dynamic, and once orders were received, the Australians had the freedom to exploit the intrinsic characteristics of speed, reach, precision and perspective to wreak havoc among the Ottoman front lines and regions beyond. On one occasion, Ross Smith and his observer strafed and destroyed a rolling stock and troop train along the railway line between Nablus and Jenin, completely unopposed. Such activity completely demoralised the Turks. In early September, the Ottoman air forces were so degraded that a senior Turkish Army officer requested they desist from operations over his part of the front; it was simply too demoralising to see the Ottoman air force shot out of the sky by the RAF. He requested they stop their infrequent operations over his part of the front, because when they were intercepted by British aircraft, the result was invariably an RAF victory.

By this stage, his forces gathered, Allenby was poised to attack.

The EEF offensive opened at 1.15am on 19 September 1918 with an air strike that would have immediate operational level consequences. No 1 Squadron AFC's Handley Page 0/400 bomber, captained by Ross Smith and armed with sixteen 112 lb bombs, destroyed the Ottoman telephone exchange at El Affule, and then destroyed the town's railway station. After daylight, No 144 Squadron's D.H.9 bombers raided Nablus, where that town's exchange was also destroyed. As a consequence of the destruction of these two centres of gravity, all Ottoman forces in the east remained completely unaware of the EEF's attack for the next two days. Allenby's land forces commenced at 4.30am with a creeping barrage delivered by 350 artillery pieces along a coastal corridor. This covered five advancing infantry divisions supported by armour. Concurrently, No 1 Squadron's Bristol Fighters ranged over the front and beyond, reporting the withdrawal of Turkish forces while also bombing and strafing the enemy below. As this occurred, the S.E.5s of No 111 Squadron set standing patrols over Jenin airfield to prevent any attempt by German aircraft to interfere with the offensive. Cutlack indicated that the EEF's offensive would end in the total destruction of the entire Ottoman army. Air power would be integral to the success; of the airmen, Cutlack wrote:

> *the victory could not have been complete without them. They prepared it in the weeks beforehand. They consummated it in the critical days. The worst scenes of destruction were their work. Many thousands of Turks believed the Bristol Fighter to be a direct instrument of Allah.*

The No 1 Squadron AFC Handley-Page 0/400 bombing aircraft with a Bristol Fighter from the same squadron at Haifa on the Palestinian coastline, mid-1918. The Bristol Fighters, big aircraft for their era, highlight the comparatively large size of the bomber and the commensurate ability to exploit the air power characteristics of reach and payload. During the opening hours of the Battle of Megiddo in September 1918, the HP400 paralysed the Ottoman communications system and railway network, thereby preventing Turkish forces from having an understanding of the wider circumstances of the battle in northern Palestine. (source: AWM B02118)

An Observation of Australian Aviators-by T.E. Lawrence

We sat around, very ready; but the watcher on the broken tower yelled 'Aeroplane up ', seeing one coming over from Derna. Our Australians, scrambling wildly to their yet-hot machines, started them in a moment. Ross Smith, with his observer, leaped into one, and climbed like a cat into the sky. After him went Peters, while the third pilot stood beside the DH9 and looked hard at me ... He was an Australian, of a race delighted in additional risks ... I seemed not to understand him. Lewis Guns, scarf mountings, sights, rings which turned, knobs which rose and fell on swinging parallel bars; to shoot, one aimed with this side of the ring or that, according to the varied speed and direction of oneself and the enemy. I had been told the theory, could repeat some of it: but it was in my head, and rules of action were only snares of action until they ran out of the empty head into the hands, by use.

A determined Australian crew of No 1 Squadron AFC pose for the camera with the squadron mascot, Charlie. These were typical of the Australian aviators that Lawrence wrote about in his memoirs. The Observer in this image, Captain Leslie Sutherland MC DCM, wrote extensively on his experiences with No 1 Squadron in Palestine after the War (source: History and Heritage Branch—Air Force).

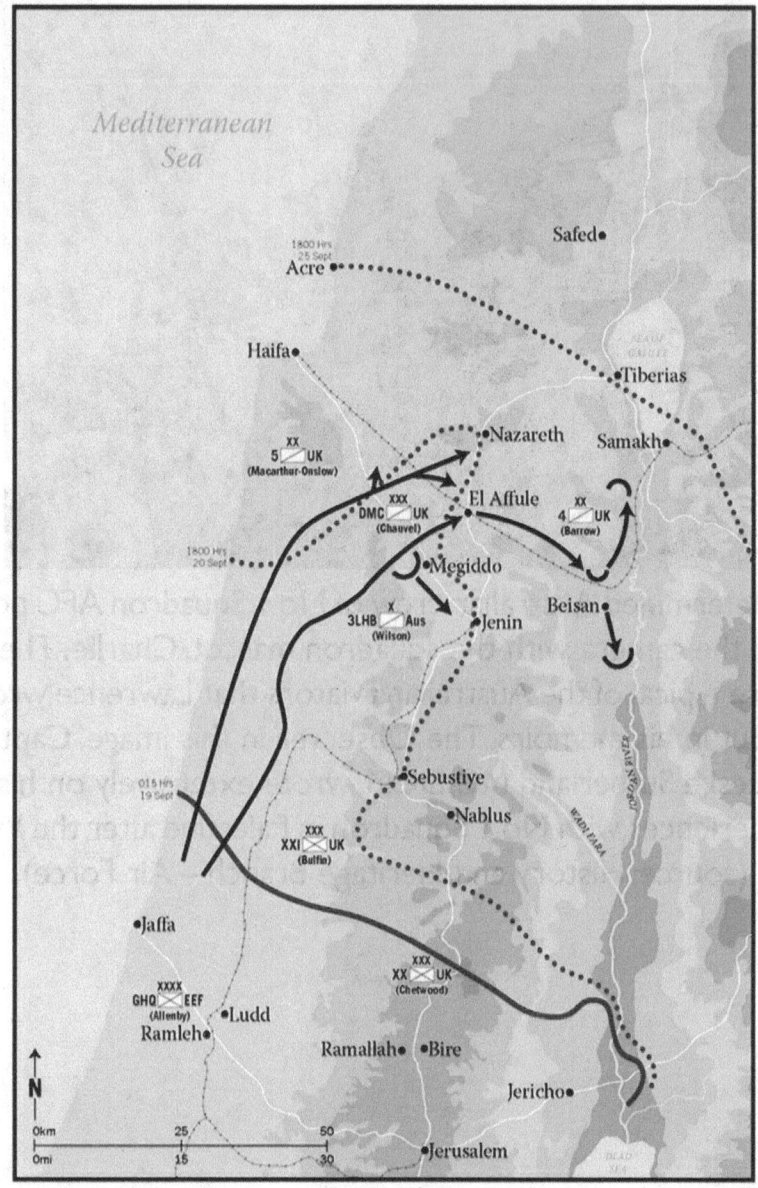

The Battle of Armageddon (Megiddo) 1918. The massive territorial gains made by Allenby's forces in in this set piece offensive across Palestine in on a few days of operations in the late summer of 1918 precipitated the defeat of the Ottoman Empire. Striking north along the Mediterranean coastline, Allenby's mounted and armoured columns turned inland and drove the Turks into headlong retreat. Harrying them all the way were aircraft of the RAF's No 40 Wing, led by the gifted Australian airman LTCOL Richard Williams. It would be on 21 September 1918 that William's aircraft trapped an Army of retreating Turks in the Wadi Fara as it fled east towards the River Jordan; there, air power would kill thousands in a single day.

Allenby's careful preparations gave his force an overwhelming advantage in every sense. The opposing Ottoman army, inflexibly fixed in entrenched positions, had no chance. During the opening hours of the offensive, the EEF drove more than twenty miles northwards along the Mediterranean coastline, cutting through the Turkish defences, before turning east to towards the ancient ruins of Megiddo, north of Nablus. The Ottoman forces, pressed on three sides, began to unravel. A gap had been punched in their front line by Allenby's infantry, armour and artillery; and the Empire mounted troops exploited the situation in a drive towards El Affule, Nazareth, and Beisan across the Plains of Sharon. With their lines of communication cut, the Turks could coordinate no response. The roads were choked, and the columns of humanity, animals and vehicles made easy targets for marauding British and Australian airmen. Flying in relays, No 40 Wing relentlessly attacked every avenue of retreat for the fleeing army. It became a rout. Williams wrote that:

> The experience of that day clearly showed what might be done from the air under favourable conditions. Animals became frantic and were completely uncontrollable while men were completely demoralised. A captured German officer stated that he had no idea the aircraft could have such an effect on ground troops.

The Turks struggled to withdraw along the main roads and railways from Nablus which ran northwards to Jenin. When they found the railway blocked, the Turks met thousands more men retreating from the attack in the west, and both groups were forced east along the Beisan road that led down the Wadi Fara towards the Jordan River. They were attacked every step of the way. No 1 Squadron AFC attacks continued into the next day.

Bombs dropped by Australian airmen bursting over the railway station at El Afule in Palestine, far behind the enemy's lines on the morning of the great attack by Allenby's forces. (source: AWM A00643)

Captain Leslie Sutherland MC DCM on the Wadi Fara

The bombs continued to rain down; the guns blazed away. And hundreds of Turks just stood—stood awaiting the bullets or shrapnel splinters that were going to end their days of war ... Thank God for a helpful thought for every one of those poor devils I kill, there'll be one less to take toll of our cavalry or infantry when they come up. But, oh, the nauseating smell of cordite, the pools of blood we could see, the desolation framed by these barren hills of Samaria. We were a tough bunch. But we were sickened. The infantry, hardened warriors that they were, were absolutely appalled when they came up.

Palestine 22 September 1918. A scene in the dust east of Megiddo during the Allenby's advance on Damascus, showing the Australian Light Horse advancing and thousands of Ottoman prisoners by the wayside. (source: AWM B00256)

On 20 September, thousands of Ottoman troops retreating north on the Jenin-El Affule road encountered the Australian Light Horse and, traumatised by the attacking aircraft, surrendered without a fight. In the Jordan Valley to the East, Lawrence witnessed the disintegration of the retreating Turkish force, though he paid homage to the German units embedded in the Ottoman Army:

> *Here, for the first time, I grew proud of the enemy who had killed my brothers. They were two thousand miles from home, without hope and without guides, in conditions mad enough to break the bravest nerves. Yet their sections held together, in firm rank, sheering through the wrack of Turk and Arab like armoured ships, high-faced and silent. When attacked they halted, took position, fired to order. There was no haste, no crying, no hesitation. They were glorious.*

Such stoicism was to no avail; Allenby's force was unstoppable. In his biography on Harry Chauvel written sixty years later, Australian historian Alec Hill pays homage to the modern methods employed by the EEF, and more so to Allenby's intellect:

> *His plan was brilliant in execution as it had been in conception; it had no parallel in France or on any other front, but rather looked forward in principle and even in detail to the Blitzkrieg of 1939.*

Flying at dawn on 21 September, two Bristol Fighters from No 1 Squadron AFC, captained by Lieutenants Stan Nunan and Allan Brown, reported thousands of Turks retreating along the narrow road through the Wadi Fara. They bombed the lead vehicles and set to work on the trapped column. Lieutenant Clive Conrick, Nunan's observer, saw his bullets hit panicked men clambering up the roadside cliffs. Then Nunan raked the length of the column. Brown and his observer, Lieutenant Garfield Finlay, did likewise. Their ammunition expended, Nunan and Brown then waited for replacement Bristol Fighters to arrive, before returning to their base to re-arm. Leslie Sutherland, in one of the arriving aircraft, said that it *'had been butchery on those two previous days. But I can think of no word to convey the dreadfulness of this action.'* Sutherland's aircraft bombed the rear of the column, trapping it, and for the rest of the day No 40 Wing bombed and machine-gunned the trapped men and horses in relays. Turkish ground fire brought down one RFC machine; whose crew survived. In general, though, the Turkish resistance quickly wilted. Sutherland indicated that he discerned a distinct change among the Turks around noon; *'they seemed resigned to their fate. White cloths and rags were waved in surrender. But even if we wanted to accept it, how could aeroplanes capture ground troops?'* The slaughter continued. When the British infantry caught up with the Turks the next day, they expected to meet a large force. What they took were about one hundred prisoners.

Aerial photograph of the township of Nablus, taken by No 1 Squadron AFC on 23 October 1918 (source: AWM B03486)

One week later, the EEF captured the city of Damascus, one hundred miles to the north of Nablus. The distance covered by Allenby's ground force in such a short space of time stood in stark contrast to operations conducted on the Western Front where territorial gains was measured in single miles. Allenby's success came in large part from his complete dominance of the air. This image was taken by No 1 Squadron AFC on 23 October 1918. (source: AWM B03526)

The name Armageddon

Armageddon—literally from the Semitic *har Megiddo* or hill of Megiddo—is mentioned once in the Book of Revelations as the site of the predicted apocalyptic battle of the end of days. The location was an important strategic township in ancient Palestine north of the modern city of Nablus and south-east of Haifa. The ruins of the fort on the hill of Megiddo were used as late as Roman times to guard the important trade route from Egypt to Syria, and they dominate views of the Plains of Sharon towards the Mediterranean Sea westwards and the Valley of Jezreel to the south. When General Sir Edmund Allenby's British Empire forces attacked across Palestine against the Ottoman Turks in 1918, his army drove its adversary eastwards towards modern day Jordan and from the plains around the *har Megiddo*. It was from this location that the 1918 battle drew its name: The Battle of Armageddon. During the battle, an AFC and two RAF squadrons attacked the retreating Turkish Seventh Army on 21

September 1918 as it negotiated its way along a dry riverbed—the Wadi Fara—leading away from Nablus. In one morning, No 1 Squadron AFC and the two RAF squadrons killed nearly 6000 Turkish troops from the air.

Scenes of absolute devastation and destruction met British ground forces when they came across the remnants of the Ottoman forces destroyed by air power in the Wadi Fara. (source: RAAF Museum)

The events at the Wadi Fara precipitated a Turkish collapse. With the Ottoman front broken, Allenby's mounted force quickly dominated the battlefields. Damascus fell on 1 October, when troopers of Chauvel's Light Horse gave way to Lawrence's Arab army which claimed the honour of entering the city first. Aleppo, the last city to fall in the campaign, fell on 26 October. In five weeks, Allenby's offensive had advanced hundreds of miles and netted over 75 000 prisoners. The Turkish Army had collapsed. The German Air Service personnel, deprived of their aircraft, retreated northwards. Both the air and ground crews were issued small arms with which to fight the oncoming EEF, though this was not required. Five days after Aleppo fell, the Ottomans sued for peace, and an armistice was struck. The war ended with the British occupying the territory that was to become Iraq, Palestine, Trans-Jordan, Syria and Lebanon. With the Ottoman Empire destroyed and Russia paralysed by civil war, Britain became the dominant power in the region.

No 1 Squadron AFC next to their Bristol Fighters, at Mejdel, Palestine in mid-1918. The officer in the foreground (with stick) is Major Richard Williams, DSO, commanding officer and 'Father of the Royal Australian Air Force'. At the war's end, Allenby praised the Australian airmen with these words:

> ...the victory gained in Palestine and Syria [he said] has been one of the greatest in the war and undoubtedly hastened the collapse that followed in other theatres. This squadron played an important part in making this achievement possible. You gained for us absolute supremacy of the air thereby enabling my cavalry, artillery and infantry to carry out their work on the ground practically unmolested by hostile aircraft. This undoubtedly was a factor of paramount importance in the success of our arms here ...

> *I congratulate not only the flying officers, but also your mechanics, for although the officers did the work in the air, it was good work on the part of your mechanics that kept a high percentage of your machines serviceable...*

(source: AWM B01472)

PARALLELS TO TODAY

The parallels to what is occurring in the Middle East today, a century after the 'war to end all wars', are striking. In World War I, Australia contributed a national force to a larger whole. Within the microcosm of the AFC, No 1 Squadron went on to achieve a degree of operational excellence equal to all other flying elements in the theatre. After years of hard fighting, the British and Arab armies then emerged victorious in Palestine. But to what end?

Volumes elsewhere write of the Allied powers mobilising Arab insurgents with promises of independence, armaments and bags of gold to throw off the yoke of a despotic regime. Yet others highlight Britain's desire for regional stability, if only to suit its own ends. A different viewpoint indicates Western—particularly British—duplicity in post-war negotiations. Like all matters, the truth is probably somewhere in the middle. Certainly, it is worth considering that in an environment beset with tribal and sectarian violence, giving self-determination to the Arab peoples may have resulted in the Balkanisation of the Ottoman Empire. This was unacceptable. Equally, if the Turks had prevailed, the Ottoman Empire would have expanded, subjecting many more Arabs to its rule. Given this, whatever Britain did or did not do, the region was destined to suffer in the coming years.

Part One of this book is about the development of Australian air power in the Middle East during World War I. However, the subject cannot be appreciated unless it is in the context of wider events. Understanding the intangibles associated with fighting a conflict in such a place—then or now—are arguably as important as the gaining of technical mastery itself. One must understand both. The characteristics of air power and the unique properties of the air domain enabled Allenby to look beyond the horizon. Understanding that air power gave Allenby the potential to generate operational—even strategic—effects to degrade the enemy and influence the outcome of his offensive is important knowledge. Appreciating the concept of airmindedness and cultivating the thinking that goes beyond the taking and holding of physical territory goes to the core of understanding what happened in the Wadi Fara. But, once more, context is everything. Almost every modern air power role was tried and tested in the Palestine Brigade during World War I—invariably with success. The precepts discovered remain true, and today, modern technical developments make the potency of air power even more profound. Australia benefited from its experiences in Palestine; the events there precipitated the formation of the RAAF only three years later. On a wider note, the war established the Australian military practice of contributing to a larger force. This remains the cornerstone of Australian foreign and defence policy. Professional military aviators need not be burdened with the responsibility of solving the intangibles highlighted in the preceding lines. What we should be responsible for is understanding how this heritage informs who we are. More so, how best we should judiciously apply this potent force in pursuit of government objectives.

A Century of Enduring Agony in Iraq

Mesopotamia is the name given to the ancient region where modern Iraq now stands. A Greek word meaning 'between two rivers', the Tigris and Euphrates, Mesopotamia was a 'fertile crescent' which gave rise to some of the earliest and most advanced ancient civilisations.

Mesopotamia featured prominently in the early history of Australian military aviation. During World War I, one of Australia's first operational contributions—the Mesopotamian Half-Flight—served in a disastrous regional campaign; and from 1916 to 1918, the AFC operated in the Palestine campaign not far to the west. A century of regional turmoil would ensue after the defeat of the ruling Ottoman Empire by the British in 1918. The following year, Britain formed the modern state of Iraq by amalgamating the three disparate provinces of Basra, Baghdad and Mosul. Although the new map made for neat borders, the Ottomans had previously kept the provinces separate for sound reasons. Their populations were internecine in their rivalry. The long-oppressed Kurds resided in the north, while a Sunni Muslim minority lived in the central region around Baghdad. In the south and west—the most populous regions—the demographic was mostly Shi'ite Muslim. To add another layer of complexity, there were also many familial and tribal affiliations across borders that had been arbitrarily drawn, with pockets of other smaller religious groups, including Christians, throughout the nation.

Despite nationhood, Iraq remained a British mandate, and the Iraqi people rankled at a foreign appointment of Feisal bin Hussein bin Ali al-Hashemi as king. Most Iraqis had not heard of Feisal—a Sunni native of Mecca on the Saudi Peninsula—who had aided the British in Palestine during the war. Feisal was oppressive, though he worked hard to unify his Arabic peoples. He was also conciliatory towards the many and varied creeds and religions in his realm, and he was able to quell much of the violence—albeit forcefully—prominent in the Middle East even a century ago. Britain ceded its mandate in 1932 and Iraq was declared independent, though with a decidedly pro-British monarchy. The monarchy remained in place until 1958 when it was overthrown in a left-wing military coup led by Abd-al-Karim Qasim. Qasim's supporters, aided by Iraqi communists, murdered the royal family, ministers and many other prominent leaders in an orgy of violence. Still, many Iraqis saw Qasim as a great reformer and Iraq subsequently renounced its pro-British ties. Qasim asserted his influence quickly, and by 1961, he was entering into armaments deals with Eastern-bloc nations, openly challenging American interests in the Middle East, and bickering with Iraq's southern neighbour, Kuwait. Washington viewed Qasim as an existential threat, so in 1963, he was ousted in a CIA-backed coup led by Baathist army officer Abdul Salam Arif. Arif then launched his own accompanying bloodbath in which a young Saddam Hussein is believed to have participated. Thousands of Iraq's educated elite were murdered.

The Baathist ideology was a revelation in a nation with fundamentalist roots. Baathism was not a religious but rather a political ideology which sought to form a greater pan-Arabic national unity under firm leadership. In this respect, it was not dissimilar to German National Socialism, but of course, Baathism also had tribal and sectarian affinities running through it. Arif's internal state police ensured the communist influence in Iraq was completely dismantled, and many communists simply "disappeared'. In 1968, Ahmad Hasan al-Bakr, assumed power—his regime was even more despotic than Arif's. Al-Bakr remained in power until 1979 when Saddam Hussein became the Baathist leader.

In the same year in neighbouring Iran, the leading Islamic cleric, Ayatollah Khomeini, overthrew the pro-American Shah. In a matter of weeks, the previously secular Persia fell into fundamentalist insularity and drew the ire of the Western world, particularly the United States. The Baathist ideology was secular, if despotic, and tension between Iran and Iraq intensified.

Saddam Hussein cashed in on Iraq's significant oil revenue to enlarge and modernise his military and then, in 1980, he attacked. The Iran-Iraq War was a brutal mix of the modern and archaic—missile strikes were juxtaposed with bayonet attacks—and Saddam even used chemical agents against the enemy. Neither side prevailed, while the West simply watched on. American sympathies lay with the Iraqis. By 1987, Iran seemed to be prevailing, so the United States supplied intelligence and logistics support to Saddam. Both sides were exhausted, and a brokered ceasefire was called in 1988. The United Nations immediately placed a peacekeeping mission—including many young Australian officers—along the border between the two countries. The war cost Iraq hundreds of thousands of lives and seriously depleted the nation's capital. Despite this, Saddam remained indefatigable. In 1990, in another attempt to recoup Iraq's losses, he invaded Iraq's southern neighbour Kuwait to acquire the small nation's coastal facilities and oil reserves. This time, the West reacted immediately.

On 29 November 1990, the UN Security Council passed Resolution 678. The resolution gave Iraq until 15 January 1991 to withdraw from Kuwait and empowered signatory states to use 'all necessary means' to force Iraq out of Kuwait after the deadline. A coalition of nations led by the United States then commenced gathering forces along the southern Saudi border. Saddam refused to comply, and military action ensued. On the night of 16 February 1991, the coalition commenced an air campaign as the opening phase of Operation DESERT STORM, with the intent of ejecting Iraqi ground forces from Kuwait. Over the following week, the coalition flew in excess of 100 000 missions, dropping 88 500 tons of munitions. Air power completely tore apart the Iraqi command and control systems, and its supply lines. Allied ground forces followed up on 24 February, overwhelming the Iraqi army in Kuwait in just 100 hours. The surviving Iraqi forces fled north. The main highway towards Iraq's southernmost city, Basra, quickly became clogged. On 27 February, Coalition aircraft and ground forces relentlessly attacked this column, destroying thousands of vehicles and killing hundreds—perhaps thousands—of Iraqi troops. The media depiction of the devastation, reminiscent of the destruction wrought in the Wadi Fara, was so profound that US President George Bush Senior was persuaded to call a halt to the hostilities. The surviving Iraqi forces escaped to live and fight another day. Though the Coalition had liberated Kuwait, it achieved little else; while Iraq was weakened, Saddam's power over the nation and its people remained intact.

In 1992, the UN Security Council implemented Resolution 687 which, besides being a cease-fire agreement, was meant to restore 'international peace and security' in the region. One of the main elements of this resolution stated that Iraq should unconditionally accept the destruction, removal, or rendering harmless under international supervision, of all weapons of mass destruction (WMD), their appurtenant infrastructure, and all related research and development programs. This included ballistic missiles with a range greater than 150 kilometres. The coalition also established 'No-Fly Zones'—codenamed Operations NORTHERN WATCH and SOUTHERN WATCH—to prevent any threat posed by Iraqi air power, as well as to protect the ethnic minorities that predominated in those regions. The Baathist power base was obdurate. It exacted a terrible toll on the population—particularly among northern Kurds—and in the decade after the Gulf War as many as 300 000 people were killed. Saddam consistently ignored the provisions of UN direction, resulting in economic sanctions being placed on Iraq in the mid-1990s. This did little other than exacerbate the suffering of the Iraqi population. Saddam continued to disregard

UN weapons mandates, consistently stymieing Western inspection parties dispatched to monitor the regime's weapon stocks. In 1998, the United States and Great Britain resorted to air strikes (Operation DESERT FOX) in an attempt to halt weapons development. Nothing changed.

The world tilted at the beginning of the twenty-first century. On 11 September 2001, the Al Qaeda network, under the leadership of Saudi national Osama Bin Laden, launched a series of coordinated asymmetric terrorist attacks in which hijacked airliners were deliberately flown into New York's World Trade Centre and the Pentagon. Four aircraft had been hijacked; three hit their targets, and the fourth came down in a rural area when an extraordinarily brave group of passengers attempted to retake control from the hijackers. Nearly 3000 people perished during the course of the day, most of them in the World Trade Centre's twin towers, both of which collapsed. The United States was galvanised by this atrocity. President George W Bush junior responded immediately by instigating a Global War on Terror. The first military efforts were decisive.

Acting on intelligence that Al Qaeda operatives were being sheltered by the Taliban regime in Afghanistan, the United States attacked. Operation ENDURING FREEDOM targeted both

Al Qaeda and the fundamentalist Taliban that had ruled most of the country since 1996. The Taliban were quickly defeated by a Western coalition, which included Australian troops. But when the Taliban withdrew into the countryside, the result was an ugly counterinsurgency that would last for the next decade. As this unfolded, Bush turned a spotlight back onto Iraq. In his State of the Union Address in 2002 he named Iran, North Korea, and Iraq as an *'axis of evil'* that posed a threat to the wider world. He emphasised that these states harboured terrorists within their borders, and that this was an avenue of supply of WMD for use in attacks on the United States and its allies.

In September 2002, the US Secretary of State, Colin Powell, informed the UN that Iraq's weapons stockpile posed a 'grave and gathering danger' to the world. British Prime Minister, Tony Blair, supported the United States and published a later-discredited dossier on Iraq's military capability. In November 2002, UN weapons inspectors returned to Iraq after a UN resolution threatened serious consequences for any dalliance or breach on Iraq's part. At the end of the tour, UN weapons inspector, Hans Blix, told the Security Council that Iraq had not fully accounted for its stocks of chemical and biological weapons and had not fully accepted its obligations to disarm. In reality, Blix did not possess concrete evidence. Saddam had simply created uncertainty and ambiguity as to whether or not he had actually had these weapons. Events unravelled quickly.

In January 2003, Secretary of Defence Donald Rumsfeld, signed orders for 62 000 troops to deploy to the Middle East Region. This was in addition to the 43 000 already in place. On 5 February 2003, Colin Powell then presented evidence to the UN Security Council of the existence of WMD in Iraq. 'Clearly, Saddam Hussein and his regime will stop at nothing until something stops him', Powell stated. His premise was that underlying 'all the facts and patterns of behaviour was Saddam Hussein's contempt for the will of the Security Council, his contempt for the truth, and most damning of all, his utter contempt for human life.' Saddam continued to openly flaunt UN attempts to monitor his weapons stockpiles. Powell declared that the USA would not run the risk that Saddam Hussein would one day use his WMD. The USA's position was clear: Iraq was a 'rogue' state. Bush argued that, by proxy, in the process of building WMD, Baathist Iraq posed an existential threat in the same way that the Taliban did. This much was problematic.

During the first week of March 2003, Britain and the USA sought UN endorsement to overthrow the Baathist regime to halt the perceived production and use of WMD, and to stabilise the region through the introduction of democratic processes. The proposal was disavowed. Britain and America then acted unilaterally. On 12 March 2003, Prime Minister Blair demanded that Saddam publicly state that his regime would not produce or retain WMD or related documentation and data, and that Iraqi officials would cooperate with UN inspectors. Blair was ignored. On 17 March, President Bush issued a warning that 'Saddam Hussein and his sons must leave Iraq within forty-eight hours. Refusal to do so will result in military conflict, commenced at the time of our choosing.' The deadline passed and Operation IRAQI FREEDOM began with a 'shock and awe' air campaign on 20 March 2003, while ground forces entered Iraq.

Over 1700 air sorties were flown during the first two days of the operation, and systematic bombing during the remainder of March paved the way for Coalition ground forces to push into Iraq. United States and British troops entered Baghdad on 5 April, and the regime fell four days later. The US declared victory on 14 April. On 1 May, President Bush famously declared the end of major combat operations while he stood in front of a banner declaring 'Mission Accomplished'. What ensued was anything but accomplished. The bombing campaign had completely destroyed Iraq's infrastructure and power grid, and upwards of a quarter of the country's population was internally displaced. Baathist officials were dismissed, and the army was disbanded as the US and its allies became an occupying force. The result was a power vacuum, an increase in religious extremism, sectarian violence and finally, a bloody insurgency. It would take eight years of continued Western occupation and eventual UN intervention for matters to stabilise enough to affect a withdrawal and handover to an elected Iraqi regime. Even then, the future was anything but clear.

In the sixteen years since US President George W Bush junior launched the Iraq War, the Middle East has suffered interminable conflict, and rightly or wrongly, America's involvement has tarnished its standing as the post-Cold War era's benevolent super-power. Professional military aviators can pass no public judgement over their role in such events; they serve simply as instruments of national power. This is, though, no Nuremberg justification; the judicious application of force and an understanding of the context of events remain central to the profession of arms. In this, perhaps, is recognition

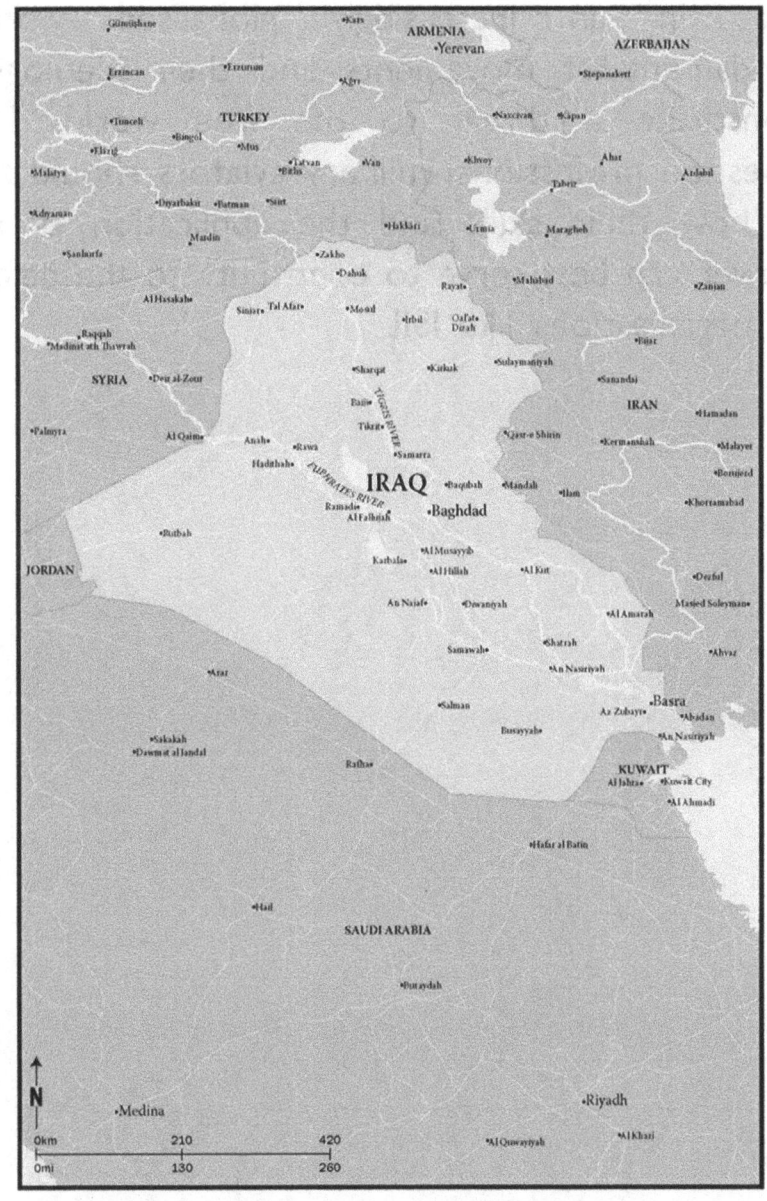

The Modern State of Iraq and surrounding states

that in an increasingly globalised world, fundamentalist movements and their ideologies constitute a threat to the free world. The question professional military aviators should ask is how their skills and the application of air power can best serve to contribute to the defeat of organisations like ISIL.

An F/A-18A Hornet preparing to undertake air-to-air refuelling over the Middle East Region. (source: Department of Defence)

Part II

OPERATION OKRA

An F/A-18F Super Horner over a city landscape in northern Iraq during Operation OKRA. (source: Department of Defence)

On the night of 8 October 2014, RAAF Boeing F/A-18F Super Hornets conducted their first strike mission in Operation OKRA, supporting the Iraqi military in its battle against the forces of the self-proclaimed Islamic State of Iraq and the Levant (ISIL). ISIL was an extremist group of Sunnis known in the West since 2013, but which has existed under various names in the years prior. Its aim was to establish an Islamic state in the Sunni-led areas of Iraq. ISIL was subsequently involved in Syria's civil war. Its leader, Abu al-Baghdadi, proclaimed a caliphate in 2014, claiming authority over all Islamic people in the region and carrying out 'ethnic cleansing' within its sphere of influence. The brutality of this fundamentalist organisation, and its wanton looting and destruction of many Near Eastern archaeological and cultural artefacts of unique significance, drew widespread criticism from the international community.

When the RAAF deployed to the region, the Chief of the Australian Defence Force, Air Chief Marshal Mark Binskin AC, stressed the importance of the mission to both Australia and the international community:

> *Disrupting and degrading ISIL will take a comprehensive and sustained effort from the international community. If we do nothing, we risk allowing the shocking acts of ISIL to further destabilise the Middle East Region and to spread beyond, where it will pose a greater threat to Australians.*

The deployment was complex and faced significant time restraints; its success depended on the employment all four core air power roles. Prior to the departure of combat aircraft, RAAF Boeing C-17A Globemaster and Lockheed Martin

C-130J Hercules aircraft began air dropping food and arms to communities besieged by ISIL in northern Iraq. On 21 September 2014, six Super Hornets from No 1 Squadron and two Airbus KC-30A air-to-air refuelling tankers from No 33 Squadron departed RAAF Amberley for RAAF Pearce in Western Australia. There they were joined by a Boeing E-7A Wedgetail Airborne Early Warning and Control aircraft from No 2 Squadron, based at RAAF Williamtown. The following day, this newly formed Air Task Group departed Pearce for Diego Garcia in the Indian Ocean, before continuing to Al Minhad, where it arrived on 24 September. In any sense of the word, this was a superb effort; from a standing start, the Australian Defence Force had despatched an Air Task Group and its support personnel to an international base over 12 000 kilometres from home where it arrived only nine days after being formed and directed to move.

The significance of deploying strike assets in support of this operation, at the invitation of a foreign government, cannot be overstated. The Australian Defence Force has an enviable reputation for fairness, honesty, integrity and respect for the rule of law. This reputation, which is a critical factor in shaping the post-conflict environment, enshrines specific obligations and responsibilities relevant to air power practitioners, particularly those involved directly in offensive operations. Air power can create devastating effects, and failure to employ this power with discrimination and proportionality can have serious adverse consequences for the individual, the Australian Defence Force and the government. These were matters front of mind to those leading this operation.

Boeing F/A-18F combat aircraft operated by No 1 Squadron Royal Australian Air Force. (source: Department of Defence)

A Boeing E-7A Wedgetail Airborne Early Warning and Control (AEW&C) aircraft operated by No 2 Squadron Royal Australian Air Force. (source: Department of Defence)

The Meaning behind the Acronyms ISIS, IS, ISIL and Daesh

As the international fight continues against the Islamic extremist group waging a bloody campaign to establish a caliphate in Iraq and Syria, there remains debate about what the group is called. When the group first came to international prominence in 2013 it was known as the Islamic State of Iraq and Syria (ISIS). This translates in Arabic to *Al-Dawla Al-Islamiya fi al-Iraq wa al-Sham*. The first three words translate to the Islamic State of Iraq while '*al-Sham*' refers to Syria and the wider surrounding area. In 2014 the group announced that it was dropping the word *al-Sham'* from its title. Henceforth it referred to itself as the Islamic State (IS: *Al-Dawla Al-Islamiya*) in recognition of its status as a self-declared caliphate.

The rest of the world has never recognised the group as a proclaimed state. When the extremists entered neighbouring Syria in 2014, the British and United States Governments commenced using the acronym ISIL, the Islamic State of Iraq and the Levant; the undefined region around Syria is historically referred to as the Levant. The area includes Syria, Lebanon, Israel, Palestine and Jordan.

Neither Britain nor the United States gave any credence to ISIL's claims for legitimate statehood and considered the old-French term Levant to accurately capture ISIL's sphere of influence. Australia has adopted the use of this acronym. The West and elements of the Arabic world have also adopted the name Daesh, sometimes spelled Da'esh, which is short for the titular *Dawlat al-Islamiyah f'al-Iraq wa alSham*. Daesh is a transliteration of the Arabic acronym formed from the English title 'Islamic State of Iraq and Syria'. While the full title is regarded as worthy by ISIL, the acronym Daesh is considered a pejorative. Acronyms used as words—neologisms—are not as prevalent in the more formal Arabic language as much as they are in English. Words such as Daesh are seen as contrived, belittling and therefore, insulting. In an organisation such as Daesh, the very word Daesh is viewed as disrespectful, and ultimately threatening of its status.

ISIS fighters. (source: wikimedia commons)

An Airbus KC-30A aircraft operated by No 33 Squadron Royal Australian Air Force. (source: Department of Defence)

The Nature of Modern Australian Air Power

When Air Commodore Steve Roberton, the first Commander of the Air Task Group, returned home, he was clear about his responsibility for the application of the air power at his disposal:

> It's worthwhile noting that everything we did over there was, and remains, about the judicious use of air power. It's no small issue to be given that legal authority for lethal effect. But to do it at the invitation of a country,

working in a large coalition, wasn't exactly smooth the whole way through.

Roberton was relating that the mere possession of high-performance platforms could not be simplistically equated with possessing capable air power. In fact, it was no guarantee of a successful outcome. Air power must be applied with discretion. Aircraft require air bases in the right locations with adequate base utilities, essential support personnel and services. Roberton had also pointed directly at the professionalism of the aviators and airmen in his command. He knew implicitly that they would be able to effectively operate and maintain the platforms and systems within his operation.

Air base support involves numerous activities: the provision of command and control, logistics, runways, hangars, maintenance, fuel, communications, financial management, administration, intelligence, firefighting, policing, airfield engineering, medical and dental, legal, pastoral, and contract support. This underlying infrastructure required to apply air power was first identified one hundred years ago, and the premise remains unchanged today.

Few nations have been able to master the complexities required for an independent aerial capability. Australia is one of the few nations that has done so. During Operation OKRA Australia demonstrated that it could deploy a balanced and self-reliant 'capability brick' in an international coalition with the capability to immediately respond and shape the battlespace when called upon.

'Flexibility' is *the* essential ingredient to this capability. The characteristic of flexibility has always made air power an attractive military instrument for a government to employ. However, the decision taken to apply air power is complicated firstly by technical matters, and secondly by the real and dynamic properties of the third dimension of air—a force of nature. Both are immutable.

Air power also encompasses more than the mere possession of aircraft; effective air power requires a particular type of 'balance' that few nations have mastered. Balance in an operational context is an ability to conduct the numerous roles and missions associated with air power simultaneously. Balanced air power demands maintaining high standards of technical, logistics and engineering functions, as well as effective command and control systems, and training.

Lesson # 8

- Air power is dependent on its supporting infrastructure at an air base; that is a reliance on first-rate support to generate, employ and sustain operations.

- Force generation and sustainment focusses on ensuring that the current force has the necessary personnel, skills and material to conduct and sustain air operations—both domestic and expeditionary—while maintaining the ability to regenerate the force during and after operations.

Alongside the need for air power to be inherently flexible and joint in nature, an overriding requirement for any small to medium force, such as the Australian Defence Force, is that it be interoperable within a wider international context. Interoperability allows Australia to deter potential threats to its sovereignty through not only the acquisition and operation of high-end capabilities that would otherwise be beyond its economic reach, but importantly through the inherently shared security interests with its major defence allies and partners

Australian security interests have always fallen under the protective mantle of 'great and powerful friends'. One hundred years ago, Australia's defence was guaranteed by its status as a Dominion in the British Empire. Today,

Australian security is underwritten by its alliance with the United States, with its most prominent manifestation being the enduring Australia, New Zealand and United States (ANZUS) Treaty of 1951. But national security does not solely mean physical security; it also comprises aspects such as economics, cultural values, military treaties and the respective interests of those in power. The term security, then:

> *is a useful term because of its elasticity. It includes not just defence against military threats ... but the economic interests that have to be secured against foreign competition ... The term 'national interest'—another usefully elastic term—therefore linked military force with the freedom to pursue commercial interests.*

Australia's ability to both interoperate with other nations and gain access to the latest international technology associated with air power stem from the nation's foreign policy. Today this occurs under the mantle of Australia's alliance with the United States of America. The relationship affords Australia both the opportunities and challenges associated with 'cutting edge' aviation technology. This makes economics a driving factor, and it is understandable that the high investment of money and resources spent in developing air power technology should yield a tangible return. In such matters air power is an appealing proposition for those who seek 'the surgical', 'the modern', 'the economic', 'the integrated' or 'the smallest footprint'. Technology refines and increases the efficiency of the enduring characteristics—*perspective, speed, reach, precision, flexibility*—which will in turn improve economy of effort.

Appreciating this context—and recognising that this has been the case since World War I—is central to professional mastery.

Air power in an Australian context means far more than this. Australia is a small nation, and investing in high-end multi-role air power technology is fundamental to the nation's support of a rules-based global order; that being:

> *a shared commitment by all countries to conduct their activities in accordance with agreed rules that evolve over time, such as international law, regional security arrangements, trade agreements, immigration protocols, and cultural arrangements.*

Australian air power is employed as an instrument of national power, in a whole-of-government 'Effects-Based Approach'. An Effects-Based Approach aims to alter an adversary's course of action, to change behaviour or to coerce—and this makes air power an extremely powerful instrument of statecraft. It follows that air power is not about technology alone, but also process, method, people, place, and an understanding of all aspects of its employment.

This concept is captured in the notion of 'airmindedness', with the Australian contribution of an Air Task Group to support operations against ISIL being a first-rate example: a technically enabled effects-based approach to operations.

A word of caution is required though. While it might be that technology has increased the utility of air power, the fundamental nature of war has not changed. Today, the air domain is simply another environment that must be considered in multi-domain warfare. History shows that when employed in isolation, air power has invariably failed to achieve a strategic outcome. This was apparent in the hard lessons learned by the United States in its disjointed application of 'strategic' and 'supporting' air power during the Vietnam War. Similar lessons have been learnt to a lesser degree in several air campaigns since. By maintaining a balanced air force and focusing on exploiting the fundamental characteristics of the air domain, modern practitioners have learned to resist an over-reliance on air power technology to fulfil strategic goals.

This lesson was no better demonstrated than during Operation DESERT STORM in 1991, when an opening air campaign was integrated with land and maritime operations in order to paralyse Iraqi forces in Kuwait. The effort included the use of unguided and precision guided munitions in a range of strategic, operational and tactical offensive counter air, and strike sorties, all of which overwhelmed the Iraqi adversaries as their air and ground capabilities were destroyed. Despite this, when air power was again used during the 2003 invasion of Iraq, the effort was marred and then completely undone by the quagmire of the occupation and insurgency.

Such analysis simply underwrites the joint nature of warfare and the need to focus on the aftermath of conflict when it occurs. In terms of air power, the notion also highlights that aircraft have the capability to produce operational and strategic effects through tactical actions. Modern Australian aviators and their close allies are well aware of this fact. Air planners today concentrate on outcomes and how they may be achieved, rather than the mechanisms and tools that enact them. This approach was intrinsic in the thinking of the aviators involved when the decision was made to utilise air power in support of the forces ranged against ISIL.

Descent into Hades: The Spread of ISIL

Iraq struggled in the years following the 2003 US-led invasion. The nation's infrastructure was virtually destroyed in the war; upwards of a quarter of the population was internally displaced; and the vacuum created by the removal of the Ba'athist regime quickly filled with sectarianism. The multi-national occupying force was challenged with a century's old dilemma: it struggled to understand the religious and ethnically diverse environment in which it found itself. The task of rebuilding the shattered nation was constantly hampered by the need to combat the numerous insurgent groups. Civilian and military casualties mounted. The escalating violence was shocking, and incidents of terrorism and indiscriminate indirect fire continued to increase until finally a massive surge of US troops in 2007 enabled the empowerment of the legitimately elected Iraqi parliament. By 2009, the efforts to rebuild Iraq appeared to be realising tangible success, with President Obama declaring a timeline for the withdrawal of US forces.

The toppling of the old order in Iraq had a regional influence. The peoples of the wider Middle East now began to protest the dictatorial rule, sham elections, state-sanctioned brutality, corruption and façades of democracy that existed in their own countries. In 2010 and early 2011, the populations of Egypt, Tunisia, and Yemen rose to throw off regimes that had been in place for decades. The Western media focussed on these events, dubbing them the 'Arab Spring'—a term borrowed from 1848 when a wave of political upheavals occurred in many European countries resulting in the overthrow of old monarchies to be replaced with more representative forms of government.

Airmindedness

By virtue of the inherent nature of air warfare, professional airmen tend to develop a distinctive perspective—fundamentally different to that of a soldier or sailor—regarding the concept, characteristics and conduct of war. Air power is a dynamic entity and history has demonstrated that it requires a fine understanding of all aspects of its employment. This understanding is termed 'airmindedness'.

The deeper understanding of the use of force in the air domains is an intangible quality that both connects airmen and optimises the employment of air power to achieve national objectives. Airmindedness cannot be inculcated through training alone; it is the product of personal perception, education, culture, organisational values and experience gained through involvement in air activities, both in peace and war. It is the instinctive ability to use the air domain to create the necessary effects that, either independently or as part of a joint force, contribute to joint campaign objectives and national security.

Commanding air power requires astute airmindedness, professional mastery and an enduring and philosophical understanding of the history, heritage, culture and values of an air force. Its leaders and commanders share a broad and unique perspective of the employment of air power. They understand the nuances of its employment that reflect the enduring nature of air power and its utility as a critical component of joint military forces.

The Crew of an E-7A Wedgetail platform collaborate closely in their provision of situational awareness across the battlespace. The airminded perspective of such crews is central to the success of modern air power operations (source: Department of Defence).

In March 2011, Iraq's neighbour Syria was challenged when pro-democracy protesters demanded an end to the authoritarian practices of President Bashar al-Assad's government regime, which had been in place more than forty years. The protests degenerated into violence and finally into an ongoing bloody civil war.

As pro-democracy uprisings grew during 2011, the United States left Iraq on the understanding that a democratically elected government would share power between the various factions that comprise Iraqi society—mainly between the Sunni and Shi'ite religious communities. Nuri al-Maliki, a Shi'ite, was elected as the Prime Minister and Tariq al-Hashemi, a Sunni, as his deputy. However, ethnic, tribal and religious affinities were never far below the surface and Iraqi Government business was conducted along similar lines. Al-Maliki distrusted Sunnis, and he replaced Sunni parliamentarians with 'friendly' Shi'ites. In 2012, the relationship between al-Maliki and al-Hashemi deteriorated when al-Maliki accused his deputy of plotting to kill him. Al-Hashemi subsequently fled to Turkey and was sentenced to death 'in absentia'.

The worsening political situation in Iraq and a bloody civil war in neighbouring Syria proved an ideal opportunity for Iraq's Sunnis. By April 2013, the levels of sectarian violence were as great as those of 2007. Events quickly unravelled, and by mid-year open warfare had broken out between government forces and Sunni insurgents, many of whom were affiliated with ISIL. The insurgents initially comprised ex-military members of Saddam's Baath Party who were supplemented by other Sunni dissidents. ISIL soon dominated both. Initially small, ISIL first gained traction in the Sunni areas of Iraq because of alMaliki 's prejudice. Concurrently, the group exerted influenced over the Sunnis in Syria by leveraging the more than forty per cent youth unemployment. As its numbers grew, ISIL raised money by profiting from captured oil production facilities. This was complemented with priceless treasures plundered from archaeological sites in the Levant.

In September 2013, a series of bombings rocked the Kurdish city of Erbil in Iraq's north. ISIL claimed responsibility and announced that it was responding to alleged Iraqi-Kurdish support for Kurds fighting against the Sunni insurgents in Syria. The group made effective use of the internet and social media to proclaim the concept of a single theocratic government, and to recruit foreign fighters to its ranks. ISIL's methods displayed a level of hitherto unknown sophistication among fundamentalist organisations, confounding the West. In November 2013, the Iraqi Government announced that October had been the deadliest month of sectarian violence since April 2008, with 900 killed. By this stage, ISIL had commenced open combat operations against the government; Iraq's military and civilian death toll for the year was approaching 7500 and matters were critical.

In January 2014, ISIL captured Fallujah and Ramadi to the west of Baghdad. Government forces recaptured both towns from the entrenched fundamentalists but could not stop

ISIL's tendrils spreading along the Euphrates River Valley to northern Iraq. Al-Maliki's party was returned to government in April, but with a minority rule. ISIL was spurred in its efforts to gain control of Northern Iraq. On 4 June, the group attacked Mosul. The Iraqi Government had nearly 60 000 troops and police in the city to defend against a 1500-strong attacking force. Despite the disparity, the insurgents were well armed with weapons stockpiled from Saddam's era and those hidden away during the post-2003 insurgency. ISIL supplemented its inventory with armour, artillery, surface-to-air missiles, and even some aircraft captured from Iraqi forces. The organisation of the fighters enabled rapid territorial expansion and facilitated the capture of additional equipment. Faced with this onslaught, the poorly led and trained Iraqi soldiers and police fled. Mosul fell to ISIL on 10 June. On 29 June, ISIL leader Abu Bakr al Baghdadi announced the formation of a caliphate stretching from Aleppo in Syria to Diyala in Iraq and renamed the group the Islamic State. Mosul gave ISIL control of the latest American weaponry left behind by the Iraqi garrison, including M1A1 Abram tanks. The northern Kurdish capital of Erbil was effectively cut off from ISIL due to the Iraqi withdrawal. The city did not fall because the Kurdish militia—the Peshmerga—rallied to resist the threat. With Erbil hosting a number of American oil companies which ran multi-billion-dollar US industries, this was an important outcome. The Peshmerga then branched into the ethnic Kurdish territory to the southeast of Mosul to stiffen the resistance against ISIL.

The barbarity associated with the ISIL offensive was profound. Mass rape, murder, looting and the wanton destruction of priceless archaeological sites was widely reported in the media. Any opposition to the caliphate or fundamentalist ideology was met with shocking violence. Mass graves were continuing to be found in Northern Iraq in late 2018, some containing thousands of slaughtered people. Tens of thousands fled amid the atrocities. Public executions were conducted, and captured Westerners were filmed as they were brutally tortured before being beheaded. The vision became choreographed propaganda—uploaded onto the internet—with the world looking on with horror.

On 7 August 2014, the United States announced that it intended to intervene in the conflict using air power, with ensuing offensive air support missions for the Iraqi Army carried out near Baghdad. Shortly afterwards, an international conference in Paris that included representatives of ten Sunni Arab states but excluded Iran and Syria, agreed to support an interventionist strategy. As these events were unfolding, Iraq's Prime Minister, Nuri al-Malaki, had come under increasing pressure to resign from his position.

His inability to halt the spread of ISIL, coupled with his reluctance to relinquish his hold on power, drew increasing criticism from both his own parliament and international commentators. Finally, on 14 August 2014, Prime Minister al Malaki announced he was stepping aside to make way for Haider al-Abadi.

The Operation Commences

On 15 August 2014, the United Nations Security Council adopted Resolution 2170 (2014) *Condemning Gross, Widespread Abuse of Human Rights by Extremist Groups in Iraq and Syria.* Australia was one of many nations concerned with ISIL's atrocities, and voted with the UN resolution to condemn both ISIL's actions and foreign nationals fighting for ISIL overseas.

On 14 September 2014, Australian Prime Minister Tony Abbott announced his government intended to deploy Australian Defence Force assets to the Middle East in preparation for operations against ISIL. The announcement had immediately followed a third televised beheading by ISIL of a captured Westerner—British aid worker, David Haines. Abbott was explicit in the Australian stance against ISIL:

> *This death cult is uniquely evil in that it does not simply do evil, it exults in evil. This death cult has ambitions way beyond those of any previous terrorist group.*

Events now moved quickly and within days of this announcement, Australia joined a coalition of countries targeting ISIL in Iraq that included the United States, Great Britain, France, Belgium, Canada, Denmark and the Netherlands. The United States also announced that together with forces from the United Arab Emirates, Saudi Arabia, Jordan, Bahrain and Qatar, it would strike targets in Syria. The international coalition committed to direct combat against ISIL in the form of air power, and special and conventional ground forces providing operational support. The ground forces were integral to a US-led 'Build Partner Capacity' mission and were to involve Australian elements deployed into Iraq itself.

Australia's commitment to destroying ISIL, codenamed Operation OKRA, was significant. Approximately 780 Australian defence personnel deployed with the Air Task Group, the Special Operations Task GroupIraq and the Task Group-Taji, and within the US-led multinational command and control facilities in the Iraqi capital, Baghdad.

Air Task Group

Operation OKRA was significant for the RAAF and the Australian Defence Force in that it was the first truly significant deployment of an Air Force combat capability since the Vietnam War. OKRA not only marked the debut of the Australian F/A-18F Super Hornets into a combat role but it was also the first time the RAAF had used its 'force multipliers'—its KC-30A air-to-air refuelling tankers and E-7A Wedgetail airborne early warning and control platforms—to provide support to strike operations. The F/A-18F Super Hornets were in time rotated out and replaced by ageing F/A-18 *Classic* Hornets. Importantly, the F/A-18Fs, KC-30As and Wedgetails represented 'cutting edge' technology in the suite of Australia's air power capability, and these platforms and their systems were interoperable with aircraft from the wider international coalition.

The RAAF had been forewarned of a potential government decision to deploy combat assets in late August 2014. By the end of the month, several senior officers including the Chief of Air Force, Air Marshal Geoff Brown, visited the Middle East to discuss with senior international leaders the roles and the rates of effort that would be required of an Australian element, the basing options, and the support that an RAAF Air Task Group would need. Amongst the delegates was the prospective commander of the group, accomplished fast jet pilot, Air Commodore Steve Roberton.

Roberton returned to Australia on the eve of Prime Minister Abbott's announcement that Australia would deploy Air Task Group 630 (ATG630), and he had only a very short period to prepare as its inaugural commander. Roberton recalled:

> *'It was pretty rapid, and it was also pretty typical of any major conflict that we have found ourselves in ... we find out, we then have to move very quickly...'*

Roberton's mission was succinct: ATG630 was to deploy to a location in the Middle East Region as an element of a US-led Coalition air force to support Iraqi Security Forces in their battle to defeat ISIL. What was noteworthy was that the deployment was not an imposition; Coalition air power was invited by the Iraqi Government because the Iraqi Security Forces needed international assistance. This mission to support Iraq in its fight against ISIL went beyond air power. As Roberton later related, the question 'Can air power win this?' was not only irrelevant, it was the wrong question. The actual question was 'At what rate can air power facilitate the Iraqi Security Forces to defeat and disrupt ISIL and facilitate a secure state within their country?' In every way it was Iraq's fight, one in which a maturing nation was struggling to leave the past behind and join the modern world. It was an invitation that Australia was obliged to respond to.

Meeting with international commanders and political representatives in the lead up to the deployment gave senior Australia defence personnel unique insights into the complicated physical and political environment into which the RAAF would deploy. The Iraqi landscape was vast and isolated, dominated by extremes of desert aridity, mountainous terrain, and the confluence of two large rivers, the Tigris and Euphrates. The disparate expanses of the Ninawah and Anbar Provinces in the north and west of the nation had become Sunni strongholds and provided ISIL the freedom to manoeuvre to sustain its operations. The countryside enabled ISIL to gain rapid control of key population centres, transport networks and border crossings at a rapid and almost unchecked pace. The entire landscape—spreading southwest from the northern city of Mosul into the Anbar Province and down the Euphrates River Valley—had developed into a network of arms caches, training grounds and communications lines that enabled ISIL unfettered manoeuvre. By capturing and holding territory, ISIL had achieved what no other terrorist organisation had ever achieved before: a sophisticated defensive system that presented significant challenges to potential adversaries.

The overarching political environment was even more intricate. The Iraqi Government—unable to combat the threat—had requested assistance; the United Nations had given its imprimatur; and United States President, Barak Obama, directed the formation of a US-led coalition which defined the end state of operations as the defeat of ISIL. What did this mean? In a military sense, defeat comprised combat operations aiming to disrupt ISIL's ability to command and control its fighters, reduce its safe havens, interdict its source of revenue, destroy its equipment, and kill its individual fighters.

The Destruction of Cultural Heritage

ISIL is a fundamentalist organisation that set out a clear agenda during the war: to completely erase the rich cultural heritage that linked the ancient region of Mesopotamia with the modern-day Sunni-dominated Muslim areas of Iraq and Syria. Mesopotamia is the fertile region of the Middle East where, five millennia ago, humanity first domesticated cattle and planted crops. The world's first cities soon followed, along with written communication. The region's five thousand years of history is a living museum, with its treasures and monuments testifying to a remarkable Semitic people. ISIL's designs for the region were egregious. It incited the wanton destruction of sites and artefacts of global cultural significance in Iraq and Syria which they regarded as 'idolatrous'. Since 2015, imagery and film has surfaced of the deliberate demolition of statues and archaeological ruins by ISIL in what was the ancient Assyria. Shockingly, the ruins of the ancient cultural capital of Nineveh, near Mosul, where the orgy of violence was captured on film as the unique site was systematically demolished with dynamite and bulldozers. Simultaneously, the hypocrisy of ISIL was exposed as its members looted museums and the unique archaeological ruins at Palmyra in modern Syria in a prelude to their destruction. The proceeds of this theft were then turned into profit for weapons procurement by ISIL and its wider nefarious activities. Following on the proceeds from oil and outright robbery, estimates suggest that this pillage was the largest revenue source for ISIL.

In 2016, the United Nations Educational, Scientific and Cultural Organisation (UNESCO) highlighted that the monuments of the ancient world, which spread across what is today Kurdistan and through the upper reaches of the Euphrates River into Syria, were likely irrevocably damaged by ISIL's reign of terror. The extent of ISIL's destruction of this history and heritage is yet to be fully gauged, if it is ever possible.

Build Partner Capacity

At the invitation of the Iraqi Government and in consultation with the US-led Combined Joint Task Force Operation INHERENT RESOLVE the ADF deployed a Build Partner Capacity 'advise and assist' mission in late 2014 in direct support of Iraqi Security Forces. A Special Operations Task Group – Iraq (SOTG-I) and Task Group Taji (TG-Taji) were central to the mission, providing military advice and assistance to building the capacity of the Iraqi Security Forces and its Counter-Terrorism Service. The trained Iraqi forces were subsequently engaged in operations against ISIL.

The SOTG-I was partnered with the Iraqi Counter-Terrorism Service which was formed on the direction of the Iraqi Prime Minister. The Headquarters and training elements of SOTG-I were stationed in a secure compound at Baghdad International Airport. The team implemented an extensive urban warfare training program for their Counter-Terrorism Service colleagues with further specialist training. Forward elements of the SOTG-I—including RAAF Combat Controllers—were deployed with Counter-Terrorism Service headquarters staff on operations against ISIL to facilitate close air support provided by coalition air power. The use of air power in this manner against ISIL forces was to prove a decisive factor in the war.

The TG-Taji mission delivered a training program that built basic skills in the form of weapons handling, tactics, counter improvised explosive device drills, building and obstacle clearing, and first aid. Trainers primarily comprised approximately 300 soldiers drawn from an Australian infantry battalion with supporting elements, and just over 100 New Zealand troops drawn from the Royal New Zealand Infantry Regiment. TG-Taji operated in conjunction with similar training groups from the United States, Great Britain and Spain.

The global nature of the mission and the conflict was best reinforced by an occasion when, in 2016 at the Taji complex, the author was

approached by an Iraqi *jundi* (private) pointing to an image of a young Arab on his mobile phone screen. In clear English he said:
Here!Look. My cousin lives in Merrylands [Sydney]. He is an Australian, too.

Australian Prime Minister Tony Abbott accompanied by the Chief of the Defence Force, Air Chief Marshal Mark Binskin, addresses the media soon after he has made the decision to commit Australian forces to the fight against ISIL. (source: Department of Defence)

On 17 October 2014, the United States Department of Defense formally established Combined Joint Task Force – Operation INHERENT RESOLVE to formalise ongoing military actions against ISIL. The breadth of the operation was impressive, encompassing the efforts and contributions of more than sixty

Coalition partners throughout the Combined Joint Operations Area of Iraq and Syria. The Combined Joint Task Force was also to degrade ISIL to a point where it would lose the physical means and/or will to fight. The goal would rapidly become problematic if Coalition support for Iraqi forces failed to act decisively, giving ISIL the space to reorganise, regenerate or evolve so it could again threaten regional and international stability. The Combined Joint Task Force's mission therefore reflected the Coalition's considered approach to the problem, as contained in this press release:

In conjunction with partner forces Combined Joint Task Force – Operation INHERENT RESOLVE is to defeat ISIS in designated areas of Iraq and Syria and sets conditions for follow-on operations to increase regional stability.

A military mission statement is generally expressed this way. A task is generally reduced to its constituent elements, the prose is sparing, and the tense reflects the urgency of the job at hand. On 15 October 2014, US Central Command released a communiqué explaining the rationale behind the name INHERENT RESOLVE:

INHERENT RESOLVE is intended to reflect the unwavering resolve and deep commitment of the US and partner nations in the region and around the globe to eliminate the terrorist group ISIL and the threat they pose to Iraq, the region and the wider international community. It also symbolizes the willingness and dedication of coalition members to work closely with our friends in the region and apply all available dimensions of national power necessary—diplomatic, informational, military, economic—to degrade and ultimately destroy ISIL.

The press release was insightful. The opening phrase *'In conjunction with partner forces...'* stressed Western acknowledgement that Iraqi Security Forces, including the Iraqi Army, the Iraqi Air Force, the Counter Terrorism Service, the Federal Police, and the Kurdish Peshmerga were the elements that would engage and defeat ISIL in Iraq. In Syria, the task would fall to the Syrian Democratic Forces and their partners, the Syrian Arab Coalition. The closing phrase *'...sets conditions for follow-on operations...'* highlighted that operations against ISIL must first defeat the organisation militarily, but then go on to reduce the group's ideology in order to stem the global flow of foreign fighters into the region. All of this was intended to improve regional stability.

RAAF Command and Control

Just how an Australian Air Task Group would fit into this organisation was significant. As Australia's contribution was relatively small, its assets would require careful management to realise their potential. Given the nature of the environment, there were always going to be challenges associated with establishing the command and control mechanism for the Air Task Group. More than a decade earlier, Prime Minister John Howard had pledged immediate support to the United States in the aftermath of the 11 September 2001 attacks. The reaffirmation of the commitment to a 'war on terrorism' by successive governments served to not only underwrite the Australian-US alliance, but also resulted in the ADF already having a sizeable presence in the region when the Air Task Group arrived. ATG630's command and control arrangements were thus predicated on the nature of Australian operations in the Middle East Region as they had been throughout the preceding decade. Notwithstanding this, there would be ongoing differences of opinion over the command arrangements that were never quite resolved during the course of the operation.

An Australian theatre headquarters commanded by a two-star Joint Force

Commander had deployed very shortly after the Australian Government's decision in 2003 to commit forces to operations in Iraq. Joint Task Force 633 (JTF633) served as the Headquarters for Australian forces in the Middle East Region and was initially established in one of Saddam Hussein's former palaces in Camp Victory adjacent to Baghdad International Airport—it came to be called 'Australia House'. The Headquarters had wide responsibilities. Headquarters JTF633 exercised *National Command* over a force of assigned elements from each of the Services. This arrangement was in place to ensure that Australian assets were always to be used in accordance with the Australian Government's direction and objectives. By 2007, Australian forces were serving across all domains in support of operations in the Persian Gulf, Indian Ocean, Iraq, Kuwait, Qatar and Afghanistan. The geographical distances and regional disparity were significant. It was about a thousand miles from the middle of the Persian Gulf to Kabul in Afghanistan, and a similar distance from the southern Gulf to the northern reaches of Iraq. Just as Iraq presented its own internal environmental challenges, the huge expanse of the wider theatre of operations posed many problems for planners and logisticians.

As Australian operations in Iraq drew down in late 2008, Headquarters JTF633 was relocated from Camp Victory to Al Minhad Air Base, near Dubai in the United Arab Emirates. Al Minhad had formerly been used by ADF elements during the invasion of Iraq in Gulf War II and then remained as a base for RAAF AP-3C surveillance aircraft. The consolidation to this one location also resulted in RAAF C130 air mobility operations relocating from Al Udeid in Qatar, and the logistics hub and Reception, Staging, Onwards-clearance and Insertion (RSO&I) facilities moving south from Ali Al Salim air base in Kuwait. RSO&I provides the final preparation for personnel before they move forward to their deployed locations, while at the same time providing acclimatisation to the new environment. These moves resulted in more than 500 ADF personnel being permanently stationed at Al Minhad in support of regional operations. While the existence of a multi-national facility at Al Minhad was in the public domain, sensitivities within the United Arab Emirates precluded the Australian Government from acknowledging its operations. This veil of secrecy was finally lifted during the course of Operation OKRA.

Commanding Military Aviation

Australian Prime Minister Tony Abbott discusses the nature of the coming mission with the crew of an RAAF F/A-18F Super Hornet. (source: Department of Defence)

The Air Force in which Air Commodore Steve Roberton serves is approaching 100 years of age. Founded by Royal decree in 1921, the Royal Australian Air Force drew heavily from the development of aviation in World War I and from the nation's status in the British Empire. After the Royal Air Force, it is the oldest independent air service in the world. The RAAF's first chief, Sir Richard Williams, was gifted, progressive and driven in his pursuit of excellence for the Service. Williams was fortunate in having a model developed by the RAF's Air Marshal Sir Hugh Trenchard on which the fledgling RAAF could be based. Trenchard's appreciation of effective air power was underwritten by six foundation stones: aviation industry, research and development, technical training, officer training, a central flying school, and a staff college system for commanders. The RAAF has maintained these elements, sometimes with difficulty, over the course of a century. Roberton, and those subsequently appointed to command the Air Task Group on Operation OKRA, were very much products of this system. They were as diverse in personality and as like-minded in their expertise as any group of focussed professionals.

There have been eleven commanders in the Commander Air Task Group role since September 2014, and today the functional position remains in Qatar. The more senior officers among this group, including Air Commodore Mike Kitcher, were products of the RAAF Academy which closed its doors in 1986 when the Australian Defence Force Academy was opened as a tri-Service establishment. Kitcher had completed the initial two years of his education at the RAAF Academy in 1984 and 1985 before graduating from ADFA in its inaugural year.

Later commanders, including Group Captain Pete Mitchell, graduated from the Defence Force Academy in the 1990s. Yet others, such as Air Commodores Terry Van Haren and Antony

Martin, were direct entry officers who had joined the RAAF without undertaking a degree qualification. Both had immediately focussed on the intricacies of their aviation qualifications. Yet another commander, Group Captain Ross Bender, qualified as an aeronautical engineer before undertaking pilot training.

The age difference across the commanders was about a decade, with all of them having previous 'deployed operational' experience and more than half on combat operations. Though most served as fast jet aircrew, their core qualifications were mixed. Martin was an Air Combat Officer with experience on exchange in the United States Navy operating the Grumman E-2C Hawkeye Airborne Early Warning and Control platform; and later the E-7A Wedgetail in Australia. Bender was a transport pilot with a great deal of experience gained flying C-130 Hercules aircraft, as an accomplished test pilot, and as former commander of the RAAF's Aircraft Research and Development Unit.

All these officers were dedicated, details-oriented, single-minded, genial, direct, precise, introspective or extroverted—aligning with their respective personalities. It is impossible to rank them in terms of command ability or experience. What can be said is that each officer was a product of an established training and education system. They were all airminded individuals who achieved excellence in their core skillsets. They each had undertaken a comprehensive staff-officer training continuum at a masters-degree level which was designed to prepare them for command. Each officer had a proven ability at commanding air power at a lower level. Even if he could not directly express the constituent elements of the evolved Trenchard air power model a century on, each commander implicitly understood the tenets of these foundations in applying air power.

A small ceremony marked the hand over command for Australia's Air Task Group, currently deployed in the Middle East Region, from AIRCDRE Steve Roberton (right) to AIRCDRE Glen Braz. (source: Department of Defence)

On 26 February 2014, the Chief of the Defence Force, General David Hurley, announced that the Australian facilities at Al Minhad Air

Force Base were to be renamed Camp Baird in honour of Victoria Cross recipient Corporal Cameron Baird who had been killed in action in Afghanistan the previous year. Hurley highlighted that while the Australian mission in Afghanistan had concluded, the Australian presence in the Middle East Region was to remain with numbers of personnel at Al Minhad to increase to approximately 800. The base and its facilities became more important as events unfolded during the year. In early September 2014, an Australian Broadcasting Commission media team reported that:

> *Australia's military presence in the UAE is reliant on our good relations and solid relationship with the ruling family, particularly the president Khalifa bin Zayed Al Nahyan. He has visited Australia a number of times, and Australian Prime Ministers have regularly dropped in for formal and informal meetings with him on their way to and from visits to the troops in Afghanistan. It is understood there are limits to what the Emirates will allow us to do there, but the planned deployment announced by Mr Abbott is obviously within those limits.*

At this time, the Al Minhad facility was principally providing command and support for two operations: Operation ACCORDION, being 'to support the sustainment of Australian Defence Force operations, [and to] enable contingency planning and enhance regional relationships in the Middle East Region'; and Operation MANITOU, which involved maritime security operations in the Middle East Region and counter-piracy in the Gulf of Aden and off the Horn of Africa. By the beginning of September 2014, nearly 800 ADF personnel were deployed in the Middle East Region—primarily at Al Minhad—conducting a variety of operative, support and enabling roles. These elements included single-Service force and combat support units; a joint movements coordination centre; a communications group; a C130 Hercules detachment; a Combined Air Operations Centre detachment; and a C-17 Globemaster support section. In addition, there were various ADF personnel embedded in several Coalition Headquarters throughout the region. These various units and elements, selected and force assigned by Headquarters Joint Operations Command at Bungendore on the outskirts of Canberra, came under the National and Operational Command of the collocated Headquarters JTF633. Operation OKRA would result in significant additions to the arrangement.

In the normal course of operational deployments, air power elements are organised into a Task Group to serve as the Task Force air component. The commander of the Task Group, an Air Component Commander, is a professional aviator who functions as the Task Force commander's principal air power adviser. In the case of ATG630, this arrangement would be entirely unsuitable for two reasons. Firstly, the Australian National Security Committee's agreement of 14 September 2014 to commit forces in support of direct combat against ISIL in Iraq would effectively double the number of Australian personnel in the Middle East Region By itself, the single RAAF Air Task Group of six F/A-18F Super Hornets, a Boeing E-7A Wedgetail aircraft, and an Airbus KC-30A tanker—to be based initially at Al Minhad—would comprise over 400 additional personnel. Aside from basing and infrastructure considerations, the National Command function of Headquarters JTF633 simply did not have the resources or structures in place to provide operational and tactical command and control for the highly specialised function of this Air Task Group. Secondly, the air power contribution to be made by ATG630 was to occur as a small element within a wider Coalition air campaign that comprised hundreds of platforms from dozens of nations conducting numerous roles and missions. ATG630 needed to remain responsive to the requirements of this Coalition.

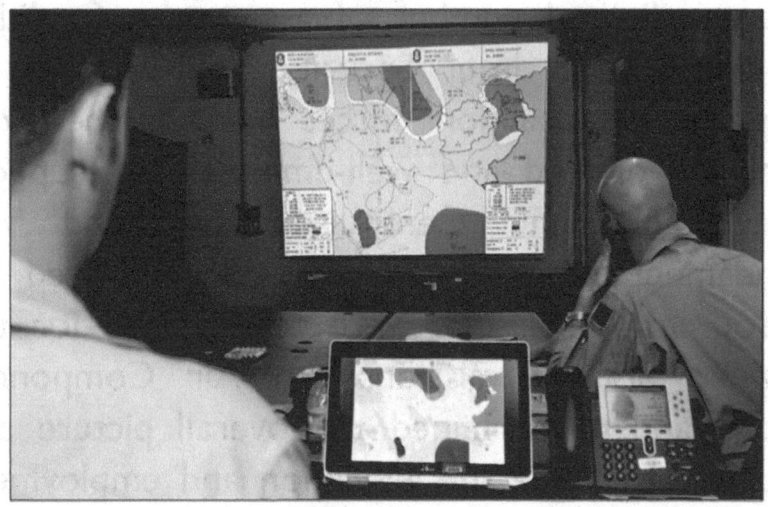

Australian aircrew in a briefing room at their facility in the MER. Digital satellite communications and real-time displays such as those depicted in this image are a feature and strength of modern air power operations. The connectivity among operating platforms, different localities and back to Australia make the transfer of time critical information virtually instantaneous. (source: Department of Defence)

The Iraqi Security Forces would require the specialist, technical support afforded by Coalition air power to defeat ISIL. It remains axiomatic that air superiority is a precondition for success in military operations. Land forces operating without it do so without the perspective, speed, reach, flexibility and precision strike afforded by air power. Deprived of such advantages, the Security Forces would have been blinded and their ability to defeat ISIL would have been significantly reduced. Fortunately, although there were a limited number of assets, the Coalition could provide Iraqi Security Forces with air superiority. Coalition forces had to be both well-coordinated and well-employed to support the Iraqi fight. Centralised command was fundamental to this premise. With limited air resources, all aircraft were to be used for the highest priority missions. An Air Component Commander maintained the overall picture and would determine the allocation and employment upon the ground commander's determination of targets and objectives. Not doing so risked allocating platforms and capabilities in a piecemeal, localised approach, in effect dissipating the very advantages that air power brought to the table.

The Coalition command and control arrangements for air power were facilitated by a Combined Air Operations Centre located outside Iraq at the Al Udeid Air Base in Qatar. The Centre enabled land and air commanders to collaborate to allocate air assets where required in the context of the entire campaign. The facility had been in place in Qatar since the beginning of the Iraq War in 2003 and embodied the notion of centralised command and decentralised execution. By 2014, the Combined Air Operations Centre's area of responsibility extended across the Middle East to Central Asia, and it was well-practiced in the art of applying air power where it was most needed. Following a precise cycle that incorporated target identification, planning and sortie execution, the Combined Air Operations Centre (CAOC) generated sorties across all air power roles and missions. To facilitate this support, the CAOC was staffed with aviation specialists from across the Coalition. Its activities and the planning and execution cycle were organised among five divisions: Strategy; Combat Plans; Combat Operations; Air Mobility; and Intelligence, Surveillance and Reconnaissance.

In comparison to the land and sea domains, air power platforms move very quickly, necessitating the Combined Air Operations Centre to maintain awareness of the rapidly changing nature of the theatre air environment. Given the speed and reach of air power, and the number and disparate location of systems and platforms involved in Operation INHERENT RESOLVE, the Centre was essential. Without it, the Coalition would not have been able to synchronise and apply positive control and coordination of all air weapons systems across the expanse of northern Iraq. Generating this situational awareness was complex and required the expertise and skills of hundreds of technical support personnel who serve in satellite communications, imagery analysis, network design, computer programming, radio systems, systems administration, medical support and other fields. The ability of these staff to ensure the Centre was able to functionally communicate imagery and information digitally in near real-time and worldwide was an outstanding achievement. Equally, the processes employed by the Centre's divisional expertise also ensured that first-class air power effects would be generated in support of Iraqi forces in the field.

Despite the overwhelming superiority of this Coalition air power support, it was important to constantly remember that this was Iraq's fight. To this end, the Combined Joint Force Land Component Command for Operation INHERENT RESOLVE was headquartered in the Iraqi capital and worked in close cooperation with the leadership of the Iraqi military. The Land Component Command supported and collaborated with the Iraqi high command in its planning activities, providing advice and assistance, training, and sustainment to elements of the field Iraqi forces.

Aside from its location, the role of the Combined Joint Force Land Component Command differed significantly from the role of the Combined Air Operations Centre and Air Component Commander. The headquarters would not command Western troops in operations against ISIL. Iraq would furnish the troops. In many cases Coalition specialists went forward with Iraqi troops and served in coordinating roles alongside the Iraqis at tactical level headquarters behind the forward edge of the battle. Among these specialists were numerous individual RAAF Combat Controllers from the SOTG-I who coordinated Coalition air strikes—sometimes with RAAF aircraft—against ISIL positions. This was as close as Coalition land elements got to the enemy.

The Combined Air Operations Centre: The Operational Nerve Centre of Contemporary Air Operations

The Combined Air Operations Centre—referred to as CAOC—is an operational command and control headquarters that ensures air power is employed to best effect across single or joint campaigns, and in accordance with the central tenet of centralised command and decentralised execution. Its functionality was envisaged within the United States Air Force and first employed during the 1991 Gulf War. The Centre's responsibilities include providing specialist advice to the Joint Commander; planning and executing air operations in support of the Joint Commander; immediate contingency planning; triggering support for operations; Search and Rescue co-ordination; integrating space and cyber in planning and execution; administering and controlling military airspace; and co-ordinating strategic Aero-Medical Evacuation. In order to realise the powerful effects that air power brings to the campaign, the Centre comprises five complimentary divisions to plan, execute and evaluate air power sorties:

- Strategy Division develops, refines, disseminates and assesses the progress of aerospace strategy and associated plans, orders, and instructions;
- Combat Plans Division develops the air tasking order for the application of resources based on guidance from Strategy Division;
- Combat Operations Division executes the air tasking order;
- Intelligence-Surveillance-Reconnaissance Division refines targeting requirements and conducts (ISR) threat and target analysis; and Intelligence, Surveillance and Reconnaissance asset management; and
- Air Mobility Division plans, integrates and directs the operation of air mobility assets.

Lesson # 9

- The command and control of air power uniquely reflects the nature of the air domain and the way that professional aviators operate and fight in it.
- Air power is most effectively utilised through the tenet of centralised command and decentralised execution. This tenet is enduring.

The Combined Joint Force Land Component Command also facilitated the provision of intelligence and strike operations for Iraq's ground forces, and this is where air power was crucial to Iraqi success. Coalition air power, including the Australian strike element, was able to provide both deliberate and dynamic targeting services in support of the ground forces operating against ISIL. Soon after it deployed, the Air Task Group would be involved in conducting deliberate deep air support interdiction missions against targets prioritised and approved by the Combined Air Operations Centre. This was to be done via a Joint Integrated Prioritised Target List (JIPTL) which was derived from sensors and intelligence sources, and the agreed targeting recommendations from each of the components. The targets were elemental to the proposed operations developed jointly between Iraqi commanders and the Combined Joint Force Land Component Command.

Targets requiring immediate attention were a different matter. Time critical targeting, particularly in support of ground troops in contact with ISIL, was actioned by a dynamic Close Air Support interdiction effort conducted by platforms 'waiting on task' to be directed to support soldiers in the fight. Both methods of targeting required precision, fidelity and close coordination at all levels.

The influence that these complexities exerted over the newly arrived Air Task Group were significant and layered. National Command of ATG630 was vested in the Commander Headquarters JTF633 who would ensure that the conduct of its operations explicitly complied with the Australian Government's endorsed rules of engagement and guidelines. For strategic oversight, this overseas headquarters was responsible directly to the Commander Joint Operations at Headquarters Joint Operations Command near Canberra. This was essential because each of the Coalition's national contingents were operating under slightly different rules of engagement meaning that the approval of Air Task Group's target list required Joint Operations Command approval.

Within the command of Commander Joint Operations provided an intermediate layer over ATG630—Operational Command. Operational Command was exercised by a one-star military aviator, the Director General-Air, who was the principle air power adviser to Commander Joint Operations and commander of the Air and Space Operations Centre at the Headquarters Joint Operations Command. The Air and Space Operations Centre focussed on matters relating to the assignment of Air Force elements to Commander Joint Operations and the subsequent employment and sustainment of assigned Air Force elements for operations and exercises. Director General-Air was therefore integral to facilitating and approving the use of air power to the deployed force. National Command and Operations Command aside, it was absolutely vital that operational control of ATG630's platforms fall under the Coalition Forces Air Component Commander in order to generate the best effects in support of the Combined Joint Force Land Component Command. This requirement was purely practical; and so, operational control organisation via the Combined Air Operations Centre quickly fell into place. Once established in locality, Australian platforms would be tasked to execute missions in accordance with the Centre's operational rhythm.

Given command and control arrangements, subordinate ATG630 commanders were mindful that they would need to be equally diplomatic and assertive as they deployed into the region. The command and control consideration required an open-minded approach from all concerned. Senior Australian leaders gave subordinate aviators a great deal of latitude. Roberton indicated that they:

> *simply imparted the mission set, what the overall strategic objectives would be, to then let us operate within that guidance, and it proved to be a great example of almost a devolution of mission command, to let us in-theatre work back ... through JOC [Joint Operations Command] ... through DGAIR [Director General-Air].*

Such organisation was straightforward at higher levels, but it generated debate amongst more junior Service personnel, with lessons from the experience still resonating today. Up to Operation OKRA, the RAAF had not applied kinetic air power on such a scale since the Vietnam War. In a matter of weeks in 2014, the RAAF was faced with the challenge of conducting complex strike operations with an intricate targeting process as an element of a joint task force over 12 000 kilometres from home, while still running domestic operations in Australia. One RAAF officer concluded:

> *To have apportioned command of Australian fighter assets any other way would have necessitated closing down the Air Force's entire air combat fleet to support OKRA alone.*

This was an over-simplification; and highlighted a degree of myopia in an Air Force that had not deployed strike assets in similar numbers for many years. Such views also did not consider the effect on Wedgetail and KC-30A platforms and crews. The lack of understanding of how air power would be employed in Iraq was just as prevalent among some middle ranking officers in the other Services, and there was a notion during Operation OKRA that the RAAF 'was going off on its own'. Isolated elements at Al Minhad—unaware even though they were serving on an air base—had no comprehension that air power was being utilised to degrade ISIL. As one member of another Service stated: 'The ADF in the Middle East is in a period of consolidation ... it is not conducting operational activity'. Yet another officer indicated that using RAAF aircraft in the manner that it was being employed was 'overkill'. He quite literally added that the ADF could do the same job with a squadron of Spitfires. Such uninformed viewpoints were thankfully infrequent. That they even occurred at all was more a reflection of the ATG's efficiency. It reinforced the fact that RAAF platforms were flying hundreds of miles from operating Emirate air bases to deliver their effects before returning for refurbishment virtually unnoticed in the course of the same day.

There were two responses to such viewpoints. The first was that Australia needed to husband its resources very carefully to be able to support multiple air operation centres and targeting processes concurrently. The effect of doing so was evident at the end of Operation OKRA: the RAAF enjoyed a mission success rate higher than ninety-eight per cent, with minimal weapon misses or issues of reputation loss for Australia. The second was one of continuing education among colleagues. The ADF is a joint organisation and this must be inculcated among all ranks across all Services consistently and continuously from the moment that they are recruited.

The point to be made is that debates over air power—especially over who commands air power—are largely irrelevant. Quite simply, in the modern profession of arms, air power is independently established, integral and vital. The only practical consideration during OKRA needed to be how to establish efficient command and control arrangements, designed to employ the advantages of air power to best effect. As ATG630 got into its 'battle-rhythm' this seemed to have been the case.

People, Platforms, Process and Place: The Core of the Mission

In late 2014, this latest generation of Australian service personnel prepared to depart for the Middle East Region to serve in the profession of arms. This time, the national commitment would last for three and a half years, with a significant historical provenance behind the deployment. When the Air Task Group departed Australia on 21 September 2014 it was precisely one hundred years since the convoys that would carry the first Australian troop commitment to World War I gathered to sail for operations at Gallipoli. It was ninety-six years to the day since No 40 Wing of the Palestine Brigade, led by Australian aviator Sir Richard Williams and spearheaded by No 1 Squadron AFC, wrought havoc in the Wadi Fara. Now, on this very same day, the same No 1 Squadron—accompanied by aircraft from two others units, Nos 2 and 33 Squadrons—were to serve in the same part of the world and to conduct the same roles and missions that their forebears had done nearly a century before.

There were, of course, vast differences between the men of the AFC and the contemporary service personnel who would be engaged in Operation OKRA. Australian society and the demographic had irrevocably altered during the century of its federated history. However, the similarities between the new and the old were striking. There was a pride in the RAAF and wider ADF that the contingent was doing a job with meaning; leaving loved ones behind—painful as it was—was necessary in order that the group could focus on the task at hand. The mateship was there: perseverance in shared adversity; fortitude; a helping hand; mutual respect at all levels for each other's professional skills; and a willingness to get on with it. Like the airmen of the AFC, the OKRA personnel were largely older and already qualified in their vocations when word came to deploy. In this, the Australian aviators, technicians and support personnel enjoyed an incredibly symbiotic, pragmatic and practical relationship.

Technicians conduct maintenance on an Australian strike platform in the MER. (source: Department of Defence)

They would soon interact and work closely with their colleagues from the Coalition member nations, particularly the personnel from the United States Air Force with whom they would share a base, operational compatibility and many cultural similarities. Even so, there were differences between the Australians and their international colleagues that the Australians wondered and marvelled at. The excesses of the American messing arrangements on big Coalition bases, where Australians would eat and socialise, were a constant source of amazement for newly arriving Air Task Group rotations. Every conceivable dish, delicacy and beverage seemed to have been catered for, with meals ranging from short-order and deep-fried to the more traditional fare. 'On base' amenities in the form of gymnasiums, movie theatres, a bar, and fast-food outlets made the station a microcosm of American society. And it was big. Thousands of personnel 'came and went' at all hours of the day and night: Americans, Britons, Danes, Belgians, and now the Australians. This all took some adjustment, but the staff of the Air Task Group did so rapidly.

In a century of military aviation much had changed, but the basics had not. The characteristics of flight, the air domain and air power were much as they were during World War I. Speed equals distance on time; fuel flow divided by ground speed equals pounds burned per nautical mile; the adiabatic lapse rate is three degrees per 1000 feet—the science was immutable.

The desert weather was also an overarching factor and was no different to what had been experience in World War I—stifling. Flight Lieutenant Paul 'Brades' Brady, a KC-30A captain, summed it up well when he arrived. 'It's very hot,' he said with laconic understatement, but then laughed and elaborated:

> *Damn hot actually. Being a Queenslander I love the heat and we live at the beach. I had never experienced heat like this until I got here and obviously hearing the stories from previous squadron members about how hot it was 'I thought that won't affect me' ... but when you see fifty degrees and ninety per cent humidity over here for weeks on end, it's impressive. And a lot of sand obviously.*

The many and varied trades of the Air Task Group staff were a manifestation of one hundred years of professional refinement of the discipline of air power. This was rightly so because the technological developments associated with air power in the century since its inception were so profound. Of course, aircrew remained the visible face of the RAAF, but they numbered perhaps barely ten per cent of the group. Tens of dozens of skilled professionals served to support, maintain, arm and operate the platforms and systems that had deployed as the core elements of the Air Task Group. Among the 'other ranks', were personnel grouped into RAAF 'musterings' broadly defined along technical and non-technical trade lines. Commissioned ranks were grouped into RAAF 'specialisations' which reflected the officer's core skills in addition to their inherent leadership and management responsibilities.

A significant consideration in the modern group was the level of education across all ranks. Since Federation, Australia had developed into a modern, vibrant, cosmopolitan and secular society. The nation has been fortunate to enjoy one of the higher education standards in the world. The RAAF is a microcosm of this society and, of course, educated personnel have underwritten the Air Force's ability to operate the sophisticated technology associated with its platforms. Both commissioned and non-commissioned personnel in the Air Task Group and wider RAAF were products of an extensive training and education system designed to prepare them for the intricacies and rigours associated with projecting air power.

All the members of the Air Task Group were professionals—motivated, highly trained and skilled at their functions. This reflected the strength of the human endeavours underpinning the Air Task Group. The organisation of the platforms, people, maintenance and logistics schedules required structure; otherwise, chaos would ensue. Air Task Group personnel were broadly apportioned according to their enabling or operative roles. Amongst the enablers, logistics support predominated; they included supply, maintenance, security and administrative staff, as well as medical, public affairs and legal specialists. Aircrew dominated the operator numbers, but they were joined by other skill groups including Ground Liaison Officers from the Army and Air Battle Managers embedded into a Coalition facility on the base. While RAAF Combat Controllers were not specifically assigned to the Air Task Group, they operated in close conjunction with the Iraqi ground forces and would liaise closely with Coalition aircrew while a strike sortie was in progress.

While these groupings worked in a broad sense, the complexities associated with supplying, maintaining and operating the platforms required far greater organisation and evolved constantly over the duration of the operation. The underwriting notion was that personnel were assigned according to the platforms that they operated or maintained, or in accordance with their function in the logistics support mechanism. Accordingly, a structured hierarchy for where personnel would be assigned to operate was already in place when the Air Task Group departed Australia for the Middle East. This required modification as the operation unfolded.

It was supported by the Australian Headquarters in-theatre and was ratified by Commander Joint Operations who had responsibility for commanding and coordinating the force assignment as well as allocation of technical and human resources from parent single Services. While the responsibility for mounting support and national command remained in place under the auspices of Headquarters JTF633 Operation ACCORDION at the Al Minhad (AMAB) facilities, the operational command arrangements for ATG630 would exist independently under the banner of Operation OKRA. However, the ATG remained responsive to the national command and support arrangements provided by HQJTF633 and HQJOC. The SOTG-I (TG632) and TG-Taji (TG633.4), also assigned to Operation OKRA were similarly organised.

All of this took some time and effort to consolidate as the air and ground campaigns unfolded, but by the height of operations against ISIL in 2016 and 2017, the structure had matured. The command and control arrangement for the Air Task Group is depicted diagrammatically at appendix 4. Subordinate Task Units within the Air Task Group had internal command and control arrangements, as did the Task Elements which were arranged in order of the roles and effects generated: strike (F/A-18A and F/A-18F); intelligence, surveillance and reconnaissance, and air battle management (Boeing E-7A Wedgetail and 'Kingpin' ground-based elements); and air mobility, and air-to-air refuelling (KC-30A).

RAAF Pilots and Air Combat Officers: Modern Air Power Specialists

All members of the Officer Aircrew specialisation serving on Operation OKRA were commissioned in either the Pilot or Air Combat Officer categories. Both categories can trace their lineage respectively to the pilots and observers who flew in the AFC: the pilot—the captain of the aircraft—is responsible for controlling the platform, its safety of flight, and operational application and integration. In multi-crewed combat platforms, the Air Combat Officer is responsible for mission command, systems operation, air-navigation, and weapons control. The pilot is the final arbiter in any decision.

The positional function of modern multi-crewed platforms is integral to the performance of the platform and its mission success. Even though personnel on a platform may be unable to perform the functions of other crew positions, the situational awareness shared among the roles aids in ensuring that the platforms can complete their assigned missions. The corollary of this is that there is no real concept of 'military rank' in an aircraft crew, other than that which is worn on their shoulders. Authority in a multi-crewed platform stems from the role of each position and from a shared commitment to a common purpose. It is common to see the captain of an aircraft as a Flight Lieutenant pilot while the mission commander can be a Wing Commander Air Combat Officer.

The Logistics support functions

Logistics support was fundamental to the air power effects being generated by the Air Task Group and comprised the mechanism for mounting and sustaining operations over an extended period. The functions central to logistics support included maintenance and supply support. Without these functions, the Air Task Group would have been ineffective.

Maintenance support was the system in place designed to maintain the aircraft and equipment in a state where it remained fit to perform its purpose. The process aimed to prolong equipment life and to minimise capability loss.

The supply support function was to provide the right support precisely when required for the duration of the air campaign. This presented challenges for a supply chain that was tasked with supporting several hundred specialist personnel and their equipment thousands of kilometres from their home airbase. It was also a diverse task and included the functions of supply, transport, movement, catering and messing. The requirements associated with all this included stock determination, procurement, inventory management and control, warehousing and distribution, and disposal.

Lesson # 10

- Sustaining a deployed force is an essential air power function.
- It affects the depth and duration of campaigns and operations, and involves the provision of maintenance, engineering, supply, combat and operational support, and coordinated international engagements.

- Effective safety and airworthiness management systems are also critical to ensure air power is sustainable and resources are preserved.

As Commander Air Task Group, Roberton and his successors would operate out of the Combined Air Operations Centre facility in Al Udeid, Qatar. Several dozen Australian personnel were assigned to specialist roles in the Centre as Combined Task Unit 630.2 (CTU630.2). Operational aircrews and other personnel were assigned to the operation under Combined Task Unit 630.1 (CTU630.1). Both Combined Task Units communicated via telephone and satellite-enabled computer technology that facilitated real-time data transfer, voice and video communication.

Initially, the Air Task Group would operate from the airfield at Al Minhad. As the operation proceeded, this would change soon. CTU630.1 provided a senior Australian aviation commander *in situ* on the Al Minhad air base and at the Australian headquarters. The first officer selected for the role, Group Captain Robert Chipman, was an experienced fighter pilot like Roberton. His function as the Commander CTU630.1 essentially placed him in a role that equated to an Officer Commanding of a Wing back home. This role entailed the higher command and operational level responsibilities associated with flying, maintenance and personnel administration.

A subordinate Task Element comprising a Task Unit Headquarters (TUHQ TE630.1.0) was collocated with the Australian platforms, and it acted as the interface to the commander of CTU630.1 and operational tasking provided by CTU630.2. To fulfil its responsibilities the TUHQ was organised along similar lines—though with fewer personnel—to the Australian JTF Headquarters and other similar Western joint headquarters.

Rather than use the designator 'J' for Joint, TE630.1.0 used 'A' for Air. The staff had an A1 cell to address administrative functions for all personnel in the Air Task Group, in addition to public affairs and liaison duties with the hosting nation. The A2 cell provided intelligence support to augment that provided by the Combined Air Operations Centre to the subordinate task elements—the strike and intelligence, surveillance and reconnaissance elements still each had their own intelligence officer assigned. An A3 cell ran an operations desk manned by staff who were on station while Australian aircraft were airborne. The A3 cell also maintained and updated a computer system with mission related data, checked the daily issued Air Task Order, prepared Escape and Evasion data packs for aircrew, and a myriad of other smaller operations related tasks. The A4 cell provided logistics support across the entire Air Task Group, facilitating spare parts request for aircraft from stores in Australia, fuel for aircraft, munitions and ordnance acquisition and storage, and fulfilling every supply demand required to operate complex military aircraft. A single officer fulfilled an A5 function which looked to short term planning for the exigencies of Operation OKRA. There was a large A6 team which was responsible for maintaining an extensive real-time communications and computer system infrastructure. A Legal Officer was assigned to help ensure that rules of engagement could be, and were, applied effectively, and to provide advice for commanders. Finally, a Warrant Officer Disciplinary served as the senior non-commissioned airman ensuring good order and discipline across the entire force, while a chaplain provided pastoral care for all personnel.

The work of the headquarters was not glamorous, but it was vital, particularly given that Group Captain Chipman's command comprised disparate platforms from different Force Element Groups which had gathered at a foreign base to conduct operations. The selection of Chipman was particularly astute. His flying qualifications were first-rate; but more so, he possessed an engaging leadership style to which all ranks responded to. Chipman was initially collocated with Headquarters JTF633 where he went to work to facilitate the operational administration that would enable the Air Task Group to commence flying. In turn, he was extremely fortunate in having Wing Commander Matt McCormack as the commander of the Task Unit Headquarters to run its day-to-day activities. McCormack was another experienced fighter pilot and, like Chipman, was well-regarded. Quietly spoken, intelligent, and completely unruffled, McCormack was the ideal commander for the responsibilities associated with the Task Unit Headquarters function. Together, Chipman and McCormack oversaw a team that enabled platform crews to focus on their operational tasks, freed from the responsibility of conducting command and administrative liaison with their international counterparts and the Australian headquarters at Al Minhad.

In addition to the Task Unit Headquarters, the other Task Elements allocated to CTU 630.1 comprised TE630.1.1 (strike), TE630.1.2 (air battle management), TE630.1.3 (air-to-air refuelling) and TE630.1.4 (ground-based air battle management). The first three elements comprised aircrews, engineers, technicians and logistics staff assigned to maintain and operate a specific platform. Each was a team, and each drew its expertise from an RAAF flying squadron in Australia.

TE630.1.1's personnel were drawn initially from No 1 Squadron operating F/A-18-F Super Hornets, a unit of No 82 Wing at RAAF Amberley. They would eventually rotate with personnel from units of No 81 Wing, operating F/A-18A *Classic* Hornets from RAAF Williamtown (Nos 3 and 77 Squadrons) and RAAF Tindal (No 75 Squadron). TE630.1.2's personnel came from No 2 Squadron within 42 Wing at RAAF Williamtown. TE630.1.3's personnel were drawn from No 33 Squadron of No 86 Wing, based at RAAF Amberley. The personnel assigned to the final element, TE630.1.4, were solely ground-based air battle management operative and air surveillance specialists, with no requirement for technical or administrative staff within their facility which was provided by an overarching USAF unit in which a wide range of Coalition staff were embedded. TE630.1.4's callsign was 'Kingpin'.

The group was large, made up of aircraft platforms, nearly four hundred personnel, and all the ordnance and maintenance equipment required to keep it functioning. The platforms of the Air Task Group comprised four different aircraft types conducting three of the RAAF's four core air power roles: strike; intelligence, surveillance and reconnaissance; and air mobility. The fourth core air power role—control of the air—had already been attained by Coalition forces prior to the Air Task Group's arrival. Even so, the RAAF strike element was capable of being 're-rolled' in mid-mission to conduct air-to-air operations if required—it never was.

The Australian platforms and systems were the best of their type in the world. The strike element of the Air Task Group initially comprised the modern, dual-seat F/A-18F Super Hornets, later replaced by the ageing, but still highly capable, single-seat F/A-18A *Classic* Hornets. Both aircraft and their systems were completely interoperable with all air elements of the Coalition.

The awesome lethality of the array of weaponry available to the Australian strike element is clearly depicted in this image of ordinance being prepared for loading on to RAAF F/A-18A Classic Hornets in the MER. (source: Department of Defence)

The platform used by the intelligence, surveillance and reconnaissance element of the Air Task Group was the E-7A Wedgetail; an aircraft based on a heavily modified Boeing 737-700 commercial airliner. The Wedgetail provided airborne early warning and control data for friendly collaborating assets to increase their situational awareness and targeting capability. Over Iraq, the Wedgetail provided air battle management for all coalition aircraft assigned to a specified combat operation during the period that it was airborne. It operated its Multi-role Electronically Scanned Array (MESA) radar, while additionally receiving data from its own communications and electronic support measures systems, and from other command and control systems. The MESA radar—fitted to the Wedgetail's dorsal surface and often returned to as its 'surfboard'—gave the platform its distinctive look. By sharing the data collected by its sensors, the Wedgetail enabled the coordination between Iraqi ground forces and supporting Coalition close air support aircraft on task, or against predetermined targets.

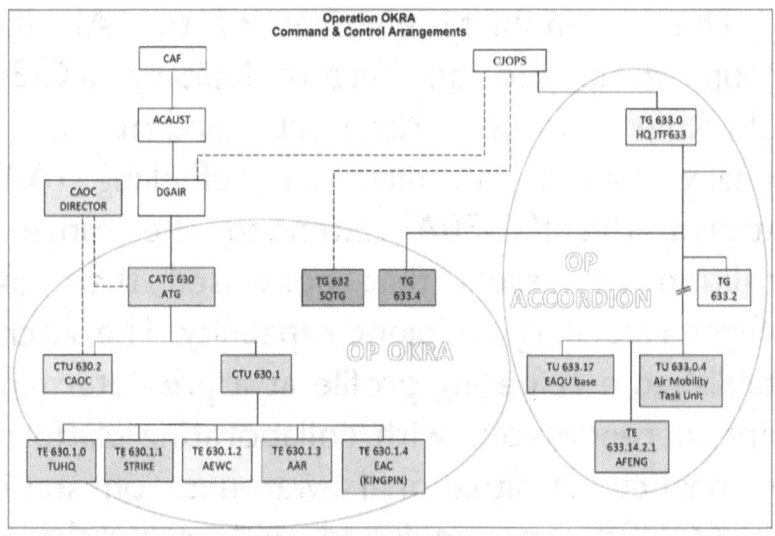

Operation OKRA: Command and Control Arrangements

The distinctive dorsal MESA radar antenna is very apparent in this image of an Australian E-7A Wedgetail as it is being marshalled in the MER. The enormous capability of the Wedgetail's electronic radar and fully digitised systems make the aircraft one of the most advanced of its type in the world. (source: Department of Defence)

The air mobility element of the Air Task Group comprised an Airbus Military KC-30A Multi-Role Tanker Transport aircraft. In its primary role as an air-to-air refuelling (AAR) platform, the KC-30A extended the range of Coalition air assets that possessed their own in-flight refuelling recipient capability. The aircraft established a refuelling profile at a pre-determined point to rendezvous with collaborating platforms. To enhance its situational awareness on station, the KC-30A was equipped with a number of radios, datalink and mission planning systems. These enabled the crews and Coalition assets to preposition between missions in anticipation of refuelling requirements over northern Iraq and Syria.

That the RAAF possessed such potent capabilities in its arsenal was integrally linked to the nation's wider defence and bilateral treaties and trade arrangements with its allies—particularly the United States. It is axiomatic that Australian air power on Operation OKRA be viewed in this context. Such arrangements all but ensured that the individual Australian platforms assigned to the Air Task Group were among the most advanced and effective platforms of their type in the world. When their systems and capabilities were integrated, they became a virtually unbeatable combination, capable of exploiting every positive characteristic of air power. The Wedgetail platform brought perspective to the fight with its 'beyond the horizon' electronic field of view. Ground-based air battle managers conducted a similar function from a Coalition facility—callsign 'Kingpin'—at the Al Dhafra Air Base in the United Arab Emirates. The KC-30A contributed exponentially to the reach of the Coalition, enabling platforms to operate in battlespace nearly one thousand nautical miles from their home bases. In terms of kinetic effect, the strike aircraft brought precision, payload and flexibility to the war. This element was enabled by precision guided munitions. The Air Task Group was able to expeditiously coordinate and concentrate force, at will, to any desired location in the battlespace. The potency of such assets was an immeasurable force multiplier for Iraqi ground forces, though the Australian contribution was dwarfed by the hundreds of similar Coalition platforms.

RAAF KC-30A conducts air-to-air refuelling with a flight of RAAF F/A-18F Super Hornets. (source: Department of Defence)

The processes involved in planning and executing a mission with these platforms were almost surgical. They were supported by voice and satellite communications systems, datalinks, and the accuracy of global positioning system-enabled navigation systems. Strike operation assignment was coordinated to exacting standards against targets developed at the Combined Air Operations Centre, with aircraft programmed to fly on deep air support interdiction sorties via the Air Tasking Order process. Others were assigned to conduct time critical close air support and target interdiction missions in support of Iraqi troops in contact with ISIL or as ISIL elements moved towards friendly forces. Australian airmen and Army ground liaison officers were embedded within the Centre to contribute to the planning and air tasking cycle. The Hornets launched and operated in packages of two or four aircraft, and always had airborne tanker and early warning and control asset support. Often, this comprised the Australian KC-30A and Wedgetail aircraft, though this was not always the case.

The KC-30A was capable of supporting a number of different types operating within the Coalition, and once it had supported the infiltration of a package of aircraft, it would remain on station in a preassigned pattern in order to receive aircraft as they completed their mission. Often, aircraft re-rolled in flight to support Iraqi troops in contact with ISIL on the ground would require fuel prior to conducting their new mission, and the KC-30A was again on station to assist.

The Australian Wedgetail aircraft and the similar Boeing E-3 AWACS of the United States Air Force were the only aircraft that operated independently to the strike and air-to-air refuelling elements. They were tasked to provide air battle management and awareness of the entire battlespace for all assets operating in-theatre.

The RAAF also maintained a Combat Support Unit as Task Unit 633.17 at the Al Minhad air base. providing logistics and ground support for aircraft assigned in support of Operations ACCORDION, HIGHROAD and OKRA. These operations comprised the ADF's total commitment to the region. Human resource management across these activities was central to the function of the Combat Support Unit, with the unit providing support for RAAF operations that included medical facilities, security, life support equipment, air load logistics, accommodation, meals, vehicles, fire services, and the maintenance of ground support equipment. The Combat Support Unit staff liaised extensively with local Emirate contractors to provide this infrastructure support, though the personnel administration and support work was done by unit staff in a headquarters facility at Al Minhad. An air movements team, facilitated by the Combat Support Unit, prepared and loaded cargo to support the parallel activities of an RAAF Air Mobility Task Unit (TU 633.0.4 AMTU) operation that flew in support of Australian activity across the entire Middle East. An airfield engineering Task Element (TE633.14.2.1) also conducted maintenance activities for the Al Minhad aerodrome facility that included runway, hardstand and navigation aid maintenance.

These detailed descriptions are important as they explain the complexity of deploying and effectively employing air power across a distance of 14 000 kilometres. All the arrangements took some time to mature in the theatre and were not as initially neat nor straightforward as populating a desktop-developed hierarchical wire diagram in an offshore location. When the Air Task Group deployed, little was organised in terms of force support. The aircraft literally grouped and flew to the established Al Minhad airbase under an existing agreement with the United Arab Emirates. Technical and maintenance personnel followed immediately behind, with all personnel in location by 23 September 2014. The three flying task elements were expected to commence flying operations over Iraq shortly afterwards. That they were ready to do so was not in question.

The Commanding Officer of No 2 Squadron and the Wedgetail detachment TE630.1.2 was Wing Commander Paul Carpenter. He was an experienced multi-engine aircraft captain and former maritime pilot who was extremely comfortable with the standard of the crew that had deployed with the airborne early warning and control aircraft. The Wedgetail was relatively new into service. In the two years prior to the deployment Carpenter had overseen No 2 Squadron conduct a continuum of local training missions with RAAF Williamtown-based F/A-18s, larger domestic exercises such as Aces North and Pitch Black in Australia's Northern Territory, Exercise Cope North in Guam, and eventually the much larger 'Red Flag' exercises conducted in Nevada and Alaska. Red Flags are perhaps the most complex high-end air warfare exercises conducted in the world. Not only had the Wedgetail platform participated in the latest iterations of this exercise, it had performed extremely well.

McDonnell Douglas F/A-18A Hornet and Boeing F/A-18F Super Hornet

The McDonnell Douglas F/A-18A Hornet is a multi-role fighter attack aircraft that first entered RAAF service in 1985 to replace the ageing Dassault Mirage III-O. Now referred to in Australia colloquially as the *Classic* Hornet, the F/A-18A is capable of prosecuting air, maritime and land targets with precision munitions through integrated systems that include radar, active warhead systems, heat seeking missiles, and an infra-red pod for targeting and sensing purposes. The aircraft is also fitted with several warning and self-protection systems that are designed to warn of, or defeat, adversary air-to-air and surface to air threats. With fitted weapons systems and sensors, the F/A-18A is designed to conduct offensive and defensive counter air operations, strategic strike, anti-surface warfare, interdiction and close air support for ground troops.

The Boeing F/A-18F Super Hornet is a later derivation of the Hornet, being larger and more capable than the earlier model. The original Hornet manufacturer, McDonnell Douglas, was merged into Boeing in 1997. Although the two types look very similar, the Super Hornet has a crew of two, is a metre longer, and has a wing area over twenty-five per cent larger than the F/A-18A. This effectively increases the type's fuel capacity and its weapons payload. The Super Hornet twin powerplants are also capable of generating about thirty per cent greater thrust than its predecessor. It is the avionics and internal systems that in particular differentiate the two platforms. The F/A-18F enjoys increased protection measures and survivability through a reduced radar signature and an integrated defensive electronic counter-measures suite.

A Royal Australian Air Force F/A-18F Super Hornet (right) and a F/A-18A Hornet aircraft await clearance for takeoff for an Operation OKRA mission out of the main air operating base in the Middle East Region. (source: Department of Defence)

F/A-18A Hornet

Artwork by Juanita Franzi

Length:	56 ft 1 in (17.1 m)
Wingspan:	40 ft 8 in (12.4 m)
Height:	15 ft 5 in (4.7 m)
Empty weight:	23 000 lb (10 433 kg)
Maximum weight:	36 970 lb (16 769 kg)
Max take-off weight:	51 900 lb (23 541 kg)
Powerplant:	Two General Electric F404-GE-402 afterburning turbofan engines
Power:	11 000 lb (49 kN) thrust each – 17 750 lb (79.0 kN) with afterburner
Cruise speed:	574 kts; 1062 km/h (660 mph)
Maximum speed:	1034 kts (1190 mph; 1915 km/h; Mach 1.8) at 40 000 ft (12 000 m)
Range:	1089 nm (1253 mi; 2017 km) without fuel
Service ceiling:	50 000 ft (15 000 m)
Crew:	One pilot (A variant)
Radar:	Hughes AN/APG-73 pulse doppler radar capable of air-to-air and air-to-surface modes
Targeting	AN/AAQ-28 (V) Litening AT electro optical targeting pod which is employed to laser designate moving targets and containing a forward-looking infrared (FLIR) sensor that displays an image of the target in the cockpit. Joint Helmet Mounted Cueing System.
Armament:	Gun: one 20 mm (0.787 in) M61A1 Vulcan nose mounted six-barrel rotary cannon, 578 rounds Air-to-Air: AIM120 AMRAAM active missile and ASRAAM heat seeking missile Air-to-Ground: Load varies according to mission profile but comprises a combination of GPS coordinate targeted or laser designated Joint Direct Attack Munitions (JDAM) including the 227kg GBU-38 JDAM, 227kg GBU-54 laser guided JDAM, 907kg GBU-31 JDAM, GBU-31 V 3B/4B Hardened Penetrator JDAM and 454kg GBU-32 JDAM.
Protection:	ALR-67 Radar Warning Receiver, electronic warfare self-protection, including directed infra-red countermeasures, chaff and flares
Communications:	HF, VHF, UHF, Link-11, Link-16, UHF SATCOM, ICS

F/A-18F Super Hornet

Artwork by Juanita Franzi

Length:	60 ft 1 in (18.31 m)
Wingspan:	44 ft 8.5 in (13.62 m)
Height:	16 ft (4.88 m)
Empty weight:	32 081 lb (14 552 kg)
Maximum weight:	47 000 lb (21 320 kg)
Max take-off weight:	66 000 lb (29 937 kg)
Powerplant:	Two General Electric F414-GE-400 turbofans
Power:	13 000 lb (62.3 kN) thrust each – 22 000 lb (97.9 kN) with afterburner
Cruise speed:	674 kts (777 mph, 1250 km/h)
Maximum speed:	1034 kts (1190 mph, 1915 km/h; Mach 1.8) at 40 000 ft (12 190 m)
Range:	1 275 nm (2 346 km) without fuel and fitted with two AIM-9X missiles
Service ceiling:	50 000 ft (15 000 m)
Crew:	Two - one Pilot and one Weapons Systems Officer
Radar:	APG-79 AESA (active electronically scanned array) radar replacing the Hughes APG-73
Targeting	AN/ASQ-228 Advanced Targeting Forward Looking Infrared (ATFLIR) surveillance and targeting pod which is employed to laser designate moving targets and containing a forward-looking infrared (FLIR) sensor that displays an image of the target in the cockpit. Joint Helmet Mounted Cueing System.
Armament:	Gun: one 20 mm (0.787 in) M61A1 Vulcan nose-mounted six-barrel rotary cannon, 578 rounds Air-to-Air: AIM- 9X Sidewinder; AIM-120 Advanced Medium Range Air-to-Air Missile (AMRAAM) active missile; and ASRAAM heat seeking missile Air-to-Ground: Load varies according to mission profile but comprises a combination of GPS coordinate targeted or laser designated Joint Direct Attack Munitions (JDAM), including the 227 kg GBU-38 JDAM, 227 kg GBU-54 laser guided JDAM, 907 kg GBU-31 JDAM, GBU-31 V 3B/4B Hardened Penetrator JDAM, 454kg GBU-32 JDAM, AGM-154 Joint Stand-Off Weapon (JSOW) and AGM-84 Harpoon Anti-Ship Missile.
Protection:	ALR-67 Radar Warning Receiver, electronic warfare self-protection, including directed infra-red countermeasures, chaff and flares
Communications:	HF, VHF, UHF, Link-11, Link-16, UHF SATCOM, ICS

Boeing E-7A Wedgetail aircraft

The E-7A Wedgetail is based on Boeing 737-700 airframe, heavily modified to include an advanced Multi-Role Electronically Scanned Array radar and ten **state-of-the-art** mission crew consoles which can track airborne and maritime targets simultaneously.

The Wedgetail is a highly advanced airborne early warning and control aircraft—currently the best of its type in the world—that provides the RAAF with an air battle management function, gathering digitized data from a suite of sophisticated sensors. The data is classified, correlated and then distributed as a recognised air picture to friendly assets in the battlespace and to participating command and control nodes beyond the battlespace. The Wedgetail data feed provides a superior level of situational awareness to friendly forces.

Boeing E-7A Wedgetail

Artwork by Juanita Franzi

Length:	110 ft 4 in (33.6 m)	Cruise speed:	530 mph (853 km/h)
Wingspan:	117 ft 2 in (35.8 m)	Range:	3500 nm (6482 km)
Height:	41 ft 2 in (12.5 m)	Endurance:	Ten hours without refuel
Empty weight:	102 750 lb (46 606 kg)	Endurance record:	16 hours 18 minutes with two air-to-air refuels
Payload:	43 720 lb (19 830 kg)	Service ceiling:	41 000 ft (12500 m)
Max take-off weight:	171 000 lb (77 564 kg)	Crew:	Two pilots and ten mission crew
Powerplant:	Two CFM International CFM56-7B27A turbofans	Protection:	Electronic warfare self-protection, including directed infra-red countermeasures, chaff and flares
Power:	27 000 lb (118 kN) each	Communications:	HF, VHF, UHF, Link-11, Link-16, UHF SATCOM, ICS

MESA Radar

MESA Radar: (multi-role electronically scanned array)	Northrop Grumman
	288 high-power transmit/receive modules
	operationally ready minutes after take-off
Wide area surveillance:	more than 340 000 square miles
Scan rate:	more than 30 000 square miles per second
	typical 10-second scan rate (but since scan rates are variable and sectors selectable, other coverage rates, ranges and priorities are programmable)
	sector-selection modes provide three to four times higher target search rates and eight to ten times higher track updates than rotating radars.

KC-30A Multi-Role Tanker Transport

The KC-30A is a heavily modified Airbus A330 airliner designed to conduct air-to-air refuelling and provide strategic air lift. It features advanced communication and navigation systems, and an electronic warfare self-protection system to protect it against threats from surface-to-air missiles. The KC-30A is the largest aircraft in the RAAF. It requires significant coordination, personnel, ground support, equipment, maintenance and logistics support to enable effective operations. The KC-30A can carry a combination of up to 270 passengers, eight military pallets and 110 tonnes of fuel. The KC-30A flies globally in all roles, tanker, cargo and passenger transport, and can be repositioned to support operations around the world within twenty-four hours.

Airbus KC-30A Tanker

Artwork by Juanita Franzi

Length:	193 ft (58.8 m)
Wingspan:	198 ft (60.3 m)
Height:	57 ft 2 in (17.4 m)
Empty weight:	102 750 lb (46 606 kg)
Payload:	99 000 lb (45 000 kg) non-fuel payload
Max take-off weight:	514 000 lb (233 000 kg)
Powerplant:	Two Pratt & Whitney PW 4170 turbofans
Power:	72 000 lb (320 kN) each
Cruise speed:	464 knots (860 km/h)
Maximum speed:	475 knots (880 km/h)
Fuel:	245 000 lb max, 143 000 lb at 1000 nm with two hours on station
Service ceiling:	42 000 ft (13 100 m)
Crew:	Two pilots, one air-to-air refuelling operator
Capacity:	Various passenger configurations are available including 291 passengers and 8 military pallets plus one 1LD6 container and one LD3 container (lower deck cargo compartments)
Communications:	HF, VHF, UHF, Link-11, Link-16, UHF SATCOM, ICS

The commanding officer of the first Wedgetail rotation, WGCDR Paul Carpenter, flying on operations over Iraq in 2014. Typical of the hundreds of personnel who would serve in ATG630, Carpenter was highly experienced, well-educated and thoroughly professional. In his circumstance, Carpenter had graduated from the Australian Defence Force Academy, and after completing pilot training had accrued thousands of hours operating maritime platforms before going on to lead No 2 Squadron. His professional, polite and reserved demeanor earned him great respect from among 2 Squadron personnel. (source: Department of Defence)

The Commanding Officer of No 1 Squadron, Wing Commander Stephen Chappell, was also the inaugural commander of Strike Element TE630.1.1 and he knew that his aviators were ready for the task at hand. They had participated in a similar suite of training exercises as No 2 Squadron. Chappell was the only aviator in his squadron with combat experience, and he reflected deeply on this. In the days leading up to the deployment he had been following the media closely, observing the events as they unfolded in Iraq, and he was encouraging his air and ground crews to do the same. When Roberton informed Chappell that his unit was going, Chappell increased the dialogue. His sense of the heritage associated with No 1 Squadron's return to this part of the world a century after Sir Richard Williams was well-developed. He organised briefings for his personnel so that they understood the nature and justification of the operation in which they would be involved. A particularly gruesome series of Daesh executions in the period leading up to the deployment served to reinforce what Chappell and his executive team sought to convey to the members of his unit.

Perhaps the least prepared of the three flying task elements was the KC-30A tanker of No 33 Squadron from RAAF Amberley. The KC-30A was so new to service that it was not yet certified for combat operations. Despite this, the TE630.3 Detachment Commander, Squadron Leader Chet Takalker, was comfortable that his platform was able to service the Australian

F/A-18Fs using the KC-30A's 'probe and drogue' fuel hose system. Probe and drogue comprised a system in which tanking hoses were extended from the KC-30A's wings onto which strike aircraft were able to join to refuel. With the proper workups, he considered the aircraft's additional boom refuelling capability would also be functional. The boom refuelling system differed to probe and drogue. It comprised a fixed stanchion (boom) that extended from the KC-30A's rear fuselage onto which certain aircraft could join to refuel. Providing both 'probe and drogue' and boom refuelling options would make the KC-30As unique amongst the other air-to-air refuelling assets within the Coalition that were limited to either one or the other method. This made the KC-30As an extremely versatile asset for Coalition operations.

The 'Probe and Drogue' refuelling system operated by the KC-30A comprises hose extensions that are extended from the aircraft into which tanking aircraft will insert a probe device to take on fuel. Here again, Australian Super Hornets are replenished in flight in the MER. (source: Department of Defence)

With literally hundreds of combat platforms from many nations contributing to the Coalition, the Australian commitment was relatively modest. However, the key point was one of comparative size of the respective contribution to their parent Services, and in this ATG630 represented a sizable portion of the RAAF's combat capability. This was further enhanced by the Group's ability to contribute effectively in an incredibly short period of time.

ISIL had spread rapidly, and Wing Commander Chappell recalled comparing the rapid advance to a World War II news reel showing Axis forces spreading like an 'ink stain' across a map of Europe or the Pacific. After receiving advice from the Chief of Joint Operations and the Air Force, the Abbott government resolved to have the Air Task Group commence kinetic operations no later than twenty-one days after it announced the deployment on 14 September—'D-Day'. This meant that flying operations would need to commence no later than 5 October 2014.

Time was of the essence with the Iraqi Army desperate for Coalition air power to enter the fray as soon as possible. The Air Task Group had planned to conduct familiarisation flights in-theatre by D+14 (28 September). These flights were essential prior to any combat operations being entertained. The timeline required that by D+9 (23 September) all elements were to have arranged logistics, communications and information systems, flying administration requirements, accommodation and administrative supporting infrastructure, explosive ordnance placement and physical security considerations as a high priority so that flying assets could be airborne within a further four days. Chipman's TU630.1 had arrived during the week prior to the task elements and was already in the process of interpreting the Air Task Group's rules of engagement and targeting directives that had been set by Headquarters Joint Operations Command. Their task was to ensure the rules of engagement and targeting directives were suitable for implementation, and to consult with Headquarters Joint Operations Command to work through any proposed amendments. This work was absolutely vital. No element of the Air Task Group would be able to fly into certain areas of the battlespace in and around Iraq without legal authority, let alone engage an adversary with lethal force. The work on establishing such clearances required further augmentation to the Combined Air Operations Centre in Qatar. Headquarters Joint Operations Command, JTF633 and Chipman's TU630.1 staff had collaborated to ensure that suitably qualified personnel were quickly put in place where they were needed at the Al Udeid facility. They were largely in place by the time that the task elements arrived at Al Minhad.

Upon arrival, virtually all the Air Task Group staff were individually ready and compliant in their medical, administrative, weapons handling and physical fitness standards. All technical and flying personnel were current in their specific functions. This made them ready to start planning for operations. Even so, this did not mean that the arrival of the Air Task Group did not present challenges.

The Al Minhad airbase—already busy—was now inundated with over three hundred more personnel. When it had relocated to the UAE, Headquarters JTF633 took with it the rigorous Reception, Staging, Onwards-clearance and Insertion (RSO&I) process designed to welcome, condition and prepare combat personnel for what they would shortly experience on operations. This was effectively a reinforcement cycle of training designed to underwrite force preparation training that an individual or formed body of personnel had already undertaken in Australia prior to deploying, and its conduct was extremely important work. It covered training in first aid for injuries sustained in close combat or from indirect fire as well as briefings on cultural sensitivities when interacting with locals, theatre-wide operations reports, conditions of service, and rules regarding alcohol consumption, dress and behavioural standards. Individual small arms (if carried) were also fired and zeroed on a range facility on the airbase. Scenarios depicting what to do if individuals encountered an improvised explosive device in their armoured vehicle were also conducted. The staff providing the briefings were experts in their fields and were either posted to Headquarters JTF633 or were contracted to the formation. However, the arrival of the Air Task Group at Al Minhad so quickly after the announcement that it would deploy gave the headquarters little time to prepare. The result was a level of friction, and it required some of the ATG personnel to take the initiative in the first days of the forthcoming operations.

The Boom system differed markedly from the 'Probe and Drogue' in that a fixed refuelling stanchion would be lowered from the tail of the KC-30A for aircraft to couple with in-flight. The fact that the KC-30A was equipped with both types of system made it an extremely versatile platform for the Coalition during Operation INHERENT RESOLVE. Here the Australian KC-30A demonstrates this versatility by refuelling a large US transport aircraft. (source: Department of Defence)

One Australian aviator, Flight Lieutenant Bryce Robinson, an E-7A Air Combat Officer, adapted very quickly to the circumstance. Studying towards a law degree part-time while in the Air

Force, he had previously served with the Australian control and reporting centre at Kandahar airfield during the 2000s. He had thousands of hours of experience, and as a Qualified Aviation Instructor he had trained many of the junior personnel with whom he now served. Most of all, Robinson was well known for his ability to focus on the practicalities of the task before him. Every aviator carried an 'escape and evasion' kit stocked with essentials in the event of being forced down. Robinson was initially perplexed as to why no one could furnish a map of Iraq for his Wedgetail crew—until it dawned on him that the ATG had arrived so quickly that there had been little time to prepare for this level of detail. As events unfolded, for the first few missions Robinson flew with a printed-out page from google maps so that he felt he at least had a chance if he found himself on the ground where he did not want to be. Other aviators were simply dumbfounded by the program that they were undertaking. As late as two years later in September 2016, half-way through the period of OKRA missions, a female RAAF Air Combat Officer—and a mother of two—who was a newly qualified member of a Wedgetail crew, had trouble reconciling how her training in detecting improvised explosive devices around a 'blown-up' Bushmaster stage-prop at Al

Minhad would assist her when flying over Northern Iraq and Syria. Yet others were far more pragmatic. They augmented the RSO&I process with their own training programs.

One young fast jet aviator was convinced that techniques on how to run long distances quickly in the desert if he was forced down in Northern Iraq were very important. This was not said in jest. In early 2015, a junior Jordanian fighter pilot had ejected in ISIL-held territory; he was captured and then barbarically executed by being burned alive in a cage. The event was filmed, and the footage was released to the media. It drew widespread condemnation around the world. Indeed, many of the aircrew serving on Operation OKRA over various rotations took to running in their off-duty hours to condition themselves for the unthinkable proposition of being forced down.

Air Commodore Roberton later indicated that Major General Craig Orme, the Australian Commander of JTF633, gave him uncategorical support in enabling the Air Task Group to commence operations. Even so, Roberton conveyed that he and Orme had numerous robust discussions on the nuances of command and control of air power on operations. The RSO&I process often came up in these discussions and centred on the fact that 'one size fits all' was no solution for preparing disparate forces for operations. As this went, the application of air power required its own inherent processes to prepare for combat. This was neither more nor less than sea or land power—it was simply different. In their dialogue, Roberton was most impressed with Orme and the outcomes between a senior aviator and an experienced senior soldier. For his part, Orme was absolutely committed to taking the fight to ISIL, and after the Air Task Group had been there for several weeks, he clearly stated in the broadest Australian vernacular that Daesh was going to get 'smacked'. However, in the last week of September 2014, none of this alleviated the urgent need for the ATG to prepare for operations.

Wing Commander Chappell recalled clearly that by 26 September his strike element's preparatory requirements had reached a critical tipping point. He had a directed timeline: TE630.1.1 now had two days to commence flying operations out of Al Minhad on 28 September 2014. There were quite literally dozens of responsibilities running through Chappell's mind—rules of engagement review, flight planning, Operation OKRA specific tactics techniques and procedural development and review, maintenance flight line establishment, preparing aircraft, building the inaugural small explosive ordnance pad, rostering, accommodation—the list was endless. Equally pressing matters faced the other elements. In the two days immediately prior to his squadron flying combat operations, Chappell was now faced with the prospect of his crews undertaking scheduled RSO&I training to 'clear' a notional field of Improvised Explosive Devices in the unlikely event they landed in such a field after ejecting in Iraq.

Chappell had conferred with Group Captain Chipman and his staff who were only too aware of the time pressure, but who were also busy trying to set the headquarters up. In the end, Chappell made the carefully considered decision to withdraw TE630.1.1 from the final two days of RSO&I training so that his element could meet the prescribed operational timeline. Of this decision, Chappell remembers:

> It was my decision to make. I did so knowing GPCAPT Chipman trusted my judgment and I knew he would support me by ensuring key stakeholders in JTF633 were aware of the reasoning behind the decision. It was simply too busy a time, with us separated at different parts of the base for twelve hours or more each day, for it to occur in a slow and linear fashion.

Chappell may or may not have been aware that ninety-eight years earlier, Sir Richard Williams had similarly petitioned his superiors on circumstances confronting No 1 Squadron. Chappell's knowledge of this is irrelevant; the point was that William's would likely have approved of the logic behind Chappell's informed thinking. It was characteristic of the moral courage that Williams had so ably displayed himself in the pioneering years of the RAAF.

Refuelling over a spectacularly lit Baghdad during the early months of Operation OKRA. Many aircrews recalled having deep introspection as they flew on combat operations over this part of the world. The landscape contrasted significantly across the length and breadth of the nation, and the fact that they were operating over the 'cradle of civilisation' was not lost on many aviators. (source: Department of Defence)

The circumstance was rushed—conditions were not ideal—but so it began. The distance from the Al Minhad facility to the southern-most city in Iraq, Basra, is nearly 600 miles in a straight line. The distance from Basra to Iraq's northern most city, Mosul, is then another 450 miles. To get to Iraq this way meant flying northwest along the length of the Persian Gulf, with onwards airways clearances being provided by air traffic control. A fighter/attack aircraft would transit the distance in about ninety minutes after climbing and refuelling. The larger aircraft, the Wedgetail and KC-30A, took only slight longer. But matters were not this simple. Transiting the route required onwards liaison with air traffic control services from Qatar, Bahrain, Saudi Arabia, Kuwait and finally Iraq. Crews also had to be sensitive of Iranian airspace which abutted their projected flight path. They had to conduct an appreciation of where they might have to divert their aircraft to along the way should they have technical or other difficulties.

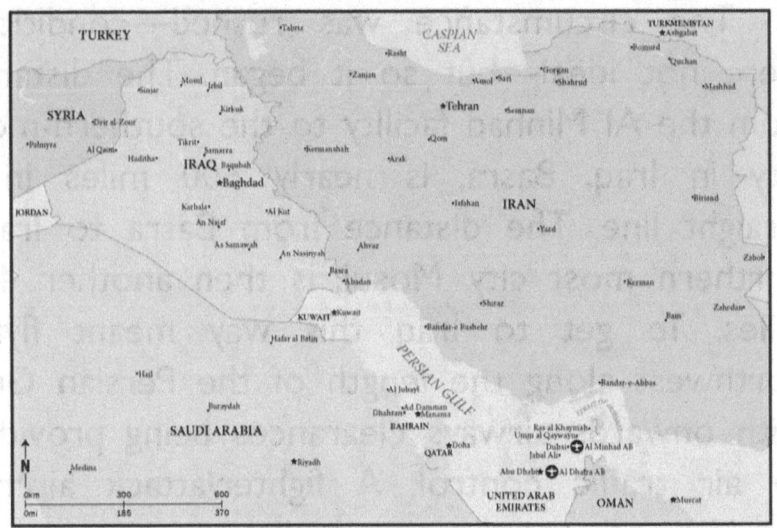

The long expanse of the Persian Gulf across which the aircraft of the ATG were required to transit enroute to their area of operations in Iraq and Western Syria. The distances flown are incredible. From the Al Dhafra airbase in the UAE, RAAF crews routinely flew the 600-mile length of the Gulf before even reaching Iraq. Should they have been tasked to operate in the northern reaches of the nation, they would then be required to fly a further 400 miles to Mosul. The focus required to plan, transit and then conduct a sortie into these austere environments pays testament to the skilled professionalism of all RAAF personnel involved.

The planning around these flights was not a straightforward matter, as aircraft as large as the KC-30A required a specified length of runway in order to safely land and take-off; Suitable airfields had to be engineered to a stipulated pavement strength so that neither the aircraft nor the surface would be damaged by heavy platforms;

and the airfields had to be equipped with refuelling, firefighting and instrument-assisted facilities. As late as mid-2016, RAAF firefighting personnel were involved in attending an Emirate aircraft accident at Al Minhad—an airfield considered modern, well-equipped with a runway nearly 13 000 feet long—in which the unfortunate pilot was killed. Not all airfields along the considerable length of the Persian Gulf would be able accommodate a platform the size of a KC-30A. In their planning considerations, crews for all platforms constantly revisited at what point in their flight, and under what circumstances, they might be required to fly to a diversionary airfield. It required accuracy, careful thought, and diplomatic finesse even before the military nature of what would occur at the furthest reach of the flight could be considered.

Having transited with civil clearance into Iraq, all Coalition assets would then switch to a military control agency. For the strike task element, this would require them to sit on station and await direction to contact a controller on the ground. This controller, generally a Coalition specialist attached to the Iraqi Army, would direct the pilot and crew to train their platform sensors into a contested area in order to reduce any detected ISIL threat. For the Wedgetail and KC-30A crews, they would establish a position at a predetermined point in order to best service what was occurring in the combat on the ground below them.

The concepts were very simple, and in the first months the processes were very rudimentary. However, it became very complicated very quickly by factors that included dozens of Coalition aircraft flying in the same airspace at the same time on different radio frequencies. The speeds at which the aircraft were operating, the night and desert flying conditions, the 'as yet' uncoordinated Iraqi airspace, the inexperience of many involved, and a multitude of other factors further compounded the situation.

The implications of these complicating factors were not as significant for the Wedgetail and KC-30A crews given the recent 'near-real' training operations that both parent squadrons had conducted prior to the deployment. TE630.1.2 (Wedgetail) would now conduct operations in which it would shadow another Coalition airborne early warning platform into Iraq while it bedded down its own operational procedures. TE630.1.3 (KC-30A) would operate in conjunction with the strike element, providing refuelling services initially via its probe and drogue capability—later this was supplemented with the boom system when it was certified for operational use.

Wing Commander Chappell was acutely aware that his strike task element would require certification with Combat Controllers in-theatre over Iraq so that they might 'prove' their ability to contribute to the fight. Chappell took this task upon himself. He later remarked:

> *I was the Commanding Officer and wanted to do my own reconnaissance of the aviation challenges my younger aircrew would face, and I was also an experienced aviator—and the only one who had previously flown in the Middle East—therefore I had a better chance of working through the procedural challenges of flying in a different part of the world.*

In late September 2014, Chappell and his Weapons Systems Officer flight-planned into Iraq, and then 'chopped' frequency to a ground controller in Baghdad who laser-designated a notional target for the fast jet. Chappell's Weapons Systems Officer adjusted the Super Hornet's sensors to detect the beam, and the aircraft launched 'notional' ordnance against a target in response to the controller's direction. TE630.1.1 was now certified to take the fight to Daesh.

By this time, all three aircraft types in the Air Task Group had conducted familiarisation flights over the Persian Gulf and northwest on the approaches to Iraq. Squadron Leader Jeremy Feldhahn was a Weapons Systems Officer in TE630.1.1 who conducted his familiarisation flight with F/A-18F captain Squadron Leader Matt Harper on 28 September. Feldhahn was an experienced Air Combat Officer with an eclectic career. This had provided him with a wide-ranging perspective of what was occurring in the battlespace around him. Having specialised as an Air Battle Manager during the early 2000s, he deployed into a headquarters function in the Middle East as a staff officer during Gulf War II. He later re-roled to an Air Combat Officer flying Super Hornets with No 1 Squadron where he flourished.

By early October 2014, TE630.1.1 was ready to fly into Iraq, and Feldhahn was allocated to make one of the first sorties. The first deep familiarisation sortie departed on 2 October and flew over Iraq as far north as Mosul. The KC-30A accompanied these flights as both elements prepared for kinetic operations. When the package tracked north over Baghdad's Coalition Camp Victory, Feldhahn looked down and reflected on where he had served as a junior officer a decade prior. In this introspective moment, he was struck by the enduring nature of what was occurring in the nation below him.

As planned, TE630.1.1 commenced operations on 5 October 2014 when a pair of armed F/A-18Fs sortied over Iraq accompanied by a KC-30A. Both Super Hornets were cleared onto an operating radio frequency, but no ordnance was released on that flight. The first use of weapons subsequently occurred on 8 October 2014 when two 500 lb bombs were dropped on ISIL facilities. The results of the eight-hour mission were successful, and within a week the Commander Joint Operations Command in Australia, Vice Admiral David Johnston, made a media announcement confirming that:

> the first Australian strike destroyed an ISIL facility and a number of ISIL members were killed in that attack ... The attack was associated with ISIL equipment, ISIL facilities and some support to troops that were on the ground.

Johnston was precise in his descriptions. In its support to the Iraqis, the Australian Government was careful to highlight that Australia's kinetic involvement was limited to targeting ISIS through air strikes. These strikes were to target ISIL's transportation network, command and control nodes, logistics and supply centres, and heavy earth-moving equipment. It was a manifestation of American air power strategist John Warden's classic 'five-rings' theory in which specific centres of gravity were targeted in an over-all plan; and in the long-term it would be unstoppable. Initially, the air strikes targeted heavy earth-moving equipment located in central Iraq which ISIL used to build berms to divert water from the Fallujah Dam. Later strikes would target further north around Mosul.

As these events unfolded, an E-7A Wedgetail of Wing Commander Carpenter's TE630.1.2 was also commencing live operations. Having sortied over the Gulf in late September, on 1 October 2014 the Wedgetail aircraft was now tasked to shadow an older USAF E-3 aircraft on a familiarisation mission over northern Iraq where it could observe the operation unfold. However, when the E-3 encountered technical difficulties early in the flight, the Wedgetail immediately assumed responsibility for the mission. It was an auspicious beginning for the very capable platform, and Coalition strike assets soon came to appreciate the fidelity of the Australian aircraft's sensors. In the coming weeks each of the elements in the Air Task Group would conduct dozens more sorties as they quickly entered a battle rhythm.

The mission stations onboard the E-7A Wedgetail are manned during a sortie over Northern Iraq in 2014. Each operator had a specific function to perform in the gathering and dissemination of mission critical data, and the interactions among the crew were almost symbiotic in nature. (source: Department of Defence)

The early missions were very dynamic in nature. Invariably, the aircraft on station responded to requests from ground commanders or on direction from intelligence, surveillance and reconnaissance assets, such as the Wedgetail or the ground-based air battle management units like TE630.1.4. These operations also occurred in response to immediate operational needs. As Squadron Leader Feldhahn had experienced, these operations led to much introspection amongst the personnel involved. Airmen involved assembling and fitting together live munitions on the ground were struck by the fact that when the F/A-18s returned from a flight the ordnance was no longer on the jet. One technician noted how 'buggered' the crews looked when their jets returned. A tanker pilot—laughing at himself as a 'deep-thinker'—recalled looking down on Baghdad's lights in the dark of the surrounding night and realising that he was flying over the cradle of civilisation. He was *right*. Yet another erudite individual observed over a sequence of sorties that a series of berms were being built by Kurdish separatists around their territory—and saw in it all a new and burgeoning nation coming of age. For others, the aesthetic was striking. The pale blue skies over sun burnished landscapes contrasted strikingly with the deep blue of the Persian Gulf. One aviator recalled seeing a spreading blanket of smoke—the result of a sabotaged oil well—from hundreds of miles away.

The aircrews were acutely aware of the dangers of coming down a thousand miles from home base. It was true that the threat of being shot down was negligible, and the Coalition had uncontested control of the skies. While ISIL had captured large numbers of anti-aircraft artillery of about 20 or 25 mm in calibre, flight tactics would ensure that strike aircraft would stay outside the envelope of these weapons. However, it would take only one round—or a piece of one round—from anti-aircraft artillery to force a fragile aircraft down; and this would mean almost certain death for the aviators involved. No one who flew against Daesh was under any illusion as to what would happen in this circumstance. Air Commodore Roberton freely recalled that such matters kept him awake at night; but he was equally assured of the professionalism of his entire staff and he implicitly knew that the skills of his technicians would almost ensure that no Australian platform would be forced down because of a mechanical or technical failure. It was very evident that there was an almost symbiotic nature in the relationship between air and ground crews. This bond enabled the air power generated by the group to respond flexibly and immediately to what was occurring in Iraq. The dynamic nature of the conflict was also reflected in the higher-level planning to defeat ISIL.

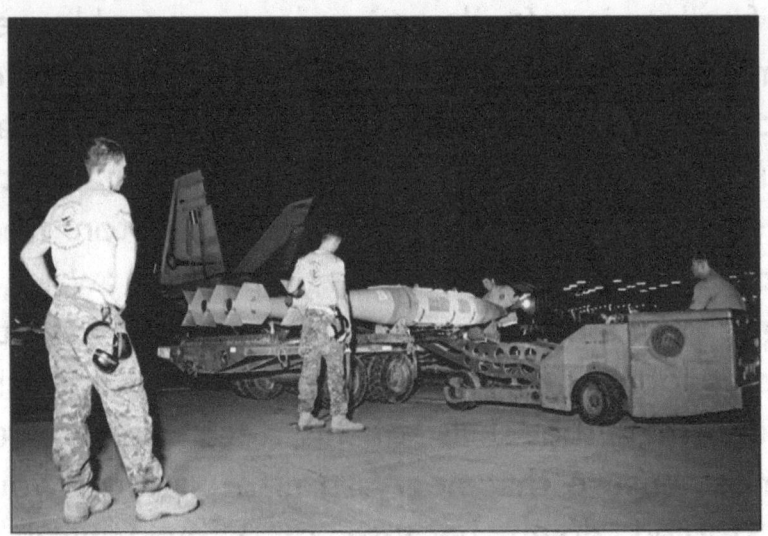

RAAF technicians prepare and arm strike aircraft in the pre-dawn darkness for coming operations against Daesh. (source: Department of Defence)

A RAAF Technician checks the armed strike aircraft for coming operations against Daesh prior to its departure. (source: Department of Defence)

By the time that ATG630 commenced kinetic operations in early October 2014, circumstances were grave for the Iraqi Government. ISIL controlled the nation's north, as far south as Tikrit, and west to the district and towns surrounding Mount Sinjar on the Syrian border. Taking advantage of the civil war in Syria, it had also crossed the border and besieged the Kurdish controlled town of Kobani. Media reports even indicated that villages from Mount Sinjar to Kobani were emptying at the approach of pickup trucks flying ISIL's black flag over fears of beheadings, mass killings and torture. Concurrently, ISIL had spread south through Western Iraq into Anbar Province to threaten the townships of Haditha and Ramadi along the Euphrates River Valley. Haditha, which had suffered in the Iraq War a decade prior, held out against Daesh. Ramadi, though, became the scene of a prolonged and pitched fight between government forces, backed by Coalition air power, and persistent attacks by ISIL forces. The battle lasted for months—well into 2015—during which time ISIL captured most of the villages surrounding Ramadi and effectively left the township besieged. In December, American advisers training Iraqi troops engaged in a firefight with ISIL elements when they attacked the Iraqis. Execution of captured Iraqi service personnel and government-friendly militiamen became a standard practice for ISIL, with hundreds of locals targeted for nothing more than simply living in the region. ISIL finally captured Ramadi on 17 May 2015, amid scenes reminiscent of the barbaric urban warfare of the Eastern Front during the World War II. Despite their valiant resistance, the hard-pressed Iraqi Government troops broke.

The vivid desert beauty of Mount Sinjar in the north western region of Iraq. The villages around Mount Sinjar were the scene of many Daesh atrocities, and the mountain became a familiar landmark to many Australian crews as they fought to stop the spread of ISIL in the first year of the campaign. (source: Department of Defence)

By the end of 2014, the stark realisation was that ISIL controlled large swathes of Iraq and Syria, with thousands of fighters armed with captured Iraqi weapons—and it was capable of holding this territory while it forcibly implemented Sharia law. Abu Bakr al Baghdadi's earlier public declaration of a caliphate was backed by practical initiatives far different to the approaches adopted by other fundamentalist groups.

Upon seizing a city, ISIL immediately commandeered police and municipal buildings and took control of the infrastructure of a district's utilities such as water and electricity. This enabled them to completely control access to vital needs. As gains were consolidated, it restored essential services normally associated with government, including medical care, security, and the judicial system. ISIL was therefore able to claim a level of legitimacy over all those living in captured territory, while at the same time demanding taxes from them. This set ISIL apart from other fundamentalist groups. In effect, the organisation was barbarically self-sufficient.

Over a six-month period, Coalition air power did the best it could to support Iraqi troops in stemming the seemingly inexorable advance of ISIL across their nation. This period would come to be known as Phase I of Operation INHERENT RESOLVE, and Chappell's analogy of the spreading ink was accurate.

Per Ardua: Through Adversity

While US Central Command was responsible for the oversight and direction of activities conducted in support of the Iraqi Government, it was the Combined Joint Task Force – Operation INHERENT RESOLVE, under US Army

Lieutenant General James Terry, that was responsible for the operational planning processes. Terry and his staff in Kuwait liaised closely with the Combined Joint Task Force Land Component Command and Iraqi staff officers in Baghdad to plan the fight against ISIL. Within weeks, they had come up with a four-phase campaign plan designed to ultimately defeat ISIL and restore Iraq's sovereignty. The planning considered the exigencies of conducting operations across the northern borders into Syria.

Like all military prose, Terry's design was pointed:

Phase I, Degrade: the CJTF [Combined Joint Task Force] will conduct air strikes against Daesh to blunt their expansion into Iraq and to begin to reduce their combat effectiveness. During this phase, the CJTF will provide training and equipping and advice and assistance to the ISF [Iraqi Security Forces] and, in a more limited role, partnered forces on the ground in Syria.

Phase II, Counterattack (Dismantle): the CJTF will support the ISF and the partnered forces in Syria as they attack to liberate territory and people under the control of Daesh. During this phase, the CJTF will conduct air strikes against Daesh fighters in support of the manoeuvre of partnered forces and in support of shaping future battles, increasing pressure and maintaining the momentum of the ground forces. The CJTF will continue the training, equipping, advising, and assisting of partnered forces, elevating the training to unit collective tasks, focused on combined arms manoeuvre.

Phase III, Defeat: the CJTF will conduct air strikes in support of the decisive battles against Daesh. ISF and partnered forces in Syria will liberate the two capitols of the self-proclaimed caliphate, Raqqah in Syria and Mosul in Iraq, and eliminate Daesh's physical means and psychological will to fight. After the liberation of Mosul and Raqqah, partnered forces will clear remaining pockets of Daesh resistance throughout both countries.

During this phase, the CJTF will conduct fires against Daesh fighters in support of the decisive manoeuvre of partnered forces, maintaining the momentum; and will continue the training, equipping, advising, and assisting of our partnered forces.

Phase IV, Support Stabilisation: the CJTF will provides security, planning, and required support to the government of Iraq and appropriate authorities in Syria.

The Combined Joint Task Force organises its tasks and missions along three lines of effort to bring about the military defeat of Daesh in

Iraq and Syria. A line of effort is a line linking multiple tasks and missions using the 'logic of purpose'—i.e., cause and effect—to focus efforts to establishing conditions at the strategic and operational levels.

The entire effort was joint, and air power was central to the success of each phase. There was no immediate air campaign plan that could be pulled 'off the shelf' with a prioritised target list developed to support Iraqi ground forces. The plan and target list had to be designed as the conflict unfolded. Compounding this, there were few Coalition troops on the ground conducting operations with the Iraqis, save those few—including Australian Combat Controllers—who were coordinating air strikes as embedded personnel. This meant that Coalition officers sitting with Iraqi commanders in Baghdad received feeds from the Iraqi Security Forces at the front, or via unmanned aerial vehicles transmitting live footage to the Combined Joint Task Force Land Component Command Headquarters. A target list was generated from this information which in turn had to be cleared with Iraqi leadership. All ordnance release required approval from the Iraqi Government.

Every planned target was scrutinised within the Combined Air Operations Centre and then cleared by the US Central Command. The

Commander of ATG630 was also required to clear targets back through the Director General-Air, Air Commodore Joe Iervasi, in Australia for ultimate approval by Commander Joint Operations. Iervasi was the ideal senior officer in Australia to undertake the function. As Director General-Air he had been involved with Operation OKRA from its inception in September 2014. Prior to this he had served as the US Central Command Combined Air and Space Operations Centre as Director. He had an appreciation and intrinsic knowledge of what was going on in the Middle-East and was ideally placed to plan for Australia's contribution in response. Iervasi would go on to remain intimately involved in the command and control arrangements for Operation OKRA and every operation that the RAAF undertook in parallel during the same period.

Despite Iervasi being an experienced fast-jet aviator, the passage of information could, of course, take time. It was critically important to get the process correct, particularly given that each Coalition air element was operating under its own national rules of engagement. Each contributing nation's rules of engagement defined the circumstances and limitations under which military force could be applied during operations. The Australian rules of engagement were expressed in a way that they complied with Australia's domestic and international laws, and the wider Laws of Armed Conflict and the Geneva Conventions. This gave the crews involved a specific set of preconditions defining on whether a target could be engaged.

Importantly, ATG630's rules of engagement were classified. Should ISIL have gained a precise knowledge of the limitations the Australian rules of engagement placed on the Air Task Group they could alter their tactics to take advantage of these limitations or endanger the lives of the aircrews involved.

The Australian contingent—like other Coalition partners—had the inherent right to hold up the euphemistically named 'red card' should circumstances preclude them from attacking an adversary. At altitude, at night, in weather, in the smoke and haze of battle, such decisions could be complicated; and this was why the Australian Government made the aircrews the final arbiter of the targeting process. Even so, there was always a Legal Officer on hand with the Commander of the Air Task Group at the Combined Air Operations Centre when operations were in progress. One such officer, Wing Commander Duncan Blake, was at constant pains to point out that the feeling that the adversary were 'inherently evil'—as Daesh were perceived to be—was not a relevant factor in the targeting process or stepping through the preconditions listed on the rules of engagement. This made an air strike even more difficult when ISIL engaged in barbaric tactics that included terrorising non-combatants, using human shields, and fighting from protected sites such as schools, hospitals, religious sites and civilian neighbourhoods.

Australian Defence Force targeting doctrine provided further guidance, going to great lengths to emphasise an operative's consideration of the principles of distinction and proportionality in targeting an adversary under such conditions. Even so, the final judgement was left to the aircrew concerned and this gave the personnel involved some level of discretionary judgement. It meant that:

> *just because collateral casualties or damage may occur or are even expected from an attack on a military objective, does not necessarily make that attack unlawful, provided those collateral effects are proportional to the military advantage.*

With such matters duly considered, Australian platforms and crews simply became another asset to task in the Air Component Commander's order of battle.

Just as the Australian assets began to be tasked, and as maintenance and logistics personnel were bedding down into a routine, the Combined Joint Task Force – Operation INHERENT RESOLVE directed the Air Task Group to relocate. The rationale was simple. While the Al Minhad airfield was large, it was not well established for fighter and strike operations. The Australian facilities could not cope with the nearly 400 extra personnel. After collaboration with the United Arab Emirates authorities, the decision was made to move all elements of the Air Task Group to the Al Dhafra airfield near Abu Dhabi, 160 kilometres to the southwest. The Wedgetail platform would provide its services across the entire operating theatre while the KC-30A, for the moment, would focus solely on support to Australian operations. At Al Dhafra, the strike and tanker platforms would operate out of a large Coalition airbase specifically supporting strike operations into northern Iraq. In many respects the move was welcomed by the airmen and airwomen of the Air Task Group.

Corporal Jason Jones was a Surface Finisher with TE630.1.1. He recalled his first thoughts on arrival at Al Minhad as how 'bloody humid' it was. His first month in-theatre had been inordinately busy. In the desert environment the Australian platforms invariably returned from a sortie with paint stripped from the exposed wing and tailplane leading edges and fuselage appendages—it was Jones's responsibility to refurbish the aircraft after every flight. The temperatures experienced approached fifty degrees Celsius—even though the Emirates was moving into autumn—and Jones spent up to twelve or fourteen hours at a time effecting repairs on the aircraft. He was comfortable with this, but also noted that he and his technical colleagues were very cramped:

> we were all just pretty much lived out of our suitcases or our bags because there were no facilities there to hang anything up or there were no facilities for anything [else] anyway.

Leading Aircraftman Hayden Phillips was an Aviation Technician also operating in TE630.1.1. His views matched Jones's. All technical staff were accommodated in the one dormitory and they came and went at all hours of the day and night as shifts commenced or finished. For the first month of operations he recalled that he and his colleagues had operated for between thirteen to sixteen hours a day in the heat, trying to maintain the delicate avionics systems in the Super Hornets. With the coming and going of maintenance crews—all with a different function—in facilities that were not fit for type, the ground crews welcomed the opportunity to move to a better location. Maintaining air power platforms required precise technical skills applied by competent and rested crews. Getting a platform safely and efficiently ready for operations was half the process that enabled ordnance to be delivered against ISIL.

The move to Al Dhafra was straightforward. There was some work involved in establishing camp facilities for the Australian Air Task Group. In preparation for the influx of personnel, slabs were laid, and large, hardy, air-conditioned tent facilities were set up for the various arriving elements. These tents could accommodate upwards of a dozen personnel with each person having his or her own storage space and wrap-around sheeted walls for some level of privacy. TU630.1 had purpose built 'Connex'-like facilities constructed for staff and administrative functions, and aircrews were allocated briefing and office space adjacent to their flight lines. Technical staff from each of the task elements had prepared 'flyaway' tool kits in Australia, and these were moved by road or air transport to the new location. Guidance systems for munitions and aircraft spares were sourced from Australia and sent directly to Al Dhafra instead of Al Minhad. Actual explosive munitions were purchased from the United States from 'in-theatre' stock; there were also purpose-built ordinance preparation facilities at the new location. Such efficiencies related directly to the RAAF's interoperability with Coalition systems.

As to facilities, the United States' presence at Al Dhafra already included more than 3500 personnel. Here, many of the younger Australian personnel, or those who had not deployed before, were introduced to the abundance of facilities provided by the United States in support of its deployed personnel. Most of the Americans personnel were members of the United States Air Force and they operated, maintained, and supported a wide variety of platforms. These included the KC-10 Extender air-to-air refuelling platform, F-22 Raptor and F-15 strike aircraft, and the RQ-4 Global Hawk, E-3 AWACS and U2 'Dragon Lady' intelligence, surveillance and reconnaissance platforms. The ground-based air battle managers would also move directly into their Coalition operating facilities with the USAF's 727th Expeditionary Air Control Squadron which also conducted its function from Al Dhafra. Briefing considerations for collocated Coalition aircrews operating in disparate aircraft packages also formed part of the decision-making process. The base was 'home' to hundreds of platforms—not just Australian and

American—from a variety of other Coalition partners contributing to the operation.

All three Australian elements relocated to Al Dhafra over one day in mid-November 2014, where operations would continue unaffected. Later, the E-7A Wedgetail would return to Al Minhad where the servicing facilities suited the larger platform, but for the moment the homogenous Air Task Group was now in place where facilities were suitable for the task at hand. Roberton paid tribute to how smoothly this took place:

> ...standing up the Air Task Group, going into theatre, starting combat operations, nearly getting it right ... and then upping stumps and then moving again and then setting it up from scratch was very hard. The site was literally a dirt paddock, a few weeks earlier. The combat support folks in the FSUs [Forward Support Units] were amazing. They did an absolutely amazing job. There are real lessons there...

The routine of operations now commenced. Days succeeded days in an often-monotonous progression as the fight against Daesh unfolded. The fundamentalist movement spread further as 2014 ended, with Australian platforms flying throughout December. Al Baghdadi proclaimed the ancient city Raqqa in Syria as the capital of his 'Caliphate'. The E-7A Wedgetail flew a

Christmas Day 2014 sortie in support of close air support activities in Iraq, and the strike and air-to-air refuelling platforms continued to be tasked.

With the Northern Hemisphere winter weather 'cooling' to averages in the high twenties, maintenance conditions were now far more hospitable. Crews flying over northern Iraq also began to see snow on the mountains. AIRCDRE Roberton returned to Australia after setting the Air Task Group up, replaced by Air Commodore Glen Braz. At the coalface, Chappell's TE630.1.1 had deployed with approximately half of his home squadron's air and ground staff, and he had been planning to rotate these personnel out early in 2015. This was sensible; not only would fresh operational and maintenance personnel enable the incumbent crews to be rested, but the invaluable experience would be shared across the wider air force.

There were plans to rotate the F/A-18F capability out of theatre at the end of the first quarter of 2015 and replace them with No 81 Wing's F/A-18A 'Classic' Hornets. The Chief of Air Force, Air Marshal Geoff Brown had collaborated closely with his counterpart at Joint Operations Command on this plan. The E7A and KC-30A were multi-crewed platforms and they would rotate in and out of theatre on a fixed schedule. Ground air battle managers serving in Kingpin flowed in and out of Al Dhafra on a schedule, while the supporting administrative, maintenance and operations staff at TU630 were on a six-month rotation.

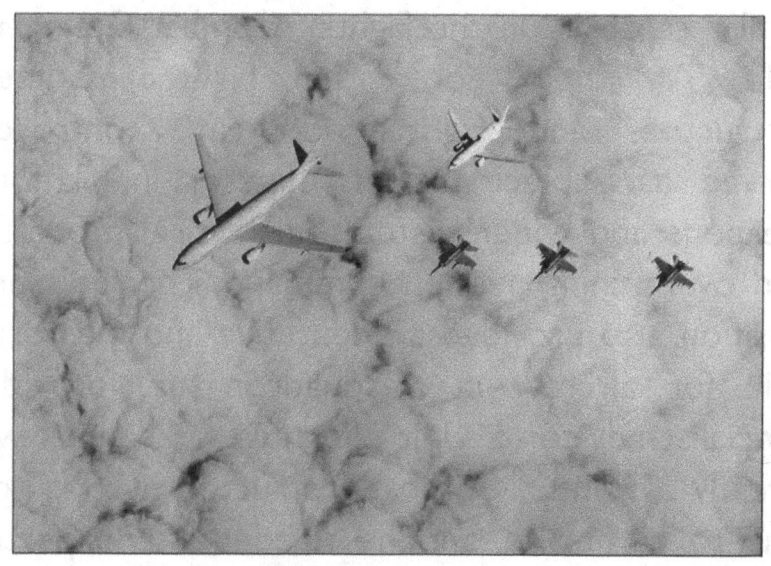

A splendid image depicting the comparative sizes of the various aircraft types that made up ATG630 during Operation OKRA (source: Department of Defence)

As his first TE630.1.1 rotation was replaced, Chappell made the conscious decision to remain with his element in-country. His experience would serve well to provide continuity across the element and ensure an effective handover when the *Classic* Hornets arrived. Chappell had worked closely with his squadron Fighter Combat Instructor whom he had tasked to establish, refine and document domestic and tactical procedures for the strike element to conduct its operations. The Fighter Combat Instructor function was a vital aircrew position in any fighter attack squadron. Ground and air-based air battle management units and squadrons also had a similar capability in the Fighter Combat Controller role. At their core, the Fighter Combat Instructors and Fighter Combat Controllers served as subject matter experts in platform weapons and wider systems, in tactical processes and overarching mission command. The functional position also provided an educative and mentoring role for aircrew in a squadron and provided specialist advice to Unit executives. Chappell was already a Fighter Combat Instructor, but his role was to command, and he needed the expertise of an individual totally focused on mission specifics. Carpenter's element also had a Fighter Combat Controller on the Wedgetail crew, and he relied heavily on this officer's expertise for the planning and conduct of every mission. Fighter Combat Instructors and Fighter Combat Controllers were selected from an already experienced pool of aviator aircrew, and in order to qualify the candidate was required to pass an intensive six-months training. The role was vital for the Air Task Group in-theatre and similar air weapons specialists in the wider Coalition air force collaborated with their Australian counterparts for joint endeavours.

The relationship between Precision and Targeting

The notion of precision encompasses the quality, condition, or fact of being exact and accurate. In the realisation of military kinetic effects, the development of precision guided munitions has added exponentially to the accuracy, lethality and discipline of air power. Today, guided munitions can be pre-programmed to strike a target and will do so irrespective of the time of day or prevailing weather conditions. The satellite enabled accuracy of global position system tracking, or laser designation ensures that modern air launched precision guided munitions will hit where they are aimed—without fail. The advanced communications suite among strike; intelligence, surveillance and reconnaissance; command and control; and terminal air control elements involved in the process simply enhances the efficiency of the kill chain—the result is that these munitions are now intrinsic to the Western way of waging war.

Just why this is so is easy to understand. Precision guided munitions are precise and proportionate. Weapons systems can be programmed, and warheads configured to yield fragmentation according to the target type, the surrounding environment and the need to avoid collateral damage. Precision guided munitions are always employed with discrimination and they may realise effects at the operational or strategic levels. During Coalition air operations over Iraq and Syria air launched precision guided munitions denied ISIL the cover of weather, shelter and darkness. Onboard sensor and tracking systems refined the process even further, enabling aircrews to match weapons and warheads to specific targets. Rules of engagement were prescriptive, and this enhanced accuracy, discrimination and proportional targeting. In the fight against ISIL, precision guided munitions were delivered with almost surgical accuracy.

Problems with ensuring success with these weapons systems occurs when they are employed without the required fidelity of targeting data. The duality of the equation—precision and targeting—will always be challenging for air power practitioners employed on strike operations. The first, precision, is a straightforward matter. Air launched precision guided munitions are enabled with technically mastery and systems that can contend with the immutable factors associated with the air domain: physics, geometry, speed, distance, time, weather, the list goes on. The more advanced the technology, the greater the mastery, the more the potential to realise a favourable effect. Such matters pertain to the accuracy of precision guided munitions. The second part of the equation—targeting—is far more complex. Targeting is a human endeavour, and nothing yet has been designed or found that can eclipse the sentient human mind. Targeting is a constantly evolving process in which an adversary or adversary centre of gravity is found, fixed, identified, tracked and destroyed. The notion of 'centres of gravity' are important. They bring to mind the concentric circles of John E. Warden's famous air power 'five-rings' theory: destroy one ring in the model (each representing a particular centre of gravity), and there is potential to realise an effect out of all proportion to the weapon employed. Over the course of its century of application, this has always been the intent behind the employment of air power. Targeting coupled with accuracy will ensure precision.

Of course, the data required in the targeting process is often perishable or time sensitive, and this means an adversary or centre of gravity is not always where a precision guided munitions is aimed or programmed to strike. The adversary may have moved, the surrounding environment may preclude an air strike, the fluidity of the battlespace is such that the fight has moved on. Such permutations are endless. All of this is problematic for strike crews who operate in this veritable 'fog of war'. The problems associated with ensuring accuracy in combat are therefore immeasurable. What do aircrew do when ISIL take shelter in a mosque or hospital? Who makes the decision about targeting an adversity who is firing from an environment considered to be of unique and priceless heritage? This much is true: when air power fails to achieve the sought-after effect, even when applied in accordance with the rules of engagement, or when the targeting is found to be faulty, the resulting media outcry and clamour of air power 'deniers' will often overshadow the thousands of more successful sorties that have been conducted.

Precision and targeting go hand in hand. Precision guided munitions and the intelligence associated with their application is a constantly evolving function in the application of kinetic air power and was central to the role of the RAAF Air Task Group in Iraq and Syria

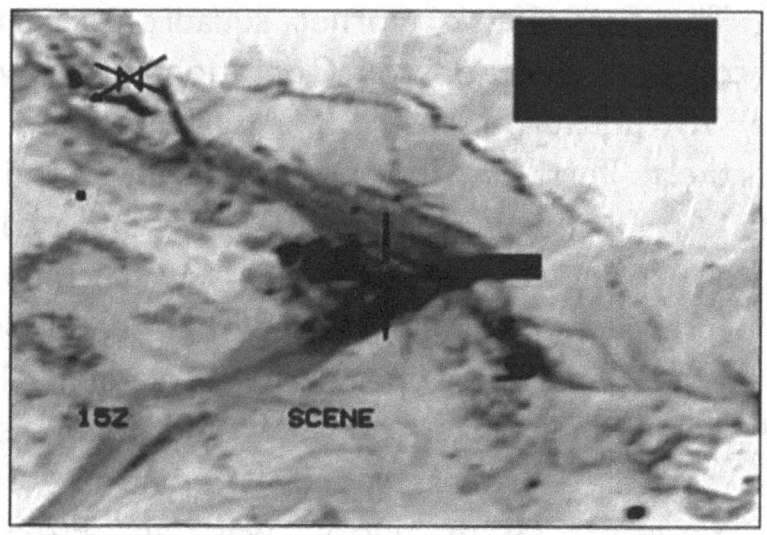

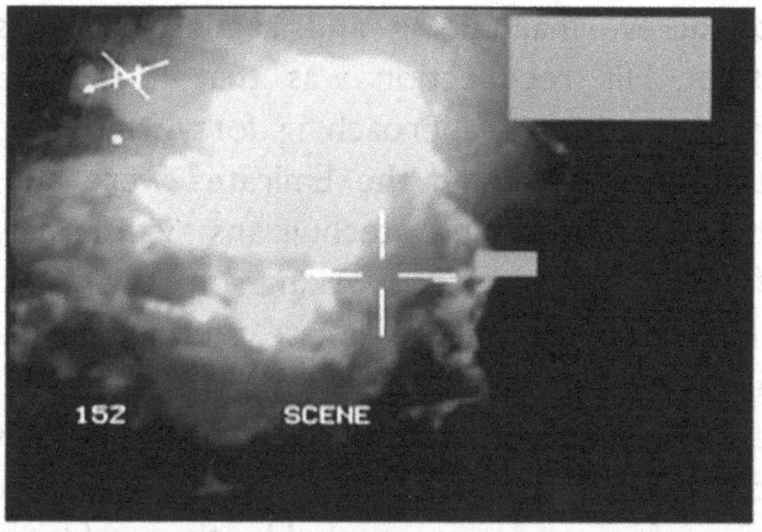

The awesome lethality of modern air launched guided weapons is depicted in imagery captured by onboard infra-red litening pod sensors. At altitude and flying in all types of weather, the RAAF strike platforms were often able to detect, track and destroy targets without the adversary even being aware that they were being watched. (source: Department of Defence)

The first *Classic* Hornet squadron selected to conduct operations on Operation OKRA was No 75 Squadron from RAAF Tindal in the Northern Territory. Its six aircraft flew straight into Al Dhafra in March 2015 as the Middle Eastern spring commenced giving way to summer. The crews immediately started their hand over with the departing Super Hornet element. The Wedgetail and tanker crews would follow suit in a staggered process shortly afterwards.

Sergeant Grant Dore was an F/A-18A technician with TE630.1.1 responsible for a groundcrew maintaining and arming the *Classic* Hornet. His recollection was that it had been very hot initially—approaching forty-five degrees Celsius—even though the Emirates were still in spring. Some of his technicians were having difficulty adjusting to working on twelve-hour shifts in the prevailing climate and Dore spent considerable effort shaping the routine of his crew on the flight line. He worked out a roster cycle and a heat management plan with the engineering executive team. He then addressed his personnel. He outlined the conditions faced by the Iraqi troops facing Daesh to his technical staff:

> They don't have the luxury of saying it's too hot or I'm too tired, they need these bombs

on target or they're going to get killed. We've got to do our job.

Dore was pleased that the group of technicians seemed to be reinvigorated after his chat with them.

Slightly smaller than the dual seat F/A-18F, the older single seat Australian F/A-18A had been constantly upgraded and well-maintained during its life of type. It was still a first-rate, high end combat capability in the war on Daesh. (source: Department of Defence)

The commanding officer of the new strike detachment was an Academy colleague of Chappell, Wing Commander Pete Mitchell. Like every officer at this rank level in the Air Task Group, Mitchell was an experienced professional. He and Chappell conducted a handover, and on 18 March 2015, Chappell and his Weapon Systems Officer, Squadron Leader Luke Warner, in a Super Hornet accompanied Mitchell in his *Classic* Hornet on a flight into Iraq. This sortie was a first; an F/A-18A and F/A-18F flying in unison on operations had not occurred before. The air task order also included an Australian KC-30A to accompany the two fighters. The tanker was captained by the TE630.1.3 Detachment Commander, Squadron Leader Greg Ferguson. In another first, all four aviators—Chappell, Warner, Mitchell and Ferguson—were Academy graduates from class of 1995. This was hardly a coincidence. They had programmed it that way—it seemed a shame not to try setting an Academy class participation record before the opportunity was lost!

By this stage the 'active' operational areas of Iraq and Syria had been apportioned into a series of battlespace grids—called 'kill-boxes' in the vernacular—by the Qatari Combined Air Operations Centre. The kill boxes gave a precise appreciation of the multi-dimensional battlespace and facilitated the allocation and command and control of strike assets operating in-theatre. From his first sortie, Mitchell recalled the green beauty of the fields around Mosul, and at altitude, seeing the snow-capped mountain ranges of Southern Turkey. This was juxtaposed by the activity observed taking place in ISIL-controlled territory where bulldozers scraped the earth to make defensive berms, and utility vehicles armed with heavy machine-guns—'technicals'—were observed moving around.

The infra-red sensing systems of both the *Classic* and Super Hornet, in addition to the arrays of radar and other sensor systems in the Wedgetail, could produce high quality imagery. Individuals carrying small arms, muzzle flashes, and vehicle silhouettes could all be distinguished by Coalition air platforms with some fidelity; and when Iraqi troops were in contact with ISIL, the strike aircraft would be called upon to coordinate with the infantry to provide close air support. In addition, unmanned aerial vehicles and satellite-based communications systems meant that compiled imagery and footage could be relayed almost instantaneously among platforms and to command and control nodes on the ground. Initially, ISIL seemed unable to reconcile the fact that Coalition air power had such accurate data at its disposal. They learned this the hard way, and there were stark recollections for some of the aviators involved.

One airman recalled Daesh attempting to disguise themselves by transporting their combatants into close proximity to the Iraqis in a taxicab. They were tracked by the Australian aircrews and positively identified before being engaged with a laser guided munition. What was strange, the aviator recalled, was despite the taxicab being destroyed and its occupants all killed, the 'Taxi' sign on top of the roof was undamaged and remained lit. On another sortie, another group of Daesh were tracked advancing along a trench line during the pitched fight for Ramadi in mid-2015. This group perhaps thought they were concealed in the trench, or in the haze of battle, but were engaged by stand-off weaponry and destroyed without knowing what had hit them. Yet another group took shelter under a bridge from potential air strikes, but the fragmentary envelope of an Australian weapon placed at ground level on the side of the bridge killed everyone below without damaging the infrastructure. Such was the awesome lethality of the firepower and systems at ATG630's disposal.

Back at Al Dhafra, Wing Commander Mark Barry had taken over from Wing Commander Matt McCormack as the Chief of Staff at TE630.1.0. Barry was an air battle management-specialised Air Combat Officer, and a qualified Fighter Combat Controller. He was assiduous, reserved, and like Chappell, this highly respected officer had a keen sense of history. Barry proudly coordinated ATG630's commemorative activities for the first Anzac Day ceremony that the group would spend in-theatre on 25 April 2015. This was the centenary of Anzac, and Barry reflected deeply on events as he was serving on operations 100 years to the day after the Gallipoli landings. Of course, the British and Canadian airmen at Al Dhafra were well-aware of the significance of this date for the Australians, and when the United States forces became aware of its meaning, they joined with the Air Task Group in a parade and commemorative barbeque. In the following years, the Anzac Day parade at Al Dhafra would grow commensurately, and it later extended to a parade on 6 July to mark the first occasion on which US and Australian personnel served together on operations during the Battle of Hamel in 1918. Throughout this period, Air Commodore Braz had worked tirelessly with his subordinate commanders in the Air Task Group and equally with Director General-Air in Australia to refine and coordinate ATG630's efforts. As summer approached in mid-2015, the complicated wiring in the E-7A—there was enough in the platform to literally stretch around the equator of the earth—was affected by the fifty degrees Celsius ambient temperatures on the flight line. This temperature quickly rose well into the seventy degrees range at noon and in the early afternoon, with the result that the Wedgetail's systems were being cooked. The platform was large and there were no facilities to keep it enclosed, so TE630.1.2 redeployed back to Al Minhad where the platform could be hangered. There it would remain for the remainder of the war.

After a hard six-months work, Braz returned to Australia and was replaced by Air Commodore Stuart Bellingham. Bellingham assumed command at a very interesting point in the campaign. His six-month tour would mark the end of the first year of operations for ATG630—as air power was starting to make a difference. By November 2015, the Coalition had conducted nearly 10 000 air strikes across Iraq and Syria, and ISIL had been effectively halted, suffering significant territorial losses in both countries. The Iraqi military had made advances, recapturing Tikrit north of Baghdad in March, and Mount Sinjar in November. Iraq would recapture Ramadi by the end of the year. The figures were fluid, though estimates counted between 8000 and 12 000 ISIL fighters killed in action or as the result of air strikes. Even so, both Mosul and Raqqa remained in the group's hands. Even though the fundamentalist group was losing territory, there was significant fight ahead.

The statistics accrued by ATG630 in its contribution to these operations were impressive. Two disparate strike platforms, the Boeing

F/A-18F Super Hornets and F/A-18A *Classic Hornets*, had been employed. The Super Hornets had conducted 418 sorties accumulating 3351 hours and releasing 278 weapons. The *Classic Hornets* had conducted 510 sorties accumulating 3747 hours and releasing 290 weapons. The E7A Wedgetail aircraft had conducted 154 missions amounting to 1268 hours. And the KC-30A had flown 442 missions, transferring nearly forty-one million pounds of fuel to Australian and Coalition aircraft.

A year in, it was evident that ISIL's well-established base of operations in Syria was enabling it to stage operations across its borders into north-western Iraq. Syria remained in the throes of a civil war that stemmed from the Arab Spring, so ISIL was able to take full advantage of Syrian President Bashar AlAssad's lack of control in his nation's eastern provinces. During its early conquests, ISIL had taken over several villages, towns and cities in eastern Syria very easily. This gave the group access to resources, but the territory also provided a level of geographic and strategic depth to ISIL's proclaimed caliphate.

This was no revelation to either the Coalition or Iraq, and the Australian Government was well-aware from the earliest days of its commitment that any plan to defeat ISIL in Iraq required a commensurate effort to combat the group in Syria. On 9 September 2015, Prime Minister Tony Abbott, in conjunction with his Defence Minister Kevin Andrews, announced that the RAAF's air strikes against ISIL would now be against targets in both Iraq and Syria. The next day, Australian Attorney-General George Brandis drew on an historical analysis when he contributed his thoughts on the matter to *The Australian* newspaper:

> The Iraqi-Syrian border is not a natural frontier—it is literally a line in the sand, the product of the division of the Middle Eastern provinces of the Ottoman Empire after World War I by the Sykes-Picot agreement. The Daesh insurgency does not acknowledge it as an international border and Daesh militias move across it without impediment. It makes absolutely no sense, from a military or strategic point of view, to be limited by an arbitrary boundary that the enemy neither recognises nor respects.

The Air Task Group was ready, with the first RAAF sortie into Syria conducted on 15 September 2015 by two F/A-18As supported by the Wedgetail and KC-30A. No ordnance was released on this flight, but in a replication of the mission the very next day, two subsequent strike aircraft identified an armoured vehicle hidden in an ISIL compound. The F/A-18As relayed the information to the Combined Air Operations Centre via the escorting E-7A and were given authorisation to engage the target. The vehicle was destroyed, and back in Australia, Defence Minister Andrews was able to announce the successful mission to Parliament almost immediately after it occurred.

This mission set a precedent, and when Mitchell's strike element rotated out during October-November 2015, the replacement F/A-18As, from No 77 Squadron at RAAF Williamtown, conducted a further twenty-one strike sorties into Syria before the end of the year. The Wedgetail would enter Syrian airspace on forty subsequent missions, and the KC-30A five times.

By October 2015, the KC-30A had firmly established itself as a Coalition force multiplier. It had received endorsement to transfer fuel to not only RAAF and US Navy strike platforms, but also US Marine Corps AV-8B Harriers, Royal Air Force Typhoons and French Armée de l'Air Rafales. It was already routinely conducting air-to-air refuelling operations with larger platforms including the Wedgetail and C-17 Globemasters. Rather than setting up a 'racetrack' pattern at a predetermined point for receivers to join, TE630.1.3 was pioneering a process whereby it accompanied strike aircraft closer to the fight on the ground so that transit times to refuel were significantly reduced. This approach was well-received across the Coalition. Flight Sergeant Col Weekes was an experienced senior non-commissioned officer employed as an air-to-air refuelling boom operator on the KC-30A. Weekes had spent nearly twenty years as an RAAF Airfield Defence Guard before 're-rolling' to an aircrew mustering—this gave him some very intuitive understanding of what was happening on the ground below. He took pride in his work and recalled that when Coalition receivers saw an Australian tanker, they understood that they would be refuelled quickly so that they could get back into the fight below.

A French Rafale strike aircraft comes off the drogue after completing refuelling with the RAAF KC-30A. The great utility of the Australian tanker was that it could cater for both 'Boom' and 'Probe and Drogue' refuelling systems. (source: Department of Defence)

Lesson#11

- There are inherent nuances to the employment of air power that reflect on an enduring understanding of the characteristics and nature of air power and its utility as a critical element of national power.

• Professional airmen and airwomen require a comprehensive understanding of air power's extensive body of knowledge and an ability to apply that knowledge to effectively employ air power.

• In addition to Centralised Command and Decentralised Execution CCDE, the tenets of concurrency and balance contribute to the optimal employment of air power.

• Concurrency and balance comprise the ability to conduct multiple operations simultaneously with an appropriate mix of platforms, capability and strategic depth.

Ad Astra: To the Stars

As 2015 concluded, ISIL had lost nearly a third of its territory back to Iraqi forces, and its sources of revenue were now being targeted directly by air power. Throughout December 2015, Coalition strike aircraft were relentless in their operations. In early December, the RAF had destroyed the oil wells at Omar in Syria, and in this one raid ISIL lost more than ten per cent of its income. On 21 December, twenty-one Coalition strike aircraft, including four RAAF

F/A-18s, attacked 137 targets across Eastern Syria. The Australian jets destroyed a large weapons cache during this sortie. ISIL was now facing attacks from a coalition of sixty-six countries led by the United States on the one hand, and the Russian-backed Syrian regime on the other. ISIL would thereafter be on the defensive. As territory was recaptured, the freed peoples came to recount appalling atrocities. ISIL had forced those in its territory to convert to a skewed understanding of the Muslim faith, and it had beheaded, slaughtered or crucified those who resisted. ISIL reintroduced slavery. Some individuals who had resisted were executed and their heads were put on spikes to warn dissenters. Mass graves were discovered as territory was recaptured.

ISIL had absolutely no legitimacy in the global order, and Al-Baghdadi's twisted interpretation of gospel was in direct contravention of Islamic teachings. He had resurrected the notion of the caliphate without the consensus of the Muslim fraternity and welcomed thousands of misguided foreign fighters into the ranks of his army. Iraqi and Coalition military leaders now commenced Phase Two of the operation to counterattack and liberate the territory and its people from under Baghdadi's control. This would be the longest and most difficult phase of the operation.

Fighting Back

The Coalition 'Build Partner Capacity' efforts on the ground had gone to some lengths to resource the Iraqi Security Force's capabilities to assist in building three Iraqi Army Divisions, three Kurdish Brigades, and an initial Tribal Force that could serve as the basis for developing an Iraqi National Guard. The nature of the air campaign in support of these fielded forces was straightforward. The Coalition would continue to target specific elements of the ISIL infrastructure to directly impact Daesh's ability to fund its activities. Deliberate air attacks were routine. Dynamic air attacks, occurring when Iraqi forces were in contact with ISIL, meant targeting terrorist vehicles, combatants, fighting positions, compounds and facilities as the circumstance warranted. By this stage in the war, such matters had been refined. Prior to jets arriving on-station in Iraq or Syria, the Combined Air Operations Centre liaised with Coalition ground liaison elements and Combat Controllers to prepare an intelligence report for the area in which the fight was taking place. This could have been at any number of localities all over Iraq and across the border into Syria.

E-7A crews had become adept at operating within the fluid nature of this battlespace; they were in high demand to provide command and control for assets across the entire Coalition air spectrum. The process ensured that strike platforms were fuelled by a tanker before arriving in-theatre. At this time, collated targeting requests were relayed to strike crews from their command and control facilities. Dynamic targets were prioritised by higher command according to whether they comprised a request for support to troops in contact with ISIL or were vehicles or hardpoints likely to impede progress during the battle. Remotely piloted aircraft and unmanned aerial vehicles also provided a live video feed to command and control facilities to aid in refining the targeting process. As soon as ISIL targets were hit, the video feeds from unmanned platforms were in position to relay images for battle damage assessment back to the Combined Air Operations Centre.

All targets were vetted in order that they complied with the rules of engagement. Before a target could be engaged, it had to fulfil the criteria detailed by the Target Engagement Authority; the veritable 'Red Card' would be played if the target did not meet the requirements listed in the rules of engagement. On numerous occasions during Operation OKRA Australian aircrew did not engage a target because these conditions were not met or because the potential for collateral damage was deemed disproportionate to the realised effect. Unfortunately, the complex nature of the conflict also resulted in error. At least twice in the conflict, Australian strike crews were implicated in the deaths of non-combatants or friendly forces. One of these events occurred in the complicated Syrian environment in September 2016 when RAAF jets were cleared to engage what they believed were confirmed ISIL combatants at the Deir al-Zor military airfield in Syria's east. In the attack, two RAAF Hornets released six weapons which killed numerous Syrian Government troops. While the RAAF accepted responsibility for the 'human error' in the targeting process, the matter was very complicated. No Australian aircrew would deliberately carry out such an act—all Coalition air strike platforms were in-theatre to combat ISIL. However, in Syria, both Assad's Russian-backed regime and the US-backed Syrian rebels were fighting ISIL, and the lack of coordination between these elements contributed to the terrible event.

In the second instance in June 2017, Australian and Coalition aircraft conducted an air strike in the Al Shafaar neighbourhood of Mosul in support of Iraqi Security Forces who were threatened with imminent loss of life or serious injury by ISIL. During this operation, two Australian aircraft released one 500 lb precision guided munition each, striking a building and a courtyard identified as enemy positions. Later it was evident that civilian casualties may have occurred as a result of the air strike, with claims of as many as thirty-five civilian deaths. Although it was unclear in the circumstances if Australian platforms had been involved in the deaths, Joint Operations Command commenced an investigation as soon as news emerged that civilians may have perished. The investigation found that the personnel involved, using the information available to them, acted in compliance with the law of armed conflict and Australian rules of engagement. The tragedy was that as many as eighteen civilians may have been accidently killed in the strike.

The commencement of the Combined Joint Task Force—Operation INHERENT RESOLVE's Second Phase of operations to dismantle and then defeat ISIL during 2016 would mean a great many more sorties generated in support of the Iraqi Security Forces. As this workup commenced, Squadron Leader David 'Doc' Martin was posted into the Combined Air Operations Centre to commence a six-month tour. He arrived in-theatre with his unrelated namesake the new Commander Air Task Group, Air Commodore Antony Martin. Both officers were highly proficient and experienced air battle managers. Air Commodore Martin was particularly personable, and his selection as the Commander reflected his leadership style and prior experience in the region. Air Commodore Martin had served on the JTF633 Headquarters staff in Baghdad during the 2007 surge, and he was familiar with the lie of the land. For his part, Squadron Leader Martin had an exceptional mix of computer-based technical skills and operative experience. He had served on exchange with the RAF's No 8 Squadron, operating the E-3 Sentry aircraft for three years, before returning to No 2 Squadron and its E-7A Wedgetails. Squadron Leader Martin was an extrovert and he got on with everyone who he worked with.

Squadron Leader Martin was impressed with the facilities at the Al Udeid Combined Air Operations Centre. From the first time he entered the room, he remembered that the operations room—about the size of a gymnasium—was a veritable hive of activity. The front wall showed an 'air picture' over Syria and Iraq, the Persian Gulf and Afghanistan. The image comprised a digitised compilation of operational assets across the vast region and was put together based on data delivered from ground and air-based radar units, other coalition aircraft, space-based systems and civil air traffic systems.

When the data was input into the combined Air Operations Centre's displays, operators had to classify and identify what their respective systems was displaying, and then place track symbology over the return on their computer screens. The 'Kingpin' facility at Al Dhafra comprised similar systems at a more localised level.

The assigned tracks conformed to a standardised system across the entire Coalition force. The tracking symbology in the E-7A, E-3, Kingpin and the Combined Air Operations Centre were instantly recognisable among all those trained to use the respective systems. They were colour coded. Blue and green symbology was assigned to Coalition military and neutral civil aircraft, while red and yellow track symbology were either non-Coalition military or unknown aircraft. The tracks also assigned a function to the associated aircraft detailing its role as a fighter; strike; air mobility; intelligence, surveillance and reconnaissance; or another role. What struck Squadron Leader Martin most was that the skies over the area of operations were covered with hundreds of tracks, and because they were constantly moving, maintaining 'situational awareness' of what track corresponded to what aircraft and where it was flying required constant vigilance. On the right-hand side wall of the room there were similar-sized screens displaying real-time video feeds from the numerous remotely piloted aircraft and unmanned aerial vehicles deployed throughout the region. The video feeds assisted team involved in the targeting decision-making process, while the front screens enabled the Defensive Operations team to make informed decisions to protect the coalition assets in-theatre. Despite his aviation experience, this was the first time Doc Martin had deployed, and he recalled a busy six-months planning for operations in the air tasking order cycle.

A No 77 Squadron F/A-18A sits in the waiting area at the Al Dhafra airbase waiting area until ground controllers give it direction to proceed. With temperatures sometimes peaking above 60 degrees Celsius on the tarmac, air and ground crew comfort was difficult to manage. (source: Department of Defence)

During his time in-theatre in 2016, Squadron Leader Martin watched a thoroughly dynamic series of combat operations evolve in parallel with the ground war. The weather had a real effect on air and maintenance operations, and this applied right across ATG630. No 3 Squadron's crews had by now rotated with No 77 Squadron crew into the strike element as spring gave way to summer. The new maintenance staff were forced to acclimatise to the harsh conditions. The new TE630.1.1 commander was a quiet and thoroughly focussed Queenslander, Wing Commander John Haly. When Operation OKRA commenced, Haly had been working in a staff role at Headquarters Air Combat Group back in Australia. Shortly afterwards he had been posted to undertake command of No 3 Squadron. With this 'insider' knowledge, Haly knew the rotation schedule for the deployment for each fast jet squadron. This gave him time to prepare for his role on operations and, like his predecessors, he would conduct a six-month tour to cover two rotations of No 3 Squadron personnel. Haly understood that the close air support and limited strike role that TE630.1.1 was conducting over Iraq and Syria encompassed a relatively narrow sub-set of the air combat role. This enabled him to use lessons from earlier rotations and employ his own experience to focus specifically on what his strike element would be doing when it arrived in-theatre. Haly and his unit executives paid attention to ensuring that his crews understood the unique rules of engagement in-theatre, and that they practiced the types of close air support that they would soon undertake for real. This required the strike aviators to refine their use of airborne sensors and communication processes with those in combat on the ground.

Both the strike and air battle management elements of the Air Task Group conducted pre-deployment training with Joint Terminal Air Controllers and Combat Controllers from No 4 Squadron at RAAF Williamtown in Australia. The function of combat control was vital. The speed, performance and abundance of sensor data in an already complex air environment required very close coordination between Coalition air assets and the Iraqi Security Forces. Combat control offered ground commanders a method to combat their adversaries with air power in a way that conventional ground forces could not. The Australian contribution came in the form of individual RAAF personnel trained as Combat Controllers. These were highly trained personnel who had a detailed appreciation of the practical application of kinetic air power. Each operated complex and portable communications systems and were responsible for integrating the complex system of intelligence, surveillance and reconnaissance; air battle management; strike; and ground elements to generate an air power effect with precision. The nature of the conflict in Iraq and Syria meant that this effect was kinetic. To be accurate meant that the controller had to be embedded with ground forces and close enough an adversary so that a target could be both visually observed and designated with a laser.

To meet this demand, Combat Controllers in the RAAF were specialist airmen selected for their acumen, spatial orientation, and specialist communications skills. As these personnel were required to operate in austere environments, often with special forces, they also undertook special forces selection and the gamut of reinforcement training, prior to focussing on the combat control skillset. At No 4 Squadron, combat control training courses provided them the skills to independently integrate air power effects with almost surgical accuracy. Australian Combat Controllers were highly regarded within Combined Joint Task Force—Operation INHERENT RESOLVE and were embedded with the Special Forces Build Partner Capacity task element in Baghdad. They deployed forward with ISF headquarters elements behind the forward edge of the battle area to provide tactical advice when Iraqi troops engaged Daesh in the field. One Australian Army Special Forces Warrant

Officer in Baghdad—a 'warrior poet' named Jason—knew his Combat Controller had been sent 'out on the plains of the Never Never'. As Jason understood the environment:

Out on the wastes of the Never Never–
That's where the dead men lie!
There where the heatwaves dance forever–
That's where the dead men lie!
Out where the grinning skulls bleach whitely
Under the saltbush sparkling brightly;
Out where the wild dogs chorus nightly–
That's where the dead men lie!

Barcroft Boake 1891

The Intricate War against ISIL in Syria

With seeming spontaneity, the 'Arab Spring' of the late 2000s promised a new age for the Middle East. Starting in Egypt and gaining momentum across the cradle of civilisation, the people of several Arabic-speaking nations defiantly rose against their corrupt and despotic leadership. The wave of defiance reached Iraq's neighbour, Syria, in 2011 and precipitated a bloody civil war that continues years later.

On one side of the conflict, the corrupt regime of President Bashar al-Assad initially seemed destined for defeat when faced by the myriad of rebel groups ranged against him. The rebels included a sizeable Kurdish population from northern Syria, whose ethnic affiliations recognise neither Syrian nor Iraqi sovereignty, and who seek an independent Peshmerga Kurdish state. By 2013, the corrupt Assad's great fortune focused the world's major global powers attention onto his nation's plight. His powers remained intact as both the United States and Russia, supporting differing sides in the conflict, vied to serve their own interests in the region. Russia, a long-time supporter of the Syrians, continued to supply Assad's regime with weaponry. America, in a show of Cold War-like defiance, opposed Russia's moves and gave support to the rebels. This resulted in a rancorous diplomatic stand-off between Washington and Moscow, while at the same time empowering Assad to establish a stranglehold over any potential rebel success.

Overshadowing all of this, when the self-proclaimed ISIL unleashed a wave of barbarism across the region in 2014, it opened a veritable 'can of worms'. ISIL claimed that it wished to establish a modern regional Islamic Caliphate in the Middle East, and it commenced a wave of fundamentalist Islamic terror attacks that threatened the bourgeoning Iraqi democracy. Not recognising the region's borders, ISIL chose to stage many of its operations out of Syria, and against Assad. It captured the Syrian city of Raqqa and proclaimed it the 'capitol' of the new caliphate.

The West, led by the United States, commenced kinetic operations in Iraq—predominantly using air power including an RAAF Air Task Group—against ISIL in 2014. It also conducted air strikes against ISIL in Syria—Australia joined in these strikes after mid-2015. The Russians—who were not a part of the Coalition—went on to commence unilateral air strikes against ISIL in support of the Assad regime in late September 2015. To confuse matters, US air operations concurrently backed rebel groups seeking to overthrow the Syrian regime. Russia purportedly targeted not only ISIL, but also other groups—including those supported by the US—ranged against Assad.

When the Australian Boeing E-7A Wedgetail flew on operations near the Iraq and Syrian border, part of its responsibility was to deconflict Coalition and Russian strike platforms which may have been operating in the theatre concurrently against ISIL but not in conjunction with each other.

This complicated three-sided war continues to devastate the region today.

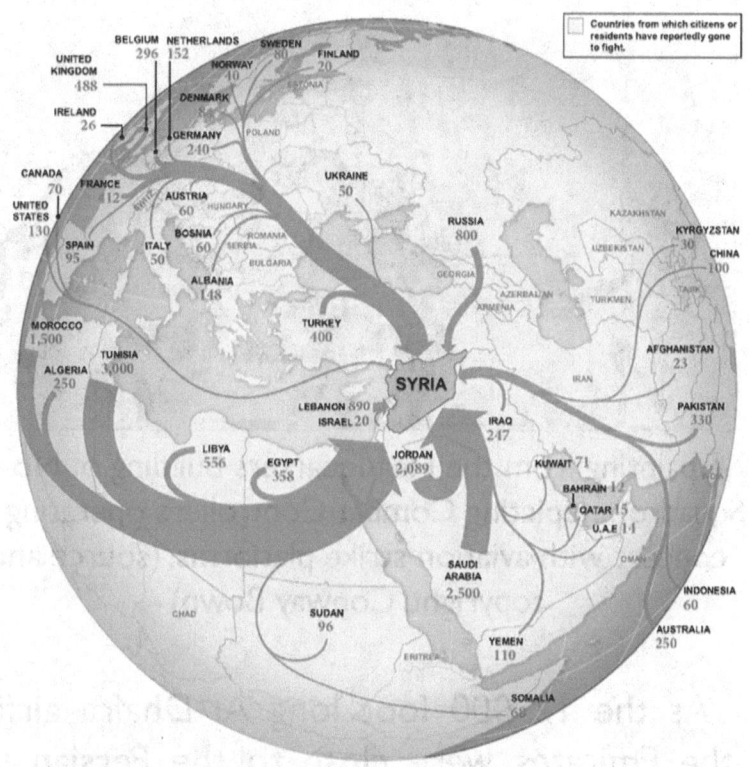

Countries where fighters came from to fight for ISIL in Syria.

From their positions in headquarters located at or just behind the frontline, Combat Controllers were able to facilitate the application of air power in support of ground commanders. Often, ATG630 air battle management and strike aircrews were pleasantly surprised to hear an Australian accent on the other end of a radio in the battlespace below them.

A painting from the Headquarters building of No 4 Squadron depicting Combat Controllers operating in concert with aviation strike platforms. (source and copyright: Conway Bown)

As the 12 000 foot long Al Dhafra airfields in the Emirates were close to the Persian Gulf, the humidity was almost unbearable—in July it hovered at eighty per cent and in August it regularly went higher. The ground was low-lying, and this meant that the water table would rise in the summer months and make the Australian accommodation facilities muddy. Conditions were very difficult, and staff had to expend considerable effort in keeping their accommodation and facilities clean from the mud that the boots of every aviator and airman and airwoman picked up. Airfield engineers eventually solved the problem by transporting tons of gravel into the Australian area for personnel to walk on.

FSGT Trudi Cox was a logistics specialist on staff at TU630 and she had spent time in the heat at Al Minhad on an earlier deployment. Even so, she could find nothing to compare with the heat and humidity that she experienced at Al Dhafra. One wit recalled that the regulatory framework surrounding what personnel could and could not wear in the prevailing conditions was ridiculous. 'There was more paperwork outlining the rules on where and when we could wear open sandals or thongs than there was on how to conduct an air strike,' he recalled with some mirth. There was grumbling about the vicissitudes and imposition of such regulations among both officers and airmen for the entire operation. There were rules about where and when hats could be worn, and where and when to salute. There were rules for what an individual could wear into the Coalition mess, irrespective of US standards. There were other rules for what one could wear when going to the ablutions block, and what colour boots went with what uniform.

Access to alcohol for Australians whilst on operations has occurred since the earliest days of World War I, but this has not always reflected well on those involved. Any claim of 'larrikinism' or the Anzac myth' rang hollow for the Air Task Group—it was there to do a job, and alcohol would inhibit its ability to do its work. At Al Minhad there was a strict no-drinking policy for all ADF personnel. At Al Dhafra, personnel were allowed three standard alcoholic drinks three times a week at a bar on the base. This differed to the US allowance. All staff at Al Dhafra generally received a pass for one day per month to go off base in pairs to visit the nearby cities of Abu Dhabi and Dubai. Again, there was a strict policy of zero-alcohol consumption on these days off. Some individuals at both airbases tested the rules. This was an infrequent occurrence, but when they were caught, the policy for such infractions was an immediate return to Australia with disciplinary action to follow. Despite some complaints, most personnel understood and accepted this measure.

As all of this went, managing personnel could at times be more onerous than managing the platforms in the Air Task Group. Squadron Leader Steve Campbell-Wright was a Personnel Capability Officer—an administration specialist—who conducted a six months rotation within TU630.1. With over thirty years' experience in the RAAF, Steve had a keen interest in the RAAF's history and heritage. Funnily, Steve bore an uncanny resemblance to a middleaged Sir Richard Williams, so much so that he was nicknamed 'Dicky'. Like his namesake, Dicky was a man who appreciated the need for robust and thorough personnel management. Campbell-Wright and a team of non-commissioned administration and clerical staff were responsible for ensuring that each task element within the Air Task Group had the right personnel structure filled with the right skills in-theatre at the right time. While the work could be mundane, time-consuming and often complex, it was also inherently important. During his tour, Campbell-Wright liaised closely with personnel and administrative staff at Headquarters JTF633.

Immigration visas posed one of the greatest challenges for Dicky's team. Air Task Group personnel were based in two different countries—at the main operating base and at the Combined Air Operations Centre. In addition, rescue crews had to be prepared to enter third countries at very short notice to recover any aircraft diverted there. With different entry and residency requirements across the countries of the Middle East Region, Dicky's team on a day-to-day basis monitored and managed both operational sorties and domestic movements. Within the Air Task Group, Campbell-Wright had an orderly room and personnel capability specialists—clerical staff—who took care of the diverse range of documentation covering pay, leave and travel requirements for each RAAF member deployed in the group. In addition, most deployed personnel had a 'Relief Out of Country Travel Fare Assistance' entitlement, which was processed by the orderly room.

Dicky's supervisor was a senior Personnel Capability Officer tasked with providing specialist administrative advice to the CATG and to manage higher-level administration, often with the Emirates host nation. For this engagement with the Emirates, the Air Task Group employed a visits and protocol officer who oversaw the visit programs by deployed Australian-based and foreign teams as well as visiting dignitaries. Notable visits from 2015 to 2017 included teams from the Australian War Memorial, located in Canberra, which assessed items for inclusion in its collection, and conducted oral history interviews with Australian deployed personnel.

In the heat of summer, Wing Commander Haly and his engineering executive paid particular attention to the welfare of their technical personnel, and went to great lengths to ensure that all personnel adhered to the mandated heat management policies for the group—these policies dictated how long personnel could operate in the extreme temperatures on the flight line and in the ordnance preparation facilities. The personnel used ice vests—literally jackets filled with fluid that were frozen to enable the wearer to have a degree of comfort when loading and maintaining an F/A-18. These vests worked for a short period though in the oppressive heat the frozen liquid melted quickly. To alleviate the situation, the TU630 commander, Group Captain Brendan Rogers, was instrumental in setting up air-conditioned maintenance tents that could be used for some aspects of the strike element's servicing regimen. The tents were erected by airfield engineers after Air Commodore Martin directly engaged his US counterpart to smooth the way for their construction on base. The tent proved to be a boon for most of the Air Task Group technicians, but the size of the KC-30A still required it to be serviced and refuelled in the open. One of the tanker captains marvelled at the resilience of the TE630.1.3 airmen as they manoeuvred the massive hoses and support equipment around the KC-30A.

At Al Minhad, the commander of the Wedgetail Detachment had similar views. Squadron Leader William Hipps was a softly spoken American-Australian who had operated Northrop Grumman E-2C Hawkeyes of the United States Navy during the 2003 invasion of Iraq. He subsequently undertook an exchange posting to the RAAF as an Air Combat Officer before deciding to settle 'down-under'. Hipps had transferred into the RAAF as the Wedgetail capability was coming into service, and his air battle management operational experience was greatly appreciated. At Al Minhad, he was in command of the seventh rotation of Wedgetail crews and was responsible for probably the most complex platform ever operated by the RAAF, a crew of up to a dozen highly specialised individuals of all ages and backgrounds, and several dozen maintenance and support staff who prepared his aircraft for the coming sortie.

While the command of a strike element on Operation OKRA could be difficult, the other task elements were no less challenged in their respective roles of maintaining their platforms and generating missions. At its core, ATG630 comprised a group of aviators, technicians and support staff who were required to project air power over a thousand miles from their deployed base. They were also required to do so within a Coalition construct and in concert with other Allied elements.

The coordination of such effects 'in time and through airspace' has been unchanged since the time of Sir Richard Williams. However, the technology enabling aircraft to be used as a means in warfare has exponentially evolved over the century. This change *was* extraordinary for the Air Task Group in that air power effects could be generated so quickly in battlespace at a distance so far away. The array of sensors at the disposal of Coalition platforms resulted in any adversary movement likely being subject to immediate scrutiny. The accuracy of ordnance delivered through either laser designation or global positioning system guidance was phenomenal.

Getting the aircraft on station was only part of the task. To ensure that they arrived safely and efficiently, these aircraft were serviced, maintained and supported by a massive staff at the base. The aircrews on each platform required unique specialist training so that it could be used to best effect. Strike platforms intrinsically operated in pairs or a formation of four, so that their systems could be integrated. The Wedgetail and KC-30A crews operated slightly differently. They comprised a team within the one platform that operated in unison to generate a completely different effect. Irrespective of the mission, all the platforms were interconnected and could communicate with wider command and control contributors via satellite-enabled radio and datalink. It was an awesome and complex biosystem and it required a great deal of planning every time a mission was conducted.

A Day's Work for the Air Task Group

The work cycle for flying a mission over Iraq or Syria was driven by the air tasking order cycle and promulgated at the Combined Air Operations Centre. The air tasking order planning cycle was fixed and rolled through a targeting, planning, executing and assessment process over a seventy-two or ninety-six hour period. An 'intention' message would be issued each day at a specified time giving a generic overview of where elements would be operating on the subsequent day. Later during the same day, a Coalition-wide air tasking order would be issued. The air tasking order gave specific direction and tasks to all units, elements and command and control agencies to project sorties in support of the operation. The air tasking order generally comprised callsigns, radio frequencies, fuel and ordnance loads, rendezvous points for tankers or disparate elements, and information specific to an operation. The air tasking order received input from intelligence and targeting specialists, and from the Combined Joint Task Force Land Component Command in order that each element could refine its planning to produce the best possible air power effect. Platform maintenance planning and crew rest periods were integrated into the process and added another layer of complexity. Airspace control orders gave an overview to crews of where and when they could operate in particular areas; 'special instructions'—referred to as SPINS—gave specific guidance to task elements at a tactical level.

Wedgetail crews would conduct an overview of the entire Iraqi and Syrian battlespace because their operations might encompass this entire expanse. They would receive an intelligence update on where Iraqi Security Forces ground elements were operating and details on ISIL disposition. The crew would be tasked with gathering specific data; they would receive update briefings on their platform and their systems; and they would be provided with an appreciation of what Coalition strike and refuelling platforms could be expected in the area of operations. There was a lot of paperwork involved—much of it in cyberspace—and a lot for the crew to digest.

Because tanker transit times into operations were longer, the KC-30A would get airborne earlier than the strike platforms, often in the early hours of the morning. The E-7A would depart at any time of the day or night depending on its tasking window. For both these large multi-crewed platforms, the crews would arrive for duty two and a half hours before take-off. The routine involved the captain reviewing the weather, any notices on airfield status along the Gulf, updates to airspace restrictions, and platform serviceability documentation. As the captain checked this, the co-pilot would look at the changes to the air tasking order that may have come out in the twelve hours since its issue. Amendments would be noted, and an in-flight pack would be prepared as a reference document for the sortie. The Wedgetail preparation also involved the air battle management mission commander who would have responsibility for command and control activities in the battlespace.

The strike crews followed a slightly different routine. Because the pre-flight administrative duties were so comprehensive, strike aviators had their equivalent packs prepared by off-duty aircrew. This freed the strike crew to prepare for weapons loading and other specific systems checks on their platforms. Ground and maintenance crews worked separately to fuel, load and prepare the individual aircraft for the coming sortie.

Closer to take-off time the various crews met independently to conduct a briefing. During the briefing the crew would discuss the domestic arrangements of departure and transit and receive an intelligence overview of potential threats and operations in the region over which they would operate. Mission specifics would be reiterated as well as what actions would be taken should the platform be forced to divert or come down. The crew would then depart for the flight line.

The multi-crewed platforms all had safety equipment vests containing multiple pockets with rations, water, maps and other useful items in case they were forced down. Strike aircrew had the added task of donning a G-suit and additional safety equipment. Every aircrew member carried a sidearm. The captain of the aircraft signed for the platform and conducted a walkaround of the aircraft while the other crew initiated the systems required for the mission.

Once the crews of the E-7A and KC-30A arrived at their aircraft, it took about forty-five minutes before they would be ready to taxi out and take-off. The strike aircraft took about twice as long depending on its mission profile. Strike platforms would undertake air-to-air refuelling once or twice prior to arriving in the area of operations, and again upon their arrival. After crossing the Iraqi coast, the element would be assigned to a command and control agency—either ground-based or airborne—and strike crews could find themselves receiving instructions from any number of nationalities that might include American, British, Danish or Australian accents. The airborne controlling agencies were predominantly American but often the Australian E-7A would operate with the Australian strike element. Strike crews on station would then hold and wait to be directed by their command and control authority to contact a Combat Controller or Joint Tactical Air Controller on the ground.

Australian Classic Hornets cross the coastline after tanking enroute to Iraq. The contrast between the deep blue waters of the Arabian Gulf and the aridity of the landscape is very evident in this image. (source: Department of Defence)

After executing the mission, the strike platform would return to its airborne hold position where it would await further direction. Invariably, an unmanned aerial vehicle or remotely piloted vehicle would capture initial imagery of what was occurring in the fight below and this would be relayed to the Combined Air Operations Centre. Sensors on the individual platforms would also record what had occurred, and this data would be downloaded when the aircraft returned to base. If a strike aircraft required refuelling, it would be directed by its command and control agency on to an air-to-air refuelling aircraft, enabling it to return to the fight if called upon.

After several such iterations, the two or four-ship strike elements would return southeast along the Persian Gulf to recover back to Al Dhafra. An average strike mission took approximately eight hours, with about an hour in the seat before take-off and about fifteen minutes upon landing. The flights were longer for the larger E-7A and KC-30A aircraft, being airborne between ten and thirteen hours. Every moment of this time required intense focus, and it was not uncommon for the technicians to assist strike aircrew from the cockpit on return.

The individual aircraft would be signed back in by the captain, and the crew safety equipment returned for storage. After a quick debrief the airmen would disperse before meeting again the next day to collate any reporting and mission data from the flight.

Retaking Iraq

October 2016 marked the end of the second year of Australia's contribution to Operation INHERENT RESOLVE. Iraqi Security Forces and Coalition air power had managed to halt the expansion of ISIL in Iraq. However, ISIL still held huge swathes of territory along the Euphrates River Valley up into eastern Syria where it maintained its capital in Raqqa, and it continued to occupy the northern Iraqi city of Mosul. One thing was certain. ISIL's powerful fielded force, though diminished, maintained a capacity to fight and the Coalition understood that retaking territory from ISIL was going to be a bitter and prolonged affair. But for now, it was important that they had been stopped.

On 17 October 2016, the Associated Press announced:

> *Lt. Gen. Stephen Townsend, commander of Combined Joint Task Force Operation INHERENT RESOLVE, says the US-led coalition is providing wide support for the Iraqi and Kurdish forces in the battle for Mosul. 'The thousands of ground combat forces who will liberate Mosul are all Iraqis, ' he stated. Townsend's statement came shortly after Iraqi Prime Minister Haider al-Abadi announced the start of operations on Monday to liberate the*

northern city of Mosul from Islamic State militants.

Even as Townsend relayed this message the Iraqis had commenced to liberate Mosul, and this signalled a definitive point in the war against ISIL. The fight was not over, but Phase II of the Combined Joint Task Force—Operation INHERENT RESOLVE would now turn to the offensive. In the preceding weeks the staff of the Combined Joint Task Force Land Component Command had collaborated closely with their counterparts in the Iraqi Security Forces and the Iraqi Government, and the Combined Air Operations Centre developed plans to provide Coalition air support coming operations.

Air Commodore Phil Gordon had been in-theatre for two months as this got underway. He had assumed command of the Air Task Group from Air Commodore Martin in July and was ready for the coming ordeal. Gordon brought an incredible array of skills to his function. He was an Academy graduate who had progressed immediately to flying the F/A-18A Hornet after completion of his flying training courses. Prior to his arrival in-theatre, Gordon had served as the Officer Commanding No 81 Wing in Australia. It was his responsibility in this function to establish the regimen for strike squadron workups and rotation into Operation

OKRA. Over twenty-five years, Gordon had maintained his currency in operating the F/A-18A and he knew exactly the intricacies of the command that he was stepping into. Air Commodores Gordon and Martin were both consummate professionals. They were precise, focussed, and looked to the welfare and high performance of their subordinates. Yet, there were differences, too. Where Martin was affable, Gordon was earnest. His keen intellect and passion for flying underwrote the high standards that he set for himself. Gordon expected these same standards of his personnel, and because he held currency on the Hornet, he would also fly on operational strike missions. Indeed, he would be the first Australian 'air rank' officer to conduct a combat sortie since World War II.

In the weeks leading up to the attack on Mosul, Coalition air power concentrated on key ISIL facilities to prepare the path ahead for Iraqi troops. Estimates of ISIL fighting strength in the city varied from eight to twelve thousand, all well-armed and dug in. For its part, the Iraqi Security Forces fielded over 100 000 troops. More than half of these comprised Iraqi regular and special forces; the remainder were Kurdish Peshmerga and a force of Shia paramilitary supported by the Iraqi Government. The offensive would commence across three axes: the Kurds from the north and northwest, the militia from the east, and the Iraqi Army from the south. When the operation commenced on 17 October 2016, the fighting was immediately barbaric. Throughout November the Iraqi Security Forces drove into regions surrounding Mosul and engaged adversaries who were dug-in and determined to hold their territory. For its part, Coalition air power conducted hundreds of sorties in support of the effort. The going was hard. Observers soon likened the operation to the horrors of urban warfare in the battles on the Eastern Front in World War II, and air power was critical to the Iraqi Security Forces' success. The Air Task Group reported that although the profiles that aircraft flew mitigated the risk that strike aircraft could be engaged from the ground, this didn't eliminate the risk entirely, and RAAF aircraft were fired upon 'reasonably regularly'.

ISIL's acknowledgement that Coalition air support was having the desired effect was soon manifested in the group's changing tactics. Where Daesh was once arrogant in declaring its presence in the territory that it had captured, Coalition air forces now observed that its adversaries would attempt to camouflage and conceal their presence whenever they heard aircraft overhead. Flying Officer Sean Gardner was a Wedgetail air battle manager, operating a world away from country New South Wales where he had grown up. Gardner had flown in the preparatory phases for the battle that was now occurring. He respected the ingenuity of the Daesh combatants he 'observed' on operations, and the lengths to which they went to conceal themselves from Coalition aircraft. He was equally laconic in his resolve to see them thoroughly defeated.

The differences between Gardner and his fellow crew member, Flying Officer Melody Sadler-Barker, were striking. Sadler-Barker was slight and spoke with a cultured English accent. She had served in the Royal Air Force for some years before she and her husband made the decision to emigrate to Australia where she commissioned into the RAAF. Sadler-Barker had worked extraordinarily hard in training when she arrived in Australia. She was justifiably proud of her achievements and missed her young family very much while she was serving overseas. Where Sadler-Barker was quiet and assiduous Gardner was a larrikin. However, they had trained and worked together, and both had a mutual respect for the other's achievements as military aviators.

The Tigris River is the eastern-most of the two great tributaries that define Mesopotamia. It flows south from the mountains of southern Turkey through Iraq, travelling all the way to Baghdad; from there it meets with the Euphrates River to continue onto Basra on the Persian Gulf. On its path south from Turkey, the Tigris bisects Mosul. By December 2016, the Iraqi Security Forces had recaptured the eastern suburbs of Mosul and were two kilometres from the river. The fighting was particularly brutal around the metropolitan Salam Hospital east of the Tigris, and the facility was captured and lost by both sides several times during the fighting that took place in the middle of the month.

A Strike Aviator's View: The Fight over Mosul

I typically had three hours on station [over or near Mosul] and at the end of each hour the formation refuelled with the tanker before returning to its station. Refuelling was a delicate manoeuvre, and because we were concentrating so much, I was constantly sweating. In this one sortie, I refuelled from an Australian tanker, an Italian tanker, a German tanker and a Canadian tanker. It was a truly real coalition effort. While I was on station, our element spoke to Belgian and American air battle managers, and I was in the Close Air Support stack with French Mirage fighters. I could see Reaper drones circling below me and there were American F-15 Eagles scheduled to replace me. While I circled over the fight, I could see all types of unmanned systems and manned fighters at all levels. Air battle managers and joint terminal controllers called in with an attack brief. In the interaction, we would talk to them about what we could see to help identify targets. As the fight progressed, the troops in contact in the fight would request support, and we would be briefed by a nine-liner [tasking order] to conduct an attack. Then it' on! I dial all of the coordinates into the systems on the aircraft there are literally dozens of numbers. I double check, triple check and make sure all the systems are functioning. Is the GPS [global positioning system] locked on? Do the guided munitions have the right coordinates? Are all systems within the right parameters? Does the target meet the criteria for rules of engagement? Then, I conduct the attack, release the bombs. I film the footage of the bomb impact and the bomb damage assessment. And then I go and do it again.

A Royal Australian Air Force F/A-18F Super Hornet flies over Mosul, Iraq, during an Operation OKRA mission. (source: Department of Defence)

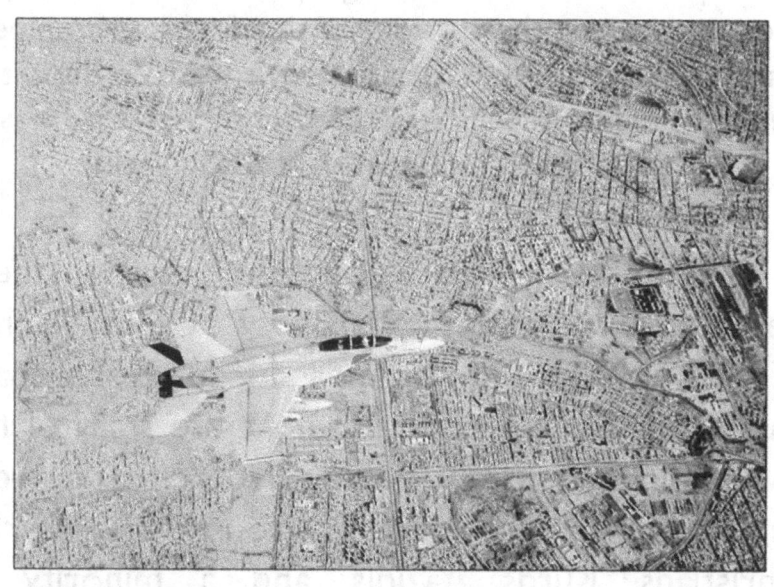

A splendid pair of images depicting an F/A-18F over a city landscape in northern Iraq during Operation OKRA. Despite the urban setting, the austerity of the desert environment is striking, and many Australian crews were consistently reminded of just how foreign this part of the world was to them. (source: Department of Defence)

What was very apparent during these operations was that the barbarity of ISIL's defence of the city had no bounds. Mosul traditionally had had a diverse population. At the start of the twenty-first century, most of its citizens were Arab Sunnis, with smaller groups of Assyrian Christians, Kurds, Yazidis, and a minority of Turkmen. During November, ISIL targeted them as the threat of the advancing Iraqi Security Forces grew larger. There was a mass crucifixion of nearly forty locals suspected of treason towards ISIL. Over the following month, yet more were shot, hanged or electrocuted because they were trying to flee from the fighting. Some were charged with collaborating with the Iraqi Security Forces, and yet others were killed simply because they had working mobile telephones. United Nations reports from the time indicated that ISIL used thousands of men, women and children as human shields in Mosul to deter Iraqi troops from advancing. The group carried out more atrocities further west in Syria during December when they executed workers around the ancient archaeological site of Palmyra.

Because of the nature of the urban fighting, the proximity of civilians, and the winter weather, the Air Task Group was even more judicious in its use of weapons in and around Mosul. There was a marked drop on the number of weapons deployed over late 2016 and early 2017, though the cumulative figures for ATG630's efforts for 2016 were impressive. The E-7A had flown 125 sorties, totalling over 1500 hours flying time. This equated to one aircraft flying every three days for an average of twelve hours per sortie. The KC-30A flew 385 missions accumulating more than 3800 hours and offloading nearly twenty-seven million pounds of fuel. The strike element had conducted over 900 sorties in Iraq and Syria, accumulating 7078 hours and releasing

798 weapons. Early in 2017, US Army Lieutenant General Stephen Townsend indicated that Coalition air support had reduced the estimated number of ISIL fighters by about half from their peak of 30 000 in 2015. It was evident that air power was a crucial ingredient in the war. In late January, the Iraqi Government claimed that it had liberated all territory on the eastern side of the Tigris River in Mosul, and Iraqi forces would resume their offensive there in the middle of February. Even so, ISIL remained in complete control of the remainder of the city though the group was effectively surrounded. So were thousands of non-combatants. During the subsequent battle for West Mosul, the extremes of ISIL's depravity would sink to further depths.

The human rights watch group Amnesty International highlighted in their report on the battle for West Mosul that ISIL had herded thousands of non-combatants directly into combat zones. ISIL deliberately used these people as human shields to stymie targeting by the Coalition and pro-Iraqi Government forces. Daesh trapped non-combatant residents into their homes by welding the doors shut and rigging booby traps at exits. People were summarily executed as they attempted to escape. The same reports also indicated that non-combatants were routinely denied medical care and food. If this were not bad enough, the report also found that pro-government forces were careless in their application of force, often targeting ISIL positions knowing that they were surrounded by large numbers of non-combatants; or using disproportionate force to destroy infrastructure housing ISIL fighters. Sadly, Amnesty International also claimed that Coalition air strikes were complicit in the destruction of property and the deaths of non-combatants in and around West Mosul.

It is a matter of fact that the Australian Air Task Group was involved in operations in West Mosul up until the time the city was liberated in June 2017. What is also known and verifiable is that the Australian rules of engagement; the RAAF's prescriptive targeting processes; and the accepted principles of proportionality and discrimination, all ensured that no Australian contributed to the terrible events taking place. In support of these claims, the Australian Department of Defence's published records show a proportionately low number of deployed munitions over the period from November 2016 to March 2017 when RAAF platforms were involved in the liberation of Mosul. The number of deployed munitions only spiked once more between March and June 2017 as operations in Northern Iraq moved further west and away from the more densely populated parts of the city.

When No 1 Squadron rotated back to the Middle-East in 2017 it had just celebrated a century of service. In this image the No 1 Squadron badge is depicted on the tail of an F/A-18F and provides a curious modern-day juxtaposition with the era in which Sir Richard Williams led the unit. No one envisaged that when the squadron selected the Cross of Jerusalem for its badge-based on its service in Palestine—that it would return to the same part of the world 100 years later to conduct the same type of mission. (source: Department of Defence)

By the time the battle for West Mosul was commencing, Air Commodore Mike Kitcher had rotated in behind Air Commodore Gordon. When he assumed command, Kitcher had thirty-three years of service in the RAAF. He had deployed on overseas operations several times in the past and was well-placed to take on the responsibilities associated with this command. During Kitcher's tour, No 81 Wing's F/A-18As would rotate back to Australia to be replaced once more by No 82 Wing's F/A-18Fs.

By now, several of the Wedgetail and KC-30A aircrew and technicians were on their second or even third rotations. These personnel were tired, though still fully capable. As for the strike element, while the return of the Super Hornets would provide some relief for the *Classic Hornet* fleet, it also marked a point when the Air Task Group's operations would spike. From March 2017 to the end of June, ATG630 platforms flew primarily in support of Iraqi Security Forces' operations to clear West Mosul of remaining pockets of ISIL. These sorties—comprising 286 strike; 40 intelligence, surveillance and reconnaissance; and 114 air-to-air refuelling flights—resulted in the delivery of 387 air-deployed weapons. TE630.1.1 variously targeted ISIL fighting positions, weapons caches, heavy weapons, vehicles and lines of communication.

The Iraqi Security Forces enjoyed overwhelming superiority in firepower and air power so the result for ISIL was inevitable. By the end of June 2017, after eight months bitter urban warfare, ISIL was all but defeated in Mosul.

The battle was notable for the savagery of the fighting; the destruction wrought on the urban and city landscape; and for the barbaric and unethical behaviour of ISIL—and unfortunately similar behaviours by some pro-government forces. On 9 July 2017, Iraqi Prime Minister al Abadi visited the shattered city and declared it liberated. Within a month, the total number of Coalition air strike operations over the preceding three years to August 2014 was approaching 25 000. At the same point, the Combined Joint Task Force—Operation INHERENT RESOLVE declared that Phase II of the Operation was over, and Phase III would commence.

Defeating ISIL

With the recapture of Mosul, Operation INHERENT RESOLVE now moved to defeating ISIL. For the CAOC, this required planning to provide air support to forces in Iraq and Syria to clear the remaining pockets of resistance from both countries. The Combined Joint Task Force—Operation INHERENT RESOLVE would continue to assist in training, equipping, advising, and assisting the Iraqi Security Forces while Russian support to Syrian forces moved to liberate Raqqa and the Deir al-Zor airfield in the east of the nation. In this complicated three-sided war, although Coalition and Russian air power remained unaligned, both groups were ostensibly fighting the same adversary. This required close coordination among aviators on all sides to keep air assets safely deconflicted. Potential clashes among aircraft conducting close air support for ground forces in this complicated environment was a nightmare scenario that all participants sought to avoid. The tension reached boiling point on 18 June 2017—a US Navy F/A-18 engaged a Syrian Sukhoi Su-22 strike aircraft which was attacking anti-government Syrian Democratic Forces. Fighting broke out on the ground below between the two sides—both were also fighting Daesh—and lasted until the Syrian Democratic Forces withdrew the following day. On 20 June 2017, a USAF F-15 fighter shot down an Iranian remotely piloted aircraft supporting Syrian Government troops in the same area. Each side involved was quick to condemn the other. Thankfully, some semblance of sense prevailed, and higher-level diplomatic action prevented any potential escalation in Eastern Syria.

Air planners and crews were acutely aware of the need to use aircraft systems effectively so that Russian, Syrian and Coalition aircraft did not engage each other in the intricate battlespace. As Mosul was declared liberated, a new Commander Air Task Group, Air Commodore

Terry Van Haren, rotated into theatre behind Air Commodore Kitcher. Van Haren was a fast jet aviator who had flown on operations during the 2003 Gulf War and he was acutely aware of the complexity of the fight underway in Iraq and Syria. While Daesh was reeling, the potential for fratricide in the busy battlespace was one matter that he needed to immediately address. With tens of dozens of strike aircraft operating over central and eastern Syria at once, Van Haren was pleased to note that the utility of the E-7A was central to averting any escalation among the competing factions. When he was interviewed later in his six-month tour, Van Haren went on to state of the Wedgetail capability:

> *We were using all the systems aboard the E-7A, every crew station was fully manned, and they were all very busy using those systems to work out the [air]picture—who was in that picture and where they came from ... and then controlling [Coalition] fighters and tankers and other aircraft in what was a congested very close proximity to other forces. It was something one could never replicate in training ... and we got a lot of value out of it!*

Making sense of the convoluted battlespace was a significant responsibility for TE630.1.2, with the task of commanding the detachment during the final months of Phase III falling to Squadron Leader Lee-Anne Stanway. Stanway had spent many years in her early career as an Air Surveillance Operator before commissioning as an Air Battle Manager in the early 2000s. When she did so, she was amongst the first RAAF personnel to convert onto the E-7A when it entered service. Stanway was certainly one of the first female aircrew to undertake this training and was newly promoted to Squadron Leader on her first rotation to Al Minhad in 2015. When she arrived in-theatre in August 2017 as commander of the Wedgetail detachment, it was her third rotation, and it was the twelfth rotation of crews for the aircraft. Stanway had served under three of the Australian commanders and would go on to accrue one year of active service across the entire three years of the operation. She recognised the differences among her commanders—Braz, Bellingham and Van Haren—but was impressed with each of them.

Stanway later recalled that several times during her 2015 tour, the Director General Air, Air Commodore Joe Iervasi, had telephoned her from Australia to chat about how the fight against ISIL was progressing. She was unabashed in her gratitude for Iervasi's belief in her abilities, recalling that she tried to set the same example for her three-dozen aircrew, maintenance and support staff. Certainly, Squadron Leader Stanway's technicians respected the way she let them get on with their servicing duties when they were under time constraints to ready the platform for a sortie. Equally, her Mission Commander was impressed with her cool demeanour—and particularly with her way of letting the crew get on with their duties when directing the battle.

The Mission Commander was one of the most experienced Wedgetail aircrew in the RAAF. He did not want to be named in this volume, but he had an intense and driven focus, and was incredibly skilled in his role. This officer had served with Stanway 'on and off' for years, and his seal of approval was 'money in the bank' for the entire RAAF air battle management fraternity. He worked long hours preparing and honing the Wedgetail crew in deconflicting the aircraft operating in the complex and often chaotic fight that was taking place in Eastern Syria. Such was their proficiency in this work, that when Stanway, and her crew and the platform came to be selected for an operational pause, senior officers within the Coalition petitioned the RAAF to keep the capability in-theatre. Van Haren was certainly aware of the skills within this element of his command, and he let the Wedgetail Detachment get on with its job.

The RAAF E-7A Wedgetail has arrived back in the Middle East to support Operation OKRA. The aircraft and crew provide tactical command and control of the airspace above Iraq and Syria. (source: Department of Defence)

When the height of summer arrived for a third time on Operation OKRA in 2017, ISIL had started to unravel. From May 2017, peaking in late August and September, TE630.1.1 Super Hornets of No 1 Squadron, under the command of Wing Commander Jason Gamlin, were tasked to conduct strike operations supporting the Iraqi Security Forces against Daesh positions near Tal Afar west of Mosul and around the Hawijah pocket near Kirkuk. This was during the height of Mosul's liberation and the fight in the old town. Gamlin was a highly competent strike pilot.

He had re-rolled to Super Hornets from the *Classic* Hornet fleet soon after the RAAF had acquired the newer platform, and he now served as the commanding officer of both TE630.1.1 in-theatre and No 1 Squadron back in Australia. Because of this, Gamlin found that this meant he had to make two short rotations out of theatre to attend to the responsibilities of duties at home.

Around this time, Paul Brady returned to theatre, now promoted to Squadron Leader and placed in command of the KC-30A detachment. Like Stanway, Brady's service had commenced in the 1980s. He had initially flown the RAAF's F-111 strike aircraft which were replaced by the F/A-18F but had left the RAAF in the 1990s to fly international airliners for Cathay Pacific. In his work with Cathay, and later Virgin airlines, Brady accrued thousands of hours experience. Even so, Brady was drawn back to the RAAF in 2014 after nearly two decades away, and his airline experience proved to be an ideal fit for the new KC-30A capability. His flight time, approachability and easy-going demeanour with all ranks made him an ideal commander for his role. When he had first returned to the RAAF, Brady's skills resulted in him being employed as Specialist aircrew, a role reserved for experienced aviators who set and check the flying standards for the other aircrew in the squadron. When he returned to the MER this time, Brady observed cosmetic changes to the Al Dhafra airbase facilities, but he was more taken with the way in which ISIL was being defeated across Iraq and Syria.

In one day of operations on 29 August, Hornets of TE630.1.1 supported Iraqi forces during operations near the village of Avghani in the Ninevah Province of northern Iraq. The Australian aircraft struck thirteen Daesh fighting positions with guided munitions, paving the way for Iraqi Security Forces success. The clearance of Tel Afar and Ninevah valleys in northern Iraq was largely completed by the end of August 2017.

From this time onwards, Coalition air power concurrently targeted ISIL's lines of communication, weapons caches, commanders, vehicles, fighting positions and infrastructure in the last two pockets of ISIL resistance in the country. The first was along the Euphrates River Valley; this region was the western arm of the fertile Mesopotamian crescent, and wound northwest from its confluence with the Tigris River south of Baghdad across the Anbar Province and into eastern Syria. The second pocket was in an isolated enclave north of Tikrit in central Iraq.

During a two-week period during the middle of September 2017, TE630.1.1 provided support to the Iraqi Security Forces as they fought north from Tikrit to clear and secure the townships of Baiji, Sharqat, Sagrah and Rayhanah from Daesh forces. The final clearance of the Hawijah pocket in central Iraq was declared on 5 October 2017. Further west, in five days of heavy fighting that commenced on 16 September, Australian strike aircraft supported the Iraqi Security Forces as they battled to liberate the township of Anah, northwest of Haditha, along the Euphrates River Valley. Daesh fled from the town on 21 September. These operations, particularly the liberation of Anah, were significant victories in the fight against ISIL.

At a point just north of the Anah township, the Euphrates River turned west where it flowed for 100 kilometres more through the Village of Rawa to the border city of Al Qaim before entering Syria. Over August and September, Gamlin's crews had flown 112 sorties in support of the Iraqi Security Forces and released 147 weapons against ISIL. Even a few years later, Gamlin was able to clearly recall the intensity of the fighting that had stemmed back to late May, particularly in the urban areas of Iraq's northern provinces. In some places where his aircraft were supporting ground troops, the Daesh fighters were less than sixteen metres away. The accurate delivery of ordinance under these circumstances required extraordinary skill on the part of the crews involved. Further, the effort involved in clearing ISIL from northern and western Iraq simultaneously during this extended period represented a tempo that many of his personnel had not experienced before. Gamlin was very proud of the work of TE630.1.1, and of the efforts of the wider Air Task Group. 'In many respects we were conducting operations in a way air power had never before been applied', he reflected. And in this, Gamlin was quite correct: the technology employed, the distances involved, and the precision required all reflected the work of a first-rate organisation.

F/A-18F aircrew acknowledge the cameras as they taxi out for operations at the Al Dhafra airbase. (source: Department of Defence)

As the operations in Western Iraq unfolded, Van Haren and his subordinate commanders had been forewarned that Air Task Group operations would likely undertake an operational pause late in the year. Key staff within the Australian National Security Committee in Canberra including the National Security Adviser, Greg Moriarty, and Defence Minister, Senator Marise Payne, were already conferring with the Chief of the Defence Force, Air Chief Marshal Binskin, and Commander Joint Operations, Vice Admiral Johnston. They concurred that it would be appropriate to withdraw RAAF forces from the fight against ISIL when the last pockets of resistance were overcome along the Euphrates River. Australian Prime Minister Malcolm Turnbull agreed to this logical proposal with the proviso that the Operation OKRA 'Build Partner Capacity' trainers would remain *in situ* in Iraq to assist with the follow-on stabilisation operations.

On 17 October 2017, the Syrian Army recaptured Raqqa and pushed east to effectively block the remnants of ISIL in an enclave around Al Qaim on the border. Meanwhile, Australian and Coalition air power turned its full attention to clearing ISIL from the Euphrates River Valley, west from Anah. The town of Rawa lay on the other side of the Euphrates River from Anah, and ISIL had destroyed the bridges crossing the river in order to slow the Iraqi Security Forces down. The response was straightforward. On 26 October 2017, the Iraqi Army launched an operation directly towards the city of Al Qaim, and effectively cut Rawa off. Al Qaim was declared liberated on 4 November 2017, and the Iraqi forces turned east once more to liberate Rawa which fell eleven days later. The rapidity and success of these operations was an indication of just how far ISIL had capitulated. The group was finished in Iraq, though there remained some stubborn pockets of resistance throughout the Western Desert until Prime Minister al-Abadi declared final victory over ISIL on 9 December 2017.

The austere and arid environment of the UAE airbase from which Australian aircraft operated is very clearly depicted in this image of aircraft readying for departure on an operational sortie. (source: Department of Defence)

The Air Task Group's statistics for sorties flown in the period from July to November 2017 in support of the liberation of Iraq were impressive. The KC-30A had flown 108 sorties throughout the period and offloaded more than ten million pounds of fuel for Coalition air assets. The E-7A had flown forty-six sorties, amassing more than 600 hours. The strike element had deployed more than 280 air launched weapons.

As ISIL was defeated in the weeks leading up to November 2017, Squadron Leader Stanway recalled that there was some confusion as whether it would be the KC-30A or the Wedgetail returning home on an operational pause. Having defeated ISIL, the plan was to set the two platforms up on a rotational basis so that one was in-theatre for six months while the other was back in Australia. 'It was really confusing for everyone over there,' Stanway said afterwards. 'Both platforms were in high demand, and no one, not even DGAIR, could tell us what was going on as we were awaiting a decision from the government.' When Stanway was briefed that a replacement crew for the E-7A was arriving in mid-November, she thought matters had been settled.

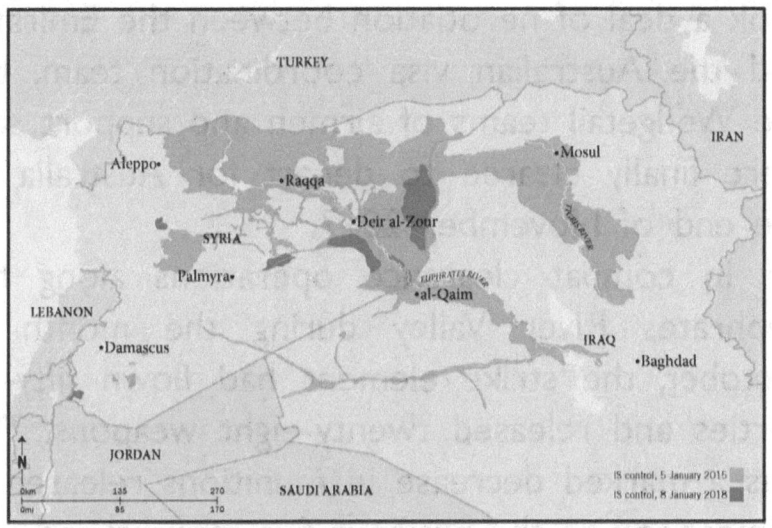

A map depicting ISIL's territorial losses during the period from 2015 to the end of 2017. The fighting to take back this territory was almost entirely the province of Iraq's newly reconstituted security forces but was wholly supported by Coalition air power.

Air Commodore Van Haren saw her at Al Minhad around the same time because he was rotating out early as the strike operations wound down. Both believed that the Wedgetail was staying, and the new crew duly arrived on the weekly replenishment flight into theatre. Van Haren was scheduled to leave on the same aircraft when it flew back to Australia. A day after the aircraft left, Stanway was informed that the new Commander Air Task Group, Air Commodore Rob Denney, had just been informed that the E-7A would be returning to Australia, and the KC-30A would be remaining behind. It took a deal of negotiation between the Emirates and the Australian visa coordination team, but the Wedgetail teams of airmen and support staff were finally cleared to depart for Australia by the end of November 2017.

In combat clearance operations along the Euphrates River Valley during the month of October, the strike element had flown fifty-six sorties and released twenty-eight weapons. This was a marked decrease in munitions released in comparison to the previous five months; and was an indication that ISIL was finished. In November and December, the strike element's sortie rate was similar—forty-eight and forty-six missions respectively. However, the weapons launch statistics showed that the job was all but complete—six weapons in November, and seven in December 2017.

The KC-30A continued to fly in December—twenty-six sorties in total, amassing over 200 hours and offloading two million pounds of fuel. For this platform, it was business as usual. Beside the KC-30A in Al Dhafra, the commander of CTU630.1, Group Captain Ross Bender, commenced rapidly downsizing in the lead up to Christmas.

On 22 December 2017, Defence Minister, Senator Marise Payne, formally announced the decision to cease TE630.1.1 strike aircraft operations in the Middle East. Two sorties were flown by Gamlin's crews in early January, but no ordnance was released. His element commenced drawing down, with the last strike element personnel arriving back at RAAF Amberley during the third week in January 2018. Air Commodore Denney had carefully overseen the drawdown of the Air Task Group, and when the strike and support elements departed, he was in a position to hand over the smaller command to Group Captain Bender, who assumed responsibility as CATG.

Bender's command in CTU630.1 had shrunk almost overnight from more than 200 personnel to a quarter of the number, and for the time being only the KC-30A remained in-theatre. Bender would rotate back to Australia after a few months to be replaced by Pete Mitchell, who had now been promoted to Group Captain.

The crews, the technicians, the support personnel—all of whom made up ATG630—numbered nearly 1800 over the three years of operations. They came and went, performing their duties professionally and responsibly. Nothing they did can be altered now.

Aftermath

In just over a year the RAAF—the second oldest air force in the world—will turn one hundred. This seems an appropriate point to pause and reflect.

A single century has elapsed since air power wrought destruction in the Wadi Fara. In this time, the air domain has become integral to the conduct of warfare; and often central to the wider campaign. Air power has altered the tactical and operational battlespace—particularly during the last twenty-five years. Air power has also achieved strategic outcomes, often controversially, but always decisively. Technology has been a central factor in the advances and developments that air power has enjoyed over these years.

Only a century ago, the most advanced combat aircraft were made of wood and doped linen. They were armed with machine guns and had a top speed of about 100 knots. The current combat strike platforms are made of carbon fibre and have weapons systems that operate beyond visual range. They can fly at 1.3 times the speed of sound and can transmit and receive enormous amounts of data via satellite communications. The pace of development has been phenomenal. Modern air power has an unprecedented level of situational awareness and the ability to apply force rapidly, accurately, and precisely. Notwithstanding this, the air power roles conducted by these platforms are highly specialised and little understood—and perhaps as equally little appreciated—outside the technical 'stovepipes' of those who operate or maintain these aircraft.

Air power has been inherently 'joint' since its inception. This concept has been reinforced time and time again. Air power possesses a unique capacity to achieve a strategic end state with maximum efficiency and minimum cost. Imperial and Coalition air power was the decisive factor in defeating an adversary in the Wadi Fara a century ago. It was equally important in the fight against ISIL. One hundred years ago, if the Turkish Army had escaped, the Ottoman Empire may have prevailed for a significantly longer period. We dare not consider what would be happening in Iraq today if Coalition air platforms had not halted ISIL. These are the 'facts' on which professional aviators and airmen will most reflect.

While the Iraqi Prime Minister may have declared victory over Daesh in December 2017, this did not represent the end of the battle. Indeed, al Abadi was only correct in terms of numbers. In December 2014, ISIL held sway across much of Iraq and Eastern Syria. It dominated eight million people. By December 2017, it held no territory and subjugated no one. At one point during ISIL's rampage in late 2014 and early 2015, the group may have had as many as 50 000 armed fighters. In December 2017 any fighters that were left in Iraq were imprisoned or dead. There is no claim here that air power did this—however, air power facilitated the Iraqi claims to victory. Even so, such matters are statistics.

Victory over ISIL cannot be measured in this way. Only the Iraqi people—and soon the Syrians—can move positively into the void left in the aftermath of these tragic years. The restoration of the ruins around Mosul, the rejuvenation following the destruction along the Euphrates Valley and the shattered landscape—all these now provide an almost overwhelming task ahead for Iraq's feeble government. The West wrought destruction in 2003 and went on to spectacularly fail in the years of occupation that followed. Now the questions of what to do are almost unanswerable. How does Iraq tackle the problems of reconstruction, governance, and counterinsurgency across the sectarian divide? What comes first? How can a Shi'ite-dominated government in Iraq restore state control in the Sunni regions? In October 2018, a new Iraqi

Prime Minister, Adil Abdul-Mahdi, son of a Shi'ite cleric, was given responsibility for the task. Abdul-Mahdi faces daunting tasks. The questions are his to answer. He must overcome the sectarianism and restore Iraq's fortunes.

There *should* be questions about all of this and why Australia committed forces the way it did. The threshold for committing the lethal firepower at the disposal of the Air Task Group should be extraordinarily high before a decision is made to employ it. However, once the decision is made, the firepower should always be—and was in this case—proportionally directed at an adversary until he is defeated.

A group portrait of the RAAF ATG taken in 2017 provides an excellent comparison of the size and types of aircraft deployed, and the number of personnel assigned to any given rotation. The image provides a splendid juxtaposition to the 1918 AFC portrait depicted earlier in the in the text showing Australian personnel at the end of World War I. Of these personnel, the Chief of the Defence Force, Air Chief Marshal Binskin, would state:

> Over more than three years, hundreds of ADF personnel have deployed to the Middle East as part of the ATG strike element. With each deployment, they have demonstrated the highest levels of skill, courage and professionalism. Our aircrew and their support crews have consistently delivered in extremely difficult and challenging conditions These personnel and their families can be proud of their achievements and their important contribution to help the Iraqi Security Forces liberate their country from Daesh. (source: Department of Defence)

The question of why Australia committed is therefore easy to answer. Firstly, it was Australia's role as a global citizen to intervene. And secondly, the deployment supported Australia's strategic interests in a rules-based global order. Both are equally relevant. The barbarism of Daesh could only be halted in the forceful manner that it was, and Australia made the decision to do so in concert with like-minded nations.

Future historians will pore over the quandary of this conflict in far-greater detail. In doing so, air power proponents will write innumerable lists of lessons learned, while detractors will continue to oppose the discipline's independence and utility. One argument in this debate will be irrelevant. Nothing will change the fact that air power—the youngest of the domains—is here to stay. And in this most recent conflict, it is clear that air power enabled the Iraqi people to defeat the unconscionable threat of Daesh. Just what will occur in northern Iraq and Syria now that the scourge of ISIL has been driven away is yet to be seen.

Leading Aircraftman Sam Thomas gives the 'all clear' to the E-7A Wedgetail prior to a mission from the main logistics base in the Middle East. (source: Department of Defence)

Appendix I

TIMELINE OF EVENTS

April 2013: Abu Bakr Al Baghdadi, head of the Al Qaida-linked Islamic State of Iraq, announces in an online recording the creation of a group called the Islamic State of Iraq and the Levant (also referred to to as Daesh).

January 2014: ISIL conquers Syria's northern city of Raqqa after fierce fighting with rival militants. It is the first provincial capital to fall from regime control and becomes the militants' main stronghold.

June 2014: ISIL declares a 'caliphate' in territories it has seized in Iraq and Syria and declares its chief Al Baghdadi 'caliph' and 'leader of Muslims everywhere'. ISIL rampage across north-western Iraq, seizing second city Mosul and a belt of territory bordering the autonomous Kurdistan region. Tens of thousands of Christians and Yazidis, a religious minority, flee.

August 2014: ISIL conquers Kurdish towns of Sinjar and Zumar, forcing thousands of Yazidi civilians to flee their homes. ISIL takes control of the Mosul Dam. President Obama announces air strikes against ISIL in Iraq to defend Yazidi citizens stranded in Sinjar. ISIL kills American journalist James Foley. ISIL militants seize Taqba airbase in Raqqa. Al Maliki steps down and Haider al Abadi takes over.

15 August 2014: UN Security Council Adopts Resolution 2170 (2014) Condemning Gross, Widespread Abuse of Human Rights by Extremist Groups in Iraq, Syria

September 2014: ISIL releases a video depicting beheading of journalist Steven Sotloff. ISIL posts video of the execution of British aid worker David Haines. ISIL advances on the Syrian border town of Kobani and thousands of refugees flee into Turkey. ISIL spokesman Abu Muhammad al Adnani calls for attacks on citizens of the United States, France and other countries involved in the coalition to destroy the group. First air strikes against ISIL in Syria.

15 September 2014: Australia joins US-led Coalition to assist Iraq in its fight against ISIL, now euphemistically known as Daesh.

21-22 September 2014: RAAF Air Task Group 630 (ATG630), comprised of six F/A-18F, one E-7A and one KC-30A, deploys from Australia and arrives at Al Minhad airbase in United Arab Emirates.

23-28 September 2014: Coalition air power commence air strikes on Kobani. ATG630 commences familiarisation flights out of Al Minhad.

October 2014: ISIL releases a video showing the beheading of British aid worker Alan Henning. Coalition increases air strikes in and around Kobani to counter ISIL advances. The Pentagon names the campaign against ISIL 'Operation Inherent Resolve.'

7-8 October 2014: First Australian sortie. First Australian air strike.

15 November 2014: ATG630 relocates from Al Min had to Al Dhafra airbase United Arab Emirates.

30 December 2014: ISIL takes responsibility for a suicide attack during a funeral north of Baghdad that killed sixteen people and wounded thirty-four others.

January 2015: ISIL is driven from the Syrian border town of Kobani after more than four months of fighting led by Kurdish forces backed by coalition air strikes.

February 2015: ISIL releases a video of Jordanian military pilot Moaz al Kasasbeh being burned alive. ISIL abducts at least 200 Assyrian Christians in north-eastern Syria. Coalition launches airstrikes in the same area.

March 2015: Iraq announces the liberation of Tikrit, north of Baghdad. ISIL had controlled Tikrit for nearly ten months.

May 2015: ISIL captures Ramadi, Iraq. ISIL captures ancient Syrian city of Palmyra. The group plunders or destroys priceless antiquities. The on-site archaeologist is executed.

June 2015: Kurdish fighters expel ISIL from the strategic Syrian town of Tal Abyad on the Turkish border. ISIL fighters kill at least 145 civilians in an attack on Kobani, Syria.

September 2015: Russia begins airstrikes in Syria. It claims to target ISIL, but Coalition officials allege that many of the strikes target civilians and Western-backed rebel groups.

October 2015: ISIL makes significant gains in north-western Syria, seizing six villages near Aleppo. Iraqi forces recapture the Baiji refinery, the largest oil refinery in the country, from ISIL.

November 2015: Kurdish forces recapture Sinjar, Iraq, from ISIL. ISIL carries out a series of attacks in Paris, killing 130 people. French conduct air strikes in retaliation in Raqqa, Syria.

December 2015: US announces that airstrikes killed ISIL finance minister Abu Saleh and two other senior leaders in Tal Afar, Iraq. Iraqi military forces seize Ramadi from ISIL.

February 2016: Iraqi forces capture Ramadi, overrun by militants the previous May. In June, they retake Fallujah, which spent two and a half years out of their control.

August 2016: The Syrian Democratic Forces coalition of Arab and Kurdish fighters, backed by US air strikes, recaptures the northern town of

Manbij. Turkish troops and Syrian rebels retake the border town of Jarabulus.

October-November 2016: Iraq and US-led coalition forces begin their campaign to liberate Mosul. ISIL fighters launch an attack on the Iraqi city of Kirkuk, killing eighteen security force members and power station workers. Security forces fend off the assault and regain full control of the oil-producing city, according to Iraqi state television. Iraqi forces retake Qaraqosh, a Christian area southeast of Mosul, which had been under ISIL rule since 2014. UN report states ISIL fighters are using tens of thousands of men, women and children as human shields in Mosul to prevent Iraqi troops from advancing. ISIL fighters are reportedly stockpiling dangerous chemicals in Mosul and have executed many more people in the city. The Iraqi Counterterrorism Service captures the Mosul state television station from the Islamic State. This is the first building taken from ISIL since the Mosul campaign began. ISIL leader Abu Bakr al Baghdadi releases his first statement in almost a year, addressing 'soldiers of the Islamic State,' specifically citing Algeria, Tunisia, Libya and other countries where ISIL has established affiliates and provinces.

December 2016: Estimates count some 15 000 ISIL fighters have been killed over two years of operations. Even so, ISIL recaptures Palmyra from Syrian Government forces, despite intensive Russian air strikes. Although the group is no longer expanding, ISIL remains entrenched and an existential threat across the region.

January 2017: Numerous car bombs throughout the month kill over a hundred people in wider Baghdad. The Islamic state claims responsibility for the attacks. ISIL attack two police stations in Samarra, killing at least seven policemen. Iraqi special forces reach the eastern bank of the Tigris river in Mosul for the first time in the campaign to recapture the city. ISIL attacks Syrian Government territory in the city of Deir Ezzor. At least eighty-two people are killed in the fighting. ISIL executes at least twelve people and destroys the Tetrapylon monument and the facade of its Roman theatre in the city of Palmyra.

February 2017: The Turkish army announces it has taken full control of Al Bab, the last ISIL bastion in Aleppo province.

March 2017: Syrian troops backed by Russian jets complete the recapture of the historic city of Palmyra.

July 2017: Iraqi Prime Minister Haider Al Abadi announces the 'liberation' of Mosul, the last urban stronghold of ISIL in Iraq, after a nearly nine-month offensive spearheaded by 100 000 government or pro-government troops backed by Coalition air strikes. The Iraqi Security Forces commence clearing operations along the Euphrates River Valley.

August 2017: Syrian regime forces recapture Al Sukhna, the last ISIL stronghold in Homs province and on the road to the eastern city of Deir Al Zor, where a government garrison has been under ISIL siege since early 2015.

October 2017: Al Abadi announces the recapture of Hawija, one of the few remaining ISIL holdouts. The Syrian Democratic Forces announce the full recapture of Raqqa after more than four months of fighting.

November 2017: Iraqi forces enter Al Qaim, the main town in the group's last bastion in the country. Syria's army seizes Deir Al Zor, driving the militants from the last major city where they had a presence.

Dec. 9: Iraqi Prime Minister Haider al Abadi declared victory over the Islamic State.

Appendix 2
OPERATION OKRA STATISTICS

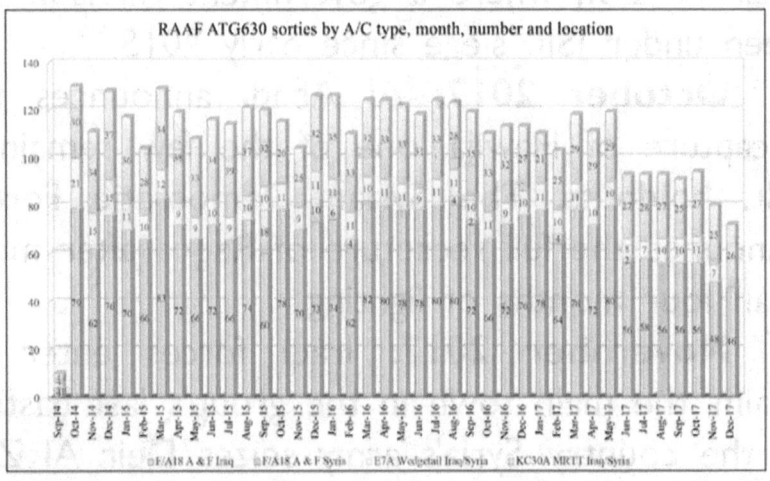

Operation OKRA: RAAF ATG630 sorties. (source: Australian Department of Defence)

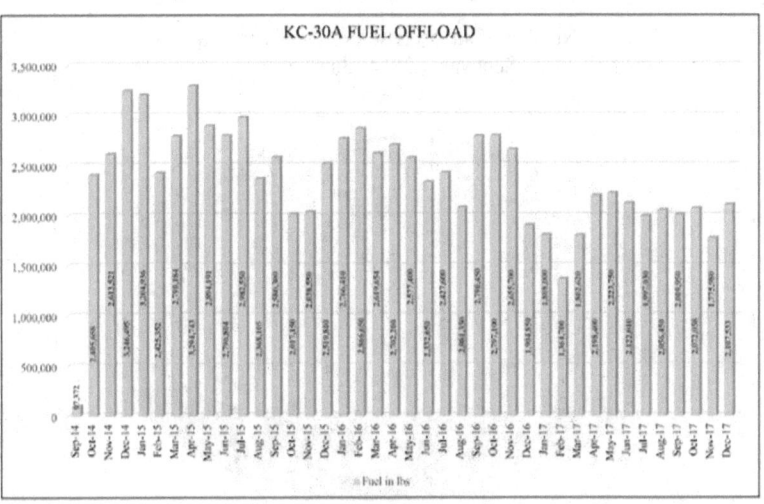

Operation OKRA: KC-30A Fuel Offload. (source: Australian Department of Defence)

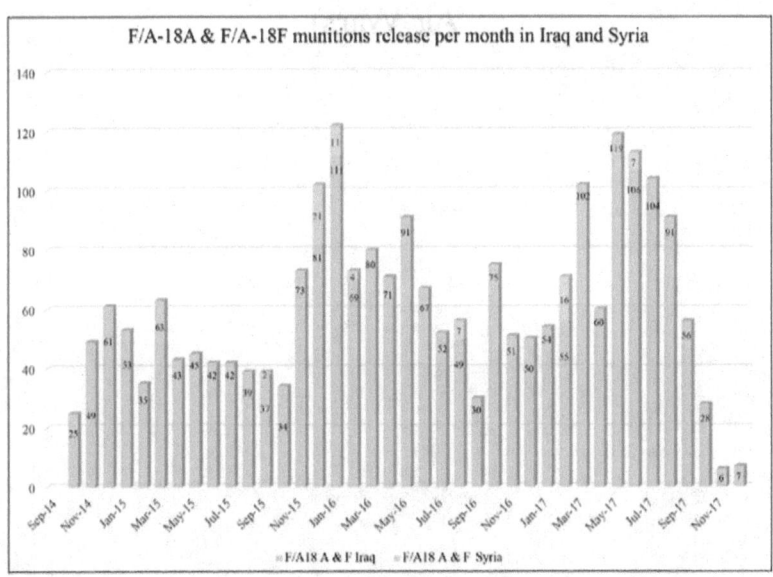

Operation OKRA: Munitions release per month in Iraq and Syria. (source: Australian Department of Defence)

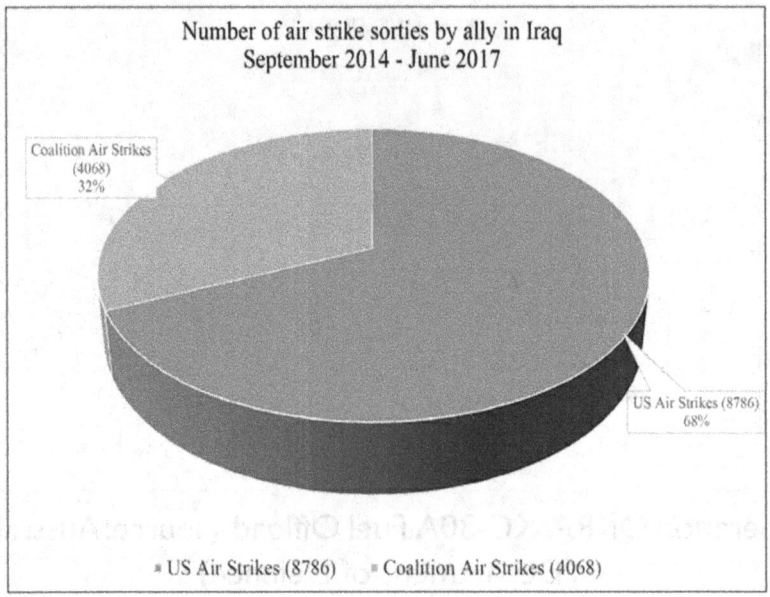

Operation OKRA: Air strike sorties by ally in Iraq. (source: Air Wars)

BIBLIOGRAPHY

Government Publications

Australian Government Department of Defence, *Global Operations: Iraq*, accessed at: http://www.defence.gov.au/Operations/Okra/

Australian Government Department of Defence, *Operation Accordion*, accessed at: http://www.defence.gov.au/Operations/OpAccordion/

Australian Government Department of Defence, *Operation OKRA*, accessed at: http://www.defence.gov.au/Operations/Okra/ATG.asp

Australian Government Department of Defence, Press Release, *Nine Months Deployed with The Air Task Group*, 13 April 2016, accessed at: https://news.defence.gov.au/media/stories/nine-months-deployed-air-task-group

Australian Government Department of Defence, Press Release, *Mammoth Milestone for KC-30A in Operation OKRA*, 30 May 2016, accessed at: https://news.defence.gov.au/media/stories/mammoth-milestone-kc-30a-operation-okra

Australian Government Department of Defence, *Defence White Paper 2016*, Canberra, 2016.

Australian Government Department of Defence, Parliamentary Press Release, Press conference with Vice Admiral David Johnston—Update on Australian Defence Force operations, 7 October 2015, accessed at: https://news.defence.gov.au/media/transcripts/press-conference-vice-admiral-david-johnston-update-australian-defence-force-0

Australian Government Parliament of Australia, Prime Minister Tony Abbott Press Release: *Humanitarian Assistance to Iraq*, 14 September 14, accessed at: https://parlinfo.aph.gov.au/parlInfo/search/display/display.w3p;query=Id:%22media/pressrel/3335348%22

Australian Government Parliament of Australia, Prime Minister Tony Abbott Press Release: *Australia to extend air operations against Daesh into Syria*, 9 September 2015, accessed at: https://parlinfo.aph.gov.au/parlInfo/search/display/display.w3p;query=Id:%22media/pressrel/4064446

Australian Government Parliament of Australia, Renee Westra, Foreign Affairs, Defence and Security Section, *Syria: Australian military operations*, 20 September 2017, accessed at: htt ps://www.aph.gov.au/About_Parliament/Parliamentary_Departments/Parliamentary_Library/pubs/

United States Central Command, Operation Inherent Resolve (OIR), accessed at: http://www.inherentresolve.mil

United States Central Command News Release, *Iraq and Syria Operations Against ISIL Designated as Operation Inherent Resolve*, accessed at: http://www.centcom.mil/MEDIA/NEWS-ARTICLES/News-Article-View/Article/884877/iraq-and-syria-operations-against-isil-designated-as-operation-inherent-resolve/

United States Air Forces Central Command, Combined Air Operations Centre Al Udeid, accessed at: http://www.afcent.af.mil/About/Fact-Sheets/Display/Article/217803/combined-air-operations-center-caoc/

Australian War Memorial

AWM4 8/4/9 Part I Diary No 1 Squadron AFC September 1918

AWM4 8/4/9 Part II Diary No 1 Squadron AFC September 1918

AWM4 8/4/9 Part III Diary No 1 Squadron AFC September 1918

AWM4 8/4/9 Part IV Diary No 1 Squadron AFC September 1918

Australian Defence Force

Australian Government Department of Defence, Australian Defence Doctrine Publication (ADDP), Operations Series ADDP 3.14, *Targeting*, Defence Publishing Service, Canberra, 2009.

Royal Australian Air Force

Australian Government Department of Defence, Royal Australian Air Force, Australian Air Publication (AAP) 1000-D, *The Air Power Manual 6th Edition*, Air Power Development Centre, Canberra, 2013.

Australian Government Department of Defence, Royal Australian Air Force, Australian Air Publication (AAP) 1001.1, *Command and Control in the Royal Australian Air Force*, Department of Defence Canberra, 2009.

Australian Government Department of Defence, Royal Australian Air Force—Air Power Development Centre, *What is Airmindedness?* Pathfinder Issue 151, Canberra, March 2011.

Australian Government Department of Defence, Royal Australian Air Force—Air Power Development Centre, *Air Force Capability Guide 2019*, Canberra, 2018.

Royal Air Force

AP 3000, *British Air and Space Power Doctrine 4th Edition*, Ministry of Defence, London, 2009.

War Office

Baldwin, J. "Experiences of Bombing with the Independent Force in 1918", in *A Selection of Lectures and Essays from the Work of Officers Attending the First Course*, the Royal Air Force Staff College, 1922-1923 His Majesties Stationary Office, Air Ministry, December 1923.

Field Service Regulations, Operations Pt 1 Section 95, His Majesty's Stationary Office, London, 1914.

Notes on Bombing Attacks, His Majesty's Stationary Office, London, December 1915.

Notes on the Interpretation of Aeroplane Photographs taken on the Palestine Front (1st and 2nd Edns), General Staff – Intelligence Branch, GHQ EEF, His Majesty's Stationary Office, London, January and June 1918.

Stationary Series (SS) 135, *Instructions for the Training of Divisions for Offensive Operations*, His Majesty's Stationary Office, London, 1916, reissued February 1918 as *The Division in the Attack*.

Royal Flying Corps, Flying Training Manual Pt 11, Chap.3, His Majesty's Stationary Office, London, June 1915.

Published Works

Aboulenein, Ahmed, Reuters, *Iraq holds victory parade after defeating Islamic State*, 10 December 2017, accessed at: https://www.reuters.com/article/us-mideast-crisis-iraq-parade/iraq-holds-victory-parade-after-defeating-islamic-state-idUSKBN1E407Z

Airwars.org.: *US Led Coalition in Iraq and Syria*, Accessed at: https://airwars.org/conflict/coalition-in-iraq-and-syria/

Amnesty International, *At Any Cost: The Civilian Cost in West Mosul, Iraq*, accessed at: https://www.amnesty.org/en/latest/campaigns/2017/07/at-any-cost-civilian-catastrophe-in-west-mosul-iraq/

Aljazeera News, *The Rise and Fall of ISIL*, 5 November 2017, accessed at: https://www.aljazeera.com/indepth/interactive/2015/02/rise-fall-isil-150212075706347.html

Atrash, N., "Mapping Palestine: The Bavarian Air Force WWI Aerial Photography", in *Jerusalem Quarterly*, 2014, 56, 95-106, at: http://www.palestine-studies.org/sites/default/files/jq-articles/JQ%2056-57%20Mapping%20Palestine.pdf

Allen, T., Berry, F. and Polmar, N., *War in the Gulf: From the Invasion of Kuwait to the Day of Victory and Beyond*, Turner Publishing, Nashville, 1991.

Andrews, William, *The Luftwaffe and the Battle for Air Superiority Blueprint or Warning? Air Power Journal*, Vol. Fall, 1995, pp.1-8.

Australian Broadcasting Commission, *Australian jets involved in US-led air strike which killed dozens of Syrian soldiers, Defence confirms*, 19 September 2016, accessed at: https://www.abc.net.au/news/2016-09-18/australian-jets-involved-in-botched-air-strike-on-syrian-army/7855610

Australian Broadcasting Commission, *Islamic State loses last occupied town as Iraqi forces capture Rawa, military says*, 17 November 2017, accessed at: https://www.abc.net.au/news/2017-11-17/iraqi-forces-recapture-last-islamic-state-held-town/9163944

Australian Defence Magazine, *A Window into the ATG's Operations in Mosul*, 18 May 2017, accessed at: http://www.australiandefence.com.au/news/a-window-into-atg-s-mosul-ops

Barr, J., *A Line in the Sand*, Simon & Schuster Ltd, London, 2012.

BBC News Services, *Islamic State and the Crisis in Iraq and Syria*, 28 March 2018, accessed at: https://www.bbc.com/news/world-middle-east-27838034

BBC News Services, *Iraqi forces launch assault on last IS bastion of al-Qaim*, 26 October 2017, accessed at: https://www.bbc.com/news/world-middle-east-41760479

Berger, J. & Stern, J., Aljazeera News, *The Rise and Fall of ISIL Explained*, 20 June 2017, accessed at: https://www.aljazeera.com/indepth/features/2017/06/rise-fall-isil-explained-170607085701484.html

Bowyer, C., *For Valour: The Air VCs*, William Kimber, London, 1978.

Brandis, G., 'It's a War of Self-Defence', in *The Australian*, 10 September 2015.

Bridge, C. & Fedorowich, K., "Mapping the British World", in *The Journal of Imperial and Commonwealth History*, 2003, 31:2, 1-15, at: http://dx.doi.org/10.1080/03086530310001705576.

Brissendon, M., Australian Broadcasting Commission (ABC), *Al MinhadAir Base: A closer look at Australia's base for operations in the Middle East*, 15 September 2014, accessed at: https://www.abc.net.au/news/2014-09-15/al-minhad:-australias-base-of-operations-in-the-middle-east/5744620

Bruce, J.M. The BE2 Series: Historic Military Aircraft. *Flight Magazine*, No 7, Part 2, 16 April 1954.

Bull, J. (edited by Mark Lax), *One Airman's War: Aircraft Mechanic Joe Bull's Personal Diaries 1916-1919*, Banner Books, Maryborough, 1997.

Callimachi, R., "Tal Afar After Liberation From ISIS: Battered but Still Standing", in *The New York Times*, 1 September 2017, accessed at: https://www.nytimes.com/2017/09/01/world/middleeast/tal-afar-mosul-islamic-state.html

Charlton, C., "American troops battle ISIS for first time as they see off' attempted attack by militants on Iraqi base" in *The Daily Mail*, 17 December 2014, accessed at: https://www.dailymail.co.uk/news/article-2878897/American-troops-battle-ISIS-time-attempted-attack-militants-Iraqi-base.html

Clark, M., *A Short History of Australia*, Penguin Publications, Ringwood, Australia, 1995.

Clodfelter, Mark, "Back from the Future: The Impact of Change on Airpower in the Decades Ahead", in *Strategic Studies Quarterly*, Fall 2009, pp.105-106.

Coker, M. and Hassan, F., "Iraq Prime Minister Declares Victory Over ISIS", in *The New York Times*, 9 December 2017, accessed at: https://www.nytimes.com/2017/12/09/world/middleeast/iraq-isis-haider-al-abadi.html

Coulthard-Clark, C., *The Third Brother: A History of the Royal Australian Air Force 1921-1931*, Allen & Unwin, Sydney, 1991.

Cutlack, F.M., *The Official History of Australia in the War of 1914-1918: The Australian Flying Corps, Vol. VIII*, first published 1923, University of Queensland Press, St Lucia, Queensland, 1984.

Delaporte, M., *Breaking Defense: Aussie Tankers Knit Coalition Forces Together*, 8 April 2018, accessed at: https://breakingdefense.com/2018/04/aussie-tankers-knit-coalition-forces-together/

Doran, M., *Australian planes involved in Iraqi airstrike which killed civilians*, Australian Broadcasting Commission, 1 February 2019, accessed at: https://www.abc.net.au/news/2019-02-01/iraqi-civilians-killed-in-airstrike-australia-involved-in/10766770

Douhet, Giulio, *The Command of the Air*, Book 1, translated by Dino Ferrari, originally published

1921, in AAPC Seminar 03 Reading 1 Page: 6, accessed 5 September 2014.

Erickson, E.J., *Ordered to Die: A History of the Ottoman Army in the First World War*, Greenwood Publishing Group, Connecticut, 2001.

Farley, Robert, *Grounded: The Case for Abolishing the United States Air Force*, The University Press of Kentucky, Louisville, 2014.

Fernandes, Clinton, *Island off the Coast of Asia: Instruments of Statecraft in Australian Foreign Policy*, Monash University Press, Melbourne, 2018.

Fishel, R. and Stein, A., 'Lessons Learned from the Air War against the Islamic State', in *War on the Rocks*, 23 February 2018, accessed at: https://warontherocks.com/2018/02/lessons-learned-air-war-islamic-state/

Ghoshal, A., "Iraq: Isis killed and crucified 40 people in Mosul for helping Iraqi forces, says UN", in The International Business Times, 11 November 2016, accessed at: https://www.ibtimes.co.in/iraq-isis-killed-crucified-40-people-mosul-helping-iraqi-forces-says-un-703589

Gordon, M. & Schmitt, E., "Officials Eye Euphrates River Valley as Last Stand for ISIS", in the *New York Times*, 31 August 2017, New York, United States. Accessed at: https://www.nytimes.com/2017/08/31/us/politics/isis-military-us-iraq-syria-euphrates.html

Greene, A., *RAAF fighters dropped six bombs on government forces in botched air strikes in Syria*, Australian Broadcasting Commission, 30 November 2016, accessed at: https://www.abc.net.au/news/2016-11-30/syria-botched-air-strikes-australian-hornets/8077588

Grey, J. et al, *The Oxford Companion to Australian Military History*, Oxford University Press, Melbourne, 1995.

Groschel, D. & Ladek, J., "Wings over the Sinai and Palestine", in *Over the Front: League of WWI Aviation Historians*, 1988, 13-1, Newport, Kentucky, United States.

Guerin, O., "Mosul: Iraq and Kurdish troops make gains in battle", in *BBC News*, 17 October 2016, accessed at: https://www.bbc.com/news/world-middle-east-37679325

Gullett, H.S., *The Official History of Australia in the War of 1914-1918: The AIF in Sinai and Palestine Vol. VII*, first published 1923, University of Queensland Press, St Lucia, Queensland, 1984.

Hallion, R., *Strike from the Sky: The History of Battlefield Air Attack*, Smithsonian Institute, Washington, 1989.

Hashim, A., "The Islamic State: from al-Qaeda affiliate to Caliphate", in *Middle East Policy*, Vol.21, No 4, 2014.

Hassan, H., "New document sheds light on the changing nature of ISIL's combat tactics", in *The National Opinion*, 20 September 2017, accessed at: https://www.thenational.ae/opinion/new-document-sheds-light-on-the-changing-nature-of-isil-s-combat-tactics-1.630289

Hassan, H., "The Battle for Raqqa and the Challenges after Liberation", in *Combatting Terrorism Centre at West Point*, June/July 2017, Volume 10 (6).

Hill, A.J., *Chauvel of the Light Horse: A Biography of General Sir Harry Chauvel, GCMG, KCB*. University of Melbourne Press, Melbourne, 1978.

Jones, H.A., *The War in the Air: Being the Story of the part played in the Great War by the Royal Air Force*, Vols. II & VI, Oxford at the Clarendon Press, London, 1937.

James, C., "Isis flags raised in Kobani near Turkish-Syrian border", in *The Guardian*, 7 October 2014, accessed at: https://www.theguardian.com/world/2014/oct/06/islamic-state-flags-reported-flying-in-kurdish-syrian-town-kobani

Kainikara, Sanu, Royal Australian Air Force Air Power Development Centre, Working Paper 18: *Air Power in the 21st Century: A Snapshot of Emerging Roles and Future Challenges*, Canberra, 2005.

Kedar, B.Z., *The Changing Land between Jordan and the Sea: Aerial Photographs from 1917 to the Present*, Yad Ben-Zvi Press, Mod Publishing House, Jerusalem, 1999.

Kenny, M., "Abbott declares war on the Islamic State 'death cult'", in *The Sydney Morning Herald*, 15 September 2014, Accessed at: https://www.smh.com.au/politics/federal/abbott-declares-war-on-the-islamic-state-death-cult-20140914-3fol3.html

Lawrence, T.E., *The Seven Pillars of Wisdom*, first published 1926, Jonathon Cape Ltd, London, 1943.

Lewis, C.E., *Sagittarius Rising*, Pen & Sword Publications, Barnsley, 2013.

Mamoun, A., ISIS Executes 300 People West of Anbar, in *Iraqi News*, 9 April 2015, accessed at: https://www.iraqinews.com/iraq-war/isis-executes-300-people-west-anbar/

McCarthy, John, *Douhet and the Decisiveness of Air Power*, in Hugh Smith (ed.), "The Strategists", Australian Defence Studies Centre, Canberra, 2001.

McLaughlin, A., *The RAAF in Operation OKRA—The Highest Levels Of Skill, Courage And Professionalism*, in Australian Aviation, 25 April 2018, accessed at: https://australianaviation.com.au/2018/04/the-raaf-in-operation-okra-the-highest-levels-of-skill-courage-and-professionalism/

McPhedran, Ian, News Corp Australia, RAAF mission against ISIS: Pilots did not drop bombs because of collateral damage risk, 8 October 2014. Accessed at: https://www.news.com.au/national/raaf-mission-against-isis-pilots-did-not-drop-bombs-because-ofcollateral-damage-risk/news-story/01d32393c58d4b52a76dfd98a670e64f

Maher, C., "Iraq launches offensive on Hawija, an Islamic State-held region near oil city Kirkuk", 21 September 2017, Reuters, accessed at: https://www.reuters.com/article/us-mideast-crisis-iraq-kirkuk/iraq-launches-offensive-on-hawija-an-islamic-state-held-region-near-oil-city-kirkuk-idUSKCN1BW0CA

Mattis, James. "USJFCOM Commander's guidance for effects-based operations," *Joint Forces Quarterly*, issue 51 (4th Quarter 2008): 105-108.

Meilinger, Phillip S. (ed.), *The Paths of Heaven—The Evolution of Airpower Theory*, Air University Press, Maxwell Air Force Base, Alabama, 1997.

Mitchell, William, *Our Air Force: the Keystone of National Defense*, E.P. Dutton & Company, New York, 1921.

Mitchell, William. *Winged Defense: the Development and Possibilities of Modern Airpower*, Putnam & Sons, New York, 1925.

Mueller, Karl P., *Air Power*, published by the Rand Corporation accessed online 06 Sep 14 at http://www.rand.org/paf/pubs.html

Newton, D., *Hell Bent: Australia's Leap into the Great War*, Scribe Publications, Sydney, 2014.

Olsen, J.E. (ed), *A History of Air Warfare*, Potomac Books, Lincoln Nebraska, 2010.

Overy, Richard, *World War II: The Bombing of Germany*, in Stephens, Alan (ed.), "The War in the Air", RAAF Aerospace Centre, Canberra, 1994.

Overy, Richard. "Air power and the origins of deterrence theory before 1939." in *Strategic Studies: A Reader*, edited by Thomas Mahnken and Joseph Maiolo, 135-155. London: Routledge, 2008.

Pape, Robert, *Bombing to Win: Airpower and Coercion in War*, Cornell University Press, New York, 1996.

Paterson, A.B. "Banjo", *Happy Despatches*, Angus and Robertson, Sydney, 1934.

Pawlyk, O., "US F/A-18E Shoots Down Syrian Su-22 in Air-to-Air Kill", in Militsry.com, 18 June 2017, accessed at: https://www.military.com/daily-news/2017/06/18/us-navy-fa18e-shoots-down-su22-over-syria.html

Rajca, Jennifer, News Corp Australia, Confirmed: Australian air strikes have killed 'multiple' ISIS targets in Iraq, 17 October 2014, Accessed at: https://www.news.com.au/national/confirmed-australian-air-strikes-have-killed-multiple-isis-targets-in-iraq/news-story/dae8eae024584f14be432ce8901e1724

Samuel, S., Farhan, S. and Lawandow, A., 'ISIS Destroyed Jonah's Tomb, but Not Its Message', in *The Atlantic*, 24 July 2017, accessed at: https://www.theatlantic.com/international/archive/2017/07/tomb-of-jonah-mosul-isis/534414/

Schmitt, E., 'Battle to Stamp Out ISIS in Syria Gains New Momentum, but Threats Remain', in *The New York Times*, 30 May 2018, accessed at: https://www.nytimes.com/2018/05/30/world/middleeast/isis-syria-battle-kurds-united-states.html

Shugerman, E., 'US air strike in Mosul killed at least 105 civilians', in *The Independent,* 25 May 2017, accessed at: https://www.independent.co.u

k/news/world/americas/mosul-us-air-strike-civilian-deaths-pentagon-latest-toll-a7755866.html

Sisk, Richard, Military News, *Airstrike Agreement Keeps US Air Controllers Away From Combat*, 29 September 2014, Accessed at: https://www.military.com/daily-news/2014/09/29/airstrike-agreement-keeps-us-air-controllers-away-from-combat.html

Siyech, M., 'Sewing the seeds of their own destruction', in *Counter Terrorist Trends and Analyses*, Vol.8, No 11 (November 2016), pp.24-28

Stephens, Alan (ed.), *The True Believers*, in "The War in the Air", RAAF Aerospace Centre, Canberra, 1994.

Stephens, Alan, *Kosovo, Or the Future of War*, in 'The use of military force in Kosovo', Working Paper (54), Air Power Studies Centre, Canberra, 1999.

Stephens, A., *The Royal Australian Air Force*, Oxford University Press, Melbourne, 2001.

Taylor, A., The Battle for Raqqa, in *The Atlantic*, 12 October 2017, accessed at: https://www.the

atlantic.com/photo/2017/10/the-battle-for-raqqa/542778/

United Nations Association of Australia, *The United Nations and the Rules Based International Order*, Canberra, 2018.

United Nations Security Council Resolution 2170 (2014) *Condemning Gross, Widespread Abuse of Human Rights by Extremist Groups in Iraq, Syria* announced on 15 August 2014. Accessed at: https://www.un.org/press/en/2014/sc11520.doc.htm

Wallin, M., Fact Sheet: "U.S. Military Bases and Facilities in the Middle East" in *The American Security Project*, June 2018, accessed at: https://www.americansecurityproject.org/wp-content/uploads/2018/06/Ref-0213-US-Military-Bases-and-Facilities-Middle-East.pdf

Warden, Colonel (USAF) John, *The Air Campaign: Planning for Combat*, National Defense University Press Publication, Washington, 1988.

Warrick, *Black Flags: The Rise of ISIS*, Penguin Books, London, 2015.

Williams, R., *These are Facts: The Autobiography of Sir Richard Williams, KBE, CB, DSO*, Australian

War Memorial and Australian Government Publishing Service, Canberra, 1977.

Youhas, A., "US-led coalition providing support for Iraqi and Kurdish fighters", in *Battle for Mosul: Isis city under attack from Iraqi and Kurdish forces—as it happened, The Guardian and Associated Press,* 17 October 2016, accessed at: https://www.theguardian.com/world/live/2016/oct/17/mosul-battle-iraq-isis-islamic-state-peshmerga-latest?page=with:block-58046999e4b01ffb8ffcc705

BACK COVER MATERIAL

The dispatch of an Ottoman Army by Australian-led Imperial air power in the Wadi Pari on 21 September 1918 occurred just five years after the advent or military aviation in Australia. In 1914, the fledgling Australian air service operated the flimsy Bristol Boxkite; four years later it was flying the far more advanced Bristol F2B Fighter. This leap forward represented a profound progress in technology that has typified the technical development of aviation, particularly in Australia ever since. Ironically, on 21 September 2014. 96 years after the events of the Wadi Fara, Australian squadrons were again deployed to the same part of the world where they would remain for more than three years on operations against extremist terrorism.

Armageddon and OKRA contrasts these events, a century apart, in the context of the development of Australian air power. The hook tracks the history where Australia has maintained a balanced air service compelling high technical, logistics and engineering standards, and effective training and command and control systems, for more than 100 years. These processes were as applicable a century ago as they are today. By examining these operational events, the author establishes the connection that access to the technology associated with air power is intrinsically linked to Australia's enduring foreign and defence policy – more so, that military power Is a means to an end, and never an end unto itself.

Index

A
Abbott, Prime Minister Tony, *185, 191, 197, 301*
Abdul-Mahdi, Adil, *370*
Abu Dhabi, *324*
AEG aircraft C.IV, *104*
aerial gunnery training, *48*
aerial photography, *13, 18*
   analysis of, *18*
      cameras, *126*
      mapping mission, *121, 123, 128*
      Pyramids of Giza, *82*
Afghanistan, *156, 200*
   counterinsurgency, *156*
Air and Space Operations Centre, *211*
air base support, *173*
Air Component Commander, *200, 202, 205, 214, 285*
air mobility, *234, 239*
Air Mobility Task Unit (TU 633.0.4 AMTU), *242*

air power, *151, 156, 221, 367, 370, 373*
allies, bilateral treaties and trade arrangements with, *239*
   balance, and, *177*
   command and control, *197, 200, 262*
   cooperation with ground power, *13*
   core roles, *234*
   discretionary application of, *173*
   'five-rings' theory, *271, 294*
   flexibility, *177*
   importance of, *45, 48, 216, 346*
   interoperable within a wider international context, *177, 180*
   Iraq, in, *214, 282*
   kinetic, *214, 239, 261, 271, 277, 296, 317*

Mosul, liberation of, *338*
nature of modern, *173, 177, 180*
obligations and responsibilities, *167*
organisation, *45*
strategy, *271*
supporting infrastructure, *173, 177*
technology, *180, 185, 367*
Air Task Group (ATG 630), *173, 180, 185, 191, 291, 370*
  see also Operation OKRA,
A' cells, *229, 231*
air mobility, *234, 239*
alcohol, access to, *324*
Anzac Day ceremony, *301*
armament technicians,
  command and control, *191, 194, 197, 200, 202, 211, 214, 224, 237*
  core air power roles, *234*
  deep air support interdiction missions, *211*
  demographic, *221, 224*
  departure from Australia, *167, 216, 242, 374*
  familiarisation flights in-theatre, *261, 271*
  flying operations, commencement, *261, 271, 275, 277, 298, 374*
  force multiplier, as, *239, 301*
  human resource management, *242*
  immigration visas, *324*
  intelligence, surveillance and reconnaissance platform, *234*
  Legal Officer, *285*
  logistics, *224, 227, 229, 231, 324*
  Operational Command, *211*
  operational pause, *356, 359, 365*

operations statistics, *301, 346, 359, 365*
planned targets, *282, 285, 311*
platforms assigned to, *239*
pre-deployment training, *317*
relocation to Al Dhafra, *285, 287*
rotations, *290, 291, 301, 314, 346, 350, 365*
RSO&I process, *261, 262, 265*
rules of engagement, *282, 285, 294, 311, 317, 341, 346*
service personnel, *216, 219, 221, 224, 262, 271, 275, 277, 287, 290, 291, 324, 327, 329, 332, 335, 346, 349, 365, 370*
skill groups, *224*
strike element, *234, 239, 290, 317*
Air Tasking Order process, *239*

air-to-air encounters German-Allied, *71, 94, 95, 118, 132*
air-to-air refuelling (AAR), *163, 224, 239, 258, 265, 290, 301, 306, 311, 332, 341*
  boom refuelling system, *258, 262*
  'probe and drogue' fuel hose system, *258, 306*
air-to-air refuelling (AAR) tankers Airbus KC-30A, *167, 185, 200, 214, 221, 224, 239, 252, 255, 258, 262, 265, 271, 285, 301, 306, 327, 329, 332, 335, 359, 365*
  McDonnell Douglas KC-10 Extender, *290*
Airborne Early Warning and Control (AEW&C) Boeing E-7A Wedgetail, *167, 183, 185, 200, 214, 224, 234, 239, 242, 249, 265, 271, 285, 290, 301, 311, 319, 329, 332, 335, 350, 353, 359, 365, 373*
  Grumman E-2C Hawkeye, *200*

Airbus aircraft KC-30A,
*167, 173, 185, 200, 214, 221,
224, 239, 252, 255, 258, 262,
265, 271, 285, 301, 306, 327,
329, 332, 335, 359, 365*
aircraft, *367*
AEG,
  see AEG aircraft,
Airbus,
  see Airbus aircraft,
Albatros,
  see Albatros fighters,
Armstrong Whitworth,
  see Armstrong
  Whitworth aircraft,
Aviatik, *71*
  Boeing,
  see Boeing aircraft,
  bracing wires, *12*
  Bristol,
  see Bristol aircraft,
  care of, *10, 12*
  Caudron,
  see Caudron aircraft,
  climate, impact of, *13,
314*
  Dassault,
  see Dassault aircraft,
  De Havilland,
  see De Havilland
  aircraft,
Deperdussin,
  see Deperdussin
  aircraft,
engines, *12*
Eurofighter,
  see Eurofighter
  aircraft,
fabric, *10*
Fokker,
  see Fokker aircraft,
General Atomics,
  see General Atomics
  aircraft,
Halberstadt, *78*
Handley Page,
  see Handley Page
  aircraft,
Lockheed Martin,
  see Lockheed Martin
  aircraft,
logs, *12*
McDonnell Douglas,
  see McDonnell
  Douglas aircraft,
Martinsyde,
  see Martinsyde
  aircraft,

Maurice Farman,
see Maurice Farman aircraft,
Morane-Saulnier,
see Morane-Saulnier aircraft,
Nieuport,
see Nieuport aircraft,
Northrop Grumman,
see Northrop Grumman aircraft,
Pfalz,
see Pfalz aircraft,
propellers, *12*
'pusher', *18*
remotely piloted vehicles, *311, 349*
Royal Aircraft Factory,
see Royal Aircraft Factory aircraft,
Rumpler,
see Rumpler aircraft,
seaplanes, *68*
Sopwith, *18*
Sukhoi,
see Sukhoi aircraft,
tyres, *12*
unmanned aerial vehicles, *311*
Vickers,
see Vickers aircraft,
woods, *10*
aircrew,
captured, *78, 94, 95*
Boeing E-7A Wedgetail, *271, 311, 327, 329, 332, 346, 350, 353, 365*
forced down, *262, 275*
modern multi-crewed platforms, *227*
No I Squadron (AFC), *49, 51*
Operation OKRA, *224, 227, 271, 275, 327, 329*
targeting, discretionary judgement, *285*
airfields,
see also by name,
accidents at, *271*
airmindedness, *45, 180, 183, 200*
Al-Abadi, Haider, *185, 336, 349, 359, 378*
Al Adnani, Abu Muhammad, *374*
Al-Assad, Bashar, *185, 301, 319*

Al-Baghdadi, Abu Bakr, *167, 185, 277, 290, 308, 374, 378*
Al-Bakr, Ahmad Hasan, *154*
Al Dhafra Air Base, *239, 285, 287, 290, 298, 301, 314, 324, 335, 359*
Al-Hashemi, Tariq, *185*
Al Kasasbeh, Moaz, *374*
Al-Maliki, Nuri, *185, 374*
Al Minhad, *167*
Air Force Base (AMAB), *194, 200, 214, 224, 231, 242, 261, 262, 271, 285, 287, 290, 301, 324, 327*
Al Nahyan, Khalifa bin Zayed, *200*
Al-Qaeda, *156*
Al Qaim, *353, 356, 359, 378*
Al Udeid, *194*
Air Base, *202, 229, 261, 314*
Albatros fighters, *78, 90, 121, 132*
   D.III, *78, 88, 94, 100, 104*
   D.IIIa, *100*
Aleppo, *151, 185, 374*
Allenby, General Sir Edmund, *49, 83, 88, 94, 100, 104, 108, 130*

air power, use of, *121, 123, 132, 151*
Armageddon offensive, *132, 134, 140, 141, 142, 145, 148, 151*
   leadership, *88, 108*
Anah, *353, 356*
Anbar Province, *185, 277, 353*
Andrews, Kevin, *301*
anti-aircraft weapons, *18, 68, 78*
Anzac Day ceremony, *301*
Anzac myth, *58, 324*
Arab forces, *121, 123, 132, 151*
   Balfour Declaration, reaction to, *109*
   insurrection, *74, 151*
Arab Spring, *180, 301, 319*
Arif, Abdul Salam, *154*
Armageddon, Battle of, *145, 148*
   historical background to name, *145*
   map, *140*
armoured cars, *100*

Armstrong Whitworth aircraft FK8, *130*
artillery creeping barrage, *134*
  mechanised, *100*
artillery spotting, *13, 30, 105, 118*
  dangers, *40, 44*
  training, *48*
Australia, New Zealand and United States (ANZUS) Treaty (1951), *177*
Australian Army AFC, and,
  Light Horse, *13, 104, 132, 142, 145, 151*
Australian Defence Force (ADF), *185*
  Academy, *197*
  international areas of operation, *194*
  Iraq, in, *214, 216*
  reputation, *167*
  targeting doctrine, *285, 346*
Australian Flying Corps (AFC), *126, 154*
  see also Royal,

Australian Air Force (RAAF) demographic, *58*
  establishment, *114, 126*
  expansion, *49*
  leadership and command, *48, 49*
  No 1 Squadron, see No 1 Squadron,
  Operation OKRA, see Operation OKRA
  structure and defined goals, *45*
  training, *45, 48, 53, 61, 63*
Australian Imperial Force (AIF) demographic, *58*
Australian national identity, *13*
Australian National Security Committee, *356*
Avghani, *353*
axis of evil, *156*
Ayatollah Khomeini, *156*
AV-8B Harrier II, *301*
C-17 Globemaster, *167, 200, 301*
F-15 Eagle, *290, 341, 349*
KC-10 Extender, *290*

air superiority, need for, *202*
airspace, *265*
AV-8B Harrier II, *301*
   C-17 Globemaster, *167, 200, 301*
   F-15 Eagle, *290, 341, 349*
   KC-10 Extender, *290*
   machine guns, *18*
   Lewis,
     see Lewis guns,
   Spandau, *78, 100*
   Vickers,
     see Vickers guns,
Army,
   see Turkish Army,
   collapse, *123, 126, 151*

B

Baathist ideology, *154, 156, 185*
Baghdad, *74, 154, 156, 185, 338*
Bahrain airspace, *265*
Baiji, *353, 374*
Baillieu, Lieutenant Reg, *78, 83*
Baird, Corporal Cameron, *200*

Balfour Declaration, *109*
Barnwell, Frank Sowter, *115*
Barry, Wing Commander Mark, *301*
Basra, *74, 154, 156, 265, 338*
Beaton, Lieutenant Edward Balfour Somerset, *68*
Bedouin Arabs, *74*
   air support, *132*
Beersheba, *56, 71, 82, 100*
   Light Brigade at, *104, 105*
Beisan, *141*
Bellingham, Air Commodore Stuart, *301, 350*
Bender, Group Captain Ross, *200, 365*
Bin Laden, Osama, *156*
Binskin, Air Chief Marshal Mark, *167, 191, 356, 370*
Bir Salem, *130*
Birmingham Small Arms (BSA) factory, *33*
Blair, Tony, *156*

Blake, Wing Commander Duncan, *285*
Blix, Hans, *156*
Boeing aircraft 737-700, *234*
   E-3 AWACS, *242, 271, 290*
   E-7 Awedgetail, *167, 183, 185, 200, 214, 224, 234, 239, 242, 249, 265, 271, 285, 290, 301, 311, 319, 329, 332, 335, 350, 353, 359, 365, 373*
Boeing aircraft, see also McDonnell Douglas,
Boelcke, Oswald, *18*
bombing operations, *13, 36, 39, 45, 68, 74, 100, 132*
   accuracy, issues with, *39, 44*
   air strikes against ISIL, *205, 271, 280, 290, 294, 296, 301, 308, 311, 319, 329, 332, 335, 374*
   Allenby's offensive, *141, 142, 145*
   CFS bomb sight, *39*
   Coalition forces, *156, 301, 341*
   collateral damage, *311, 346*
   global position system tracking, *294*
   Iraq War, *156*
   ISIL, against, *271, 294, 296*
   Notes on Bombing Attacks 1915, *36*
   opposing airfields, *71*
   precision and targeting, *294, 296*
   RAAF technicians, *275*
   sights, using, *39, 44, 45*
   training, *48*
   'X' Squadron, *104*
bombs, *36, 45*
   25 lb Cooper bomb, *36, 39, 45*
   112lb Mk 1 bomb, *36, 39*
   230lb bomb, *36, 45*
   250lb bomb, *39*
   520lb bomb, *39*
   1650lb bomb, *39*
   Hales 20lb fragmentation bomb, *36, 39, 45*

release mechanisms, 39
'Skeleton' cradle carrier, 39
Borton, Brigadier Amyas Eden 'Biffy', 123, 130
Bowden Fletcher, Howard, 68
Brady, Flight Lieutenant Paul 'Brades', 221, 353
Brandis, George, 301
Brassell, Lieutenant Jack Stanley, 90
Braz, Air Commodore Glen, 200, 290, 301, 350
Bristol aircraft Boxkite, M.1, 104
R.2A, 115
Scouts, 68, 104
Bristol Fighters 'Brisfits', 94, 100, 108, 130, 134, 145, 151
   Allenby's offensive, 132, 134
   armaments, 33, 115
   F.2a, 115
   F.2b, 7, 104, 115, 118
   reconnaissance, 132
British Army,
Desert Mounted Corps, 104
XX Corps, 83, 104
XXI Corps, 83, 104
British Empire Dominions, 177
Brooks, Captain Charles, 90
Brown, Air Marshal Geoff, 185, 290
Brown, Lieutenant Allan, 145
Build Partner Capacity, 185, 191, 308, 311, 317, 356
Bull, Joe, 78, 90
Burnett, Lieutenant Colonel Charles, 130
Bush, George (Snr), 156
Bush, George W, 156

C

Cairo, 82
Camm, Lieutenant Richard Andrew, 68
Camp Baird, 200
Camp Victory, 194
Campbell-Wright, Squadron Leader Steve 'Dicky', 324, 327

Carpenter, Wing Commander Paul, *242, 255, 271, 291*
casualties air combat, *90*
   anti-aircraft ground fire, *78*
   Baathist, *156*
civilian, *311, 314*
   ISIL, *301, 346, 378*
   sectarian violence, *156, 180*
   terrorist attacks, *374, 378*
   trainee pilots, *53*
   Turkish, *74, 141, 142, 145*
Chappell, Wing Commander Stephen, *255, 258, 262, 298, 301*
certification of aviators, *271*
   flying operations in Iraq, *298, 301*
   personnel rotation, *290, 291*
   withdrawal of TE630.1.1 from RSO&I training, *262, 265*
Charlie the dog, *68, 137*

Chauvel, Major General Sir Harry, *83, 104, 145, 151*
Chipman, Group Captain Robert, *229, 231, 261, 262*
'clock code' system, *30, 40*
Close Air Support interdiction effort, *211*
Coalition forces, *219, 317*
   Basra bombing, *156*
   Build Partner Capacity, *185, 191, 308, 311, 317, 356*
command and control arrangements, *202, 205*
   Iraqi military, working with, *205, 336*
   ISIL, against, *185, 191, 200, 202, 205, 239, 271, 277, 280, 301, 306, 308, 311, 314, 336*
   Russian forces, and, *349*
   shock and awe campaign, *156*
Cole, Lieutenant Adrian, *18, 78*
combat (WWI), *18*

combat clearance operations, *365*
Combat Controllers, *282, 317, 324*
Combat Support Unit (Task Unit 633.17), *242*
Combined Air Operations Centre (CAOC), *202, 205, 229, 239, 301, 311, 324, 329*
    defeating ISIL, *349*
    divisions, *205, 208*
    Legal Officer, *285*
    operations, *329, 332, 335*
    planned targets, *282, 285, 311*
    purpose and responsibility, *208*
    tracking symbology, *314*
combined arms operations, *301, 317*
Combined Joint Force Land Component Command (CJFLCC), *205, 211, 214*
Combined Joint Task Force (CJTF), *191, 280*
Combined Joint Task Force Land Component Command (CJTFLCC), *280, 282, 329, 336*
Combined Task Unit 630.1 (CTU630.1), *229, 261, 287*
Combined Task Unit 630.2 (CTU 630.2), *229*
command air forces, *48, 49*
    definition, *48*
communications artillery spotting, *30*
    digital satellite, *202*
    pilot training, and, *63*
    precision and targeting, *294, 296*
Conrick, Lieutenant Clive, *145*
control of the air, *234*
Counter-Terrorism Services, *185, 191*
    counterinsurgency, *156, 367*
Cox, Flight Sergeant Trudi, *324*
Cross of Jerusalem, *346*

D

dynamic targeting services, *211*
Daesh (Da'esh), *171*
  see also Islamic State of Iraq and the Levant (ISIL),
Damascus, *142, 145, 151*
Dassault aircraft,
  Mirage, *167, 171, 173, 177, 180, 183, 185, 242, 341*
  Rafale, *301, 306*
De Havilland aircraft, *18*
  Airco D.H.4, *45*
D.H.1, *68*
D.H.2, *88, 104*
D.H.9, *45, 130, 132*
De Havilland, Geoffrey, *24*
Deir al-Zor military airfield, *311, 349, 378*
Denney, Air Commodore Rob, *365*
Diego Garcia, *167*
Dier el Belah, *13, 104*
Dittmar, Oberleutnant Gustav, *94, 100*
Diyala, *185*
Dore, Sergeant Grant, *298*
dual-controlled training aircraft, *63*
Dubai, *194, 324*

E

EEF (WWI), *121, 123, 126*
effects-based approach, *180*
Egypt Arab Spring, *180, 319*
Egyptian Expeditionary Force (EEF), *74, 83, 108*
  air power, *48, 49, 71, 100, 108, 132*
  Allenby's offensive, *132, 134, 140, 141, 145*
  combined arms operations, *121, 123, 126*
El Affule, *123, 141*
El Arish, *56, 74, 82*
Erbil, *185*
'escape and evasion' kits, *262*
Euphrates River, *154, 185, 277, 336, 338, 353, 356, 365, 367*
Eurofighter aircraft Typhoon, *301*

Exercise Aces North (Northern Territory), *242*
Exercise Cope North (Guam), *242*
Exercise Pitch Black (Northern Territory), *242*

F

Falke, Oberleutnant Richard, *88*
Fallujah, *185, 374*
Fallujah Dam, *271*
Feisal bin Hussein bin Ali al-Hashemi, *74, 118, 121, 132, 154*
Feldhahn, Squadron Leader Jeremy, *271*
Felmy, Hauptman Helmuth, *98*
Felmy, Oberleutnant Gerhard, *88, 90, 94, 95, 98*
   awards, *98*
   character, *95*
Ferguson, Squadron Leader Greg, *301*
Field Service Regulations, *13*
fighter aircraft, see combat,
Fighter Combat Controller, *291*
Fighter Combat Instructor, *291*
Finlay, Lieutenant Garfield, *68, 145*
flying training standards, *61, 63*
Fokker E.III, *29*
   E-type 'Eindekker', *18, 29, 56, 71*
Fokker, Anthony, *18*
Foley, James, *374*
force multipliers, *185*
Fysh, Lieutenant Hudson, *68*
fighters, *171*

G

Gulf War, *156, 180, 208*
Gallipoli, *216*
Gamlin, Wing Commander Jason, *353, 356, 365*
Gardner, Flying Officer Sean, *338*
Garros, Roland, *18*

Gaza, *74, 100, 104, 105, 108*
   Third Battle, *98, 100, 104*
General Methods of Teaching Scout Pilots, *63*
General Atomics aircraft Reaper unmanned aerial vehicle, *341*
Geneva Conventions, *282*
German Air Service, *56, 105, 123, 151*
   FA300, *56, 68, 71, 74, 78, 82, 88, 90, 94, 95, 98*
   FA301, *104*
   FA302, *104*
   FA303, *104*
   FA304b, *104*
   logistics, *94*
   outmatched, *132, 151*
   superior aircraft, *82, 88*
German Army, *145*
German National Socialism, *154*
Global War on Terror, *156*
Gordan, Air Commodore Phil, *336, 346*
Gosport communication system, *63*
ground spotting, *30*

Gulf War, *156, 180, 208*
Gullet, Henry, *83*

H

Haditha, *277, 353*
Haifa, *145*
Haines, David, *185, 374*
Haly, Wing Commander John, *314, 317, 324*
Heavy Bomber, *130*
Harper, Squadron Leader Matt, *271*
Hawijah, *353*
Hawley, Lieutenant Frederic Cecil, *68*
Headquarters Joint Operations Command, *200, 211, 261*
heat management policies, *327*
Heliopolis, *82*
Henning, Alan, *374*
Hipps, Squadron Leader William, *327*
Howard, John, *191*
Hurley, General David, *200*
Hussein, Sherif of Mecca, *74*

Hyam, Lieutenant William, *78*

I

Iervasi, Air Commodore Joe, *282, 350*
Immelmann, Max, *18, 29*
Improvised Explosive Devices, *262*
infra-red litening pod sensors, *296*
insurgency Arab, *74, 151*
Iraq, *156, 180, 185, 277, 367, 370*
intelligence (core air power), *234*
interrupter gear, *18, 29*
Iran, *156*
Iran-Iraq War, *156*
Iraq, *156, 180, 185, 277, 367, 370*
   airspace, *265, 271*
   Australian theatre of operations, *194*
   battlespace grids ('kill-boxes'), *301*
   climate, *290*
   Coalition invasion of, *156, 180, 194*
   distances, *265*
   formation of, *154*
   insurgency, *156, 180, 367*
   map, *160*
   occupation, *180, 367*
   post-WWI, *154, 156*
   reconstruction, *367*
   sanctions, *156*
   sectarian violence, *156, 180, 185*
   US withdrawal from, *185*
Iraqi Counter-Terrorism Service, *185*
Iraqi National Guard, *308*
Iraqi Security Forces, *185, 202, 280, 308, 311, 317, 336, 353, 356, 359*
   Mosul, liberation of, *336, 338, 341, 344, 346, 349, 374, 378*
   timeline of events, *374, 378*
Islamic State (IS), *171, 185*
Islamic State of Iraq and the Levant (ISIL), *156, 167, 180, 258, 301*

air strikes against, *205, 271, 280, 290, 294, 296, 301, 308, 311, 319, 374*
barbarity, *185, 262, 277, 285, 308, 319, 346, 374, 378*
capturing cities, *277, 280*
casualties, *301, 346, 378*
Coalition forces against, *185, 191, 200, 202, 205, 239, 271, 277, 280, 301, 306, 308, 311, 314, 336*
historical and cultural heritage, destruction of, *167, 185, 374*
human shields, *285, 346, 378*
international condemnation, *185*
Mosul, battle for, *336, 338, 341, 344, 346, 349, 374, 378*
name, origin of, *171*
spread, *180, 185, 277, 280, 290*
Syria, in, *277, 301, 319, 322, 349, 350, 356, 359*
territorial losses (2015-17), *361, 367*
timeline of events, *374, 378*
unravelling, *353, 359*
investigation into civilian casualties, *314*

J

Jaffa, *121*
Jenin, *123, 132, 141*
  airfield, *132, 134*
Jerusalem, *108*
Jewish people, *108, 109*
Johnston, Vice Admiral David, *271, 356*
Joint Force Commander, *194*
Joint Integrated Prioritised Target List (JIPTL), *211*
Joint Operations Command, *211, 224, 271, 282*
Joint Task Force 633 (JTF 633), *194, 261*
  command and control, *211*
  Headquarters, *194, 200, 202, 224, 229, 231, 261, 262, 324*

Joint Terminal Air Controllers, *317*
Jones, Corporal Jason, *287*
Jones, Henry Albert, *44*
Junction Station, *130*

K

Kenny (pilot), *132*
Khamsin, *13, 51, 56*
kill-boxes, *301*
Kingpin (TE630.1.4), *224, 231, 239, 271, 290, 314*
Kirby, Lieutenant, *78*
Kirk, Lieutenant Walter Alistair, *68, 132*
Kirkuk, *353*
Kitcher, Air Commodore Mike, *197, 346, 350*
Kite Balloon Company, *104*
Kobani, *277, 374*
Kurds, *154, 156, 185*
   casualties, *156*
   militia, *185, 191, 336, 338, 374*
   Syria, *319*
Kut Al Amara, *18*
Kuwait, *154, 180*
   airspace, *265*
   Iraqi invasion, *156*

L

Lawrence, Colonel T.E. (Lawrence of Arabia), *74, 104, 118, 123, 145, 151*
   air transport, *118, 132*
   Australian aviators, on, *137*
Laws of Armed Conflict, *282*
leadership air forces, *48, 49*
Letch, Lieutenant Harold Alexander, *68*
Lewis, Captain Cecil, *24*
Lewis guns, *33*
   mounted on aircraft, *18, 24, 33, 71, 115, 137*
Lockheed Martin aircraft
   AP-3C surveillance aircraft, *194*
   C130 Hercules, *194, 200*
   C-130J Hercules, *167*
   F-22 Raptor, *290*
   U2 'Dragon Lady', *290*
Luftwaffe, *98*

M

McCormack, Wing Commander Matt, *231, 301*
McDonnell Douglas aircraft,
  see also Boeing aircraft,
McNamara, Lieutenant Frank, *78, 88*
  Victoria Cross, *78, 82*
Macpherson Smith, Captain (Sir) Ross, *33, 132*
Magdhaba, *74*
Martin, Air Commodore Antony, *200, 314, 327, 336*
Martin, Squadron Leader David 'Doc', *314*
Martinsyde aircraft, *68, 78, 90, 104*
  G100 'Elephant' bomber, *18, 36, 71, 88*
Maude, General Sir Stanley Frederick, *74*
MG08, *33*
Medjel, *105*
Megiddo, *123, 141, 145*
  Battle of, *134*
Mesopotamia, *74, 154, 185*
Mesopotamian Half-Flight, *114, 154*
Middle East Region (MER) climate, *13, 221, 290, 298, 301, 314, 324, 327*
  map, *269*
  warfare, *13*
Mission Rehearsal Exercises (MRE), *121*
Mitchell, Group Captain Pete, *200, 298, 301, 365*
Moriarty, Greg, *356*
Mosul, *154, 185, 265, 280, 301, 311, 353, 367*
  liberation of, *336, 338, 341, 344, 346, 349, 374, 378*
  population, *346*
Mount Sinjar, *277, 301*
Muir, Lieutenant Stanley, *71*
Multi-role Electronically Scanned Array (MESA) radar, *234, 239, 249*
Murray, General Archibald, *13, 48, 51, 74, 83*
Murray-Jones, Captain Alan, *88, 90*
Mustard, Lieutenant Ernest Andrew, *33, 68*

N

name, origin of, *171*
  Ismailia, *82*
Nablus, *121, 123, 132, 141, 145*
national security, *177, 180*
Nazareth, *141*
Neuve Chapelle, Battle of, *13*
New Zealand Mounted Rifles, *104, 108*
Newton, Colonel Isaac, *33*
Nieuport aircraft fighters, *130*
night landings, *63*
Ninawah Province, *185*
Ninevah, *185*
Ninevah Province, *353*
No-Fly Zones, *156*
North Korea, *156*
Northrop Grumman aircraft RQ-4 Global Hawk unmanned aerial vehicle, *290*
No 1 Squadron, *13, 53, 68, 71, 104, 128, 130, 151*
  Allenby's offensive, *132, 134*
  ATG 630, *231, 346*
  Australian Light Horse, relationship with, *51, 104, 132*
  commissioned aircrew, *49, 51*
  Egypt, arrival in, *51, 53, 56*
  establishment, *49, 51*
  German aircraft, conflict with, *88, 90*
  initial deployment, *49*
  mapping mission, *121, 123, 128*
  Operation OKRA, *167, 216, 255*
  WWI operations in Middle East, *71, 78, 82, 88, 216*
No 5 Wing, *68, 71, 74, 88, 90, 104*
  chain of command, *130*
No 40 Wing, *12, 104, 108, 114, 132, 216*
  Allenby's offensive, *141, 145*
  chain of command, *130*
  Jordan River, work at, *121, 123, 132*

mapping mission, *121, 123*
Nunan, Lieutenant Stan, *145*

O

Obama, Barak, *185, 374*
observers, *18, 44*
    air-to-air combat, *132*
    No 1 Squadron, *68*
    pilot, collaboration with, *13, 18*
    qualifications, *74*
    role, *30, 74*
    training, *51, 63*
Omar, *308*
Operation ACCORDION, *200, 224, 242*
Operation DESERT FOX, *156*
Operation DESERT STORM, *156, 180*
Operation ENDURING FREEDOM, *156*
Operation HIGHROAD, *242*
Operation INHERENT RESOLVE, *185, 191, 205, 262, 280, 282, 285, 317, 336*
    mission statement, *191*
    phases, *280, 282, 314, 336, 349*
    rationale, *191*
Operation IRAQI FREEDOM, *156*
Operation MANITOU, *200*
Operation NORTHERN WATCH, *156*
Operation OKRA, *164, 167, 185, 197, 200, 216, 242, 353*
    see also Air Task Group (ATG630), Air Combat Officers, *227*
    aircrew, *227, 271, 275, 327, 329*
    Coalitions assets, military control, *271*
    command and control, *191, 194, 197, 200, 202, 211, 214, 237, 282, 327*
    logistics support, *227, 229, 231*

mission success rate, *216*
pilots, *227*
preparation, *258, 261, 262, 265*
statistics, *380, 382*
Operation SOUTHERN WATCH, *156*
Orme, Major General Craig, *262*
Orsova (HMAT), *51*
Ottoman Empire, *151*

P

Palestine, *39, 121*
  British Mandate, *109*
  climate, *13*
Palestine Brigade, *48, 49, 104, 121, 151*
  chain of command, *130*
  control of area, *132*
  establishment, *104*
  mapping missions, *121, 123*
  No 5 Wing, see No 5 Wing,
  No 40 Wing, see No 40 Wing,
Palmyra, *185, 346, 374, 378*

Patterson, Banjo, *53*
Payne, Marise, *356, 365*
Peshmerga, *185, 191, 338*
Pfalz aircraft, *56, 68*
  E.II monoplanes, *56*
Phillips, Leading Aircraftman Hayden, *287*
photography, aerial, *13, 18*
  analysis of, *18*
Plains of Sharon, *141, 145*
post-conflict environment, shaping, *167*
Powell, Colin, *156*
  precision, *294, 296*
Prussian Army,
  8th Pomeranian, No, *68*
  Infantry Regiment, *95*

Q

Qasim, Abd-al-Karim, *154*
Qatar, *194, 202, 205, 229*
  airspace, *265*

R

Rafa, *74*
Ramadi, *185, 277, 301, 374*
Ramleh (Ramla), *128, 130*

Raqqa, *280, 290, 301, 319, 336, 349, 356, 374, 378*
Rawa, *353, 356, 359*
Rayhanah, *353*
Reception, Staging, Onwards-clearance and Insertion (RSO&I) process, *261, 262, 265*
   reconnaissance, *36, 68, 74, 132, 234*
   aerial photography, *13, 18*
   air, *13, 18*
   artillery spotting, *13, 30*
   Bristol Fighters, *132*
   cavalry, *13*
   core air power role, *234*
   ground spotting, *30*
   observers,
   see observers,
Red Cards, *285, 311*
Red Flag Exercises, *242*
religious extremism, *156*
rescues, *78, 82*
   immigration issues, *324*
resupply missions, *18*

Roberton, Air Commodore Steve, *173, 185, 197, 200, 214*
   Commander Air Task Group, *229, 255, 262, 290*
Roberts, Captain E., *5*
Robinson, Flight Lieutenant Bryce, *262*
Rogers, Group Captain Brendan, *327*
Romani, *56, 71*
   airfield, *71*
Rothschild, Lionel Walter, *109*
Royal Air Force (RAF) formation, *126, 197*
Royal Aircraft Factory aircraft B.E.2, *18, 24, 27, 56, 63, 68, 100, 115*
   B.E.2a, *18, 24*
   B.E.2b, *24*
   B.E.2c 'Quirke', *5, 24, 56, 78, 88, 104*
   B.E.2e, *104*
   B.E.12 fighter-bomber, *88, 104, 105, 121*
   F.E.2, *63*
   R.E.8, *94, 100, 104, 130*

Scouting Experimental S.E.5a fighter, *108, 121, 130, 134*
Royal Australian Air Force (RAAF),
see also Australian, Flying Corp (AFC)
  Academy, *197*
  Aircraft Research and Development Unit, *200*
  C130 air mobility operations, *194*
  deployment to Iraq, *167*
  domestic exercises, *242*
  formation, *151, 197*
  No 1 Squadron, see No 1 Squadron,
  No 2 Squadron, *167, 216, 231*
  No 3 Squadron, *231, 314*
  No 4 Squadron, *317*
  No 33 Squadron, *167, 216, 231, 255*
  No 75 Squadron, *231, 298*
  No 77 Squadron, *231, 301, 314*
  training, *261*
  uniforms, *5*
Royal Flying Corps (RFC),
  aerial photography, *13, 18*
  autonomy, *48, 49*
  demographic, *58*
  expansion, *49*
  leadership and command, *48, 49, 71*
  No 5 Wing, see No 5 Wing,
  No 14 Squadron, *51, 53, 68, 71, 78, 88, 104, 130*
  No 17 Squadron, *51, 53, 68*
  No 81 Wing, *231, 290, 346*
  No 82 Wing, *231, 346*
  No 111 Squadron, *94, 104, 108, 121, 130, 134*
  No 113 Squadron, *104, 130*
  No 142 Squadron, *130*
  No 144 Squadron, *130, 132*

No 145 Squadron, *130*
RAF, creation of, *126*
　structure and defined goals, *45*
　training, *45, 48, 61, 63*
Royal Laboratory, *36*
Royal Naval Air Service (RNAS), *68, 105, 126*
rules of engagement, *282, 285, 294, 311, 317, 341, 346*
Rumpler aircraft, *56, 68, 71, 82, 90, 132*
　C.I, *56, 104*
　C.I V, *104*
Rumsfeld, Donald, *156*
Rutherford, Captain Douglas, *78, 82*
Rutledge, Major Foster, *83*
Resolution 687, *156*
Resolution 2170 (2014), *185, 374*
　weapons inspections, *156*

S

Saddam Hussein, *154, 156, 185*
　WMD, *156*
Sagrah, *353*
Salam Hospital, *338*
Salder-Barker, Flying Officer Melody, *338*
Saleh, Abu, *374*
Salmond, Lieutenant Colonel (later Air Vice-Marshal) William Geoffrey, *68, 74, 90, 108*
　leadership and command, *48, 49, 53, 78*
Samaria, *142*
sandstorms, *74*
Sarona, *130*
Saudi Arabian airspace, *265*
Scarff Ring, *100*
　No 3, Mark II Barbette, *33*
Scarff, Warrant Officer Frederick, *33*
Schleiff, Leutnant Franz, *90*
'School of Aeronautics', *48*
scouting, *13, 18*
seaplanes, *68*
sectarian violence, *156, 180, 185*

Sharqat, *353*
Shi'ite Muslims, *154, 185*
shock and awe campaign, *156*
Sinai, *51, 53, 56, 68, 71, 74, 82*
situational awareness, *183, 205, 227, 234, 239, 249, 314, 367*
Smith, Captain Ross, *78, 132*
   Allenby's offensive, *132*
   Lawrence of Arabia, and, *132, 137*
Sotloff, Steven, *374*
Spandau Arsenal, *33*
special instructions (SPINS), *329*
Special Operations Task Group - Iraq (SOTG-I), *185, 205, 224*
Stanway, Squadron Leader Lee-Anne, *350, 353, 359, 365*
Steele, Lieutenant Norman, *5, 78*
Steele, Lieutenant Robert, *94, 100*
Stooke, Lieutenant, *132*
strafing, *45*
   opposing airfields, *71, 105*
strike (core air power), *234, 239, 290*
   weaponry, *234*
Suez Canal, *51, 53, 74, 82*
   importance of, *56*
Sukhoi Su-22, *349*
Sumner Potts, Lieutenant Leonard Malcolm, *115*
Sunni Muslims, *154, 185*
surveillance (core air power), *234*
Sutherland, Captain Leslie William, *7, 18, 68, 95, 137, 145*
   Wadi Fara bombing, *142*
Sutherland, Lieutenant R., *94*
Sykes-Picot Agreement 1916, *108*
Syria, *121, 167*
   air strikes, *301, 308, 319, 374*
   civil war, *301, 319, 349*
   historical and cultural destruction, *185, 374*

ISIL in, *277, 301, 319, 322, 349, 350, 356, 359*
Operation INHERENT RESOLVE, *280, 349*
pro-democracy protests, *185*
Russian forces, *308, 311, 319, 349, 374*
Syrian Democratic Forces, *191, 349, 374*

T

Task Elements, see Task Elements
timeline of events, *374, 378*
uniform rules, *324*
work cycle for flying a mission, *329, 332, 335*
time critical targeting, *211*
tactical and operational liaison processes, *71*
Takalker, Squadron Leader Chet, *258*
Tal Afar, *353, 374*
Taliban, *156*
Taplin, Lieutenant, *18, 121, 123*

Target Engagement Authority, *311*
targeting doctrine, *285, 346*
 global position system tracking, *294*
 planned targets, *282, 285, 311, 346*
 precision and, *294, 296*
time critical, *211*
Task Elements
deployment, *242*
TE630.1.1 (strike), *231, 255, 262, 314*
TE630.1.2 (air battle management), *231, 242, 271, 350*
TE630.1.3 (air-to-air refuelling), *231, 271, 301, 306*
TE630.1.4 (ground-based air battle management) 'Kingpin', *224, 231, 239, 271, 290, 314*
TE630.3, *255*
TE633.14.2.1, *242*
Task Group Taji (TG-Taji), *185, 191*
TG633.4, *224*

Task Unit Headquarters (TUHQ TE630.1.0), *229*
technology,
  military, *13, 180, 185, 329, 367*
terrorist attacks, *156, 374, 378*
Terry, Lieutenant General James, *280*
Thomas, Leading Aircraftman Sam, *373*
Tigris River, *74, 154, 185, 338, 353*
Tikrit, *277, 301, 353, 374*
Townsend, Major General Sir Charles, *336, 346*
Trail, Lieutenant James Hamilton, *115*
Trenchard, Air Marshal Sir Hugh, *13, 197*
  air forces training, *48, 197*
Tunisia Arab Spring, *180*
Turkish Army, *13, 56*
  No 14 Squadron, *104*
  retreating from Palestine, *74, 140*

Turnbull, Prime Minister Malcolm, *356*

U

United Arab Emirates, *194, 200, 239*
United Nations, *156, 346*
United Nations Educational, Scientific and Cultural Organisation (UNESCO), *185*
United States Australia, relationship with, *177, 180*
  US Central Command, *280, 282*
United States Air Force, *219, 290*
727th Expeditionary Air Control Squadron, *290*
  bases, *221, 287, 290*
urban fighting, *346*

V

Van Haren, Air Commodore Terry, *200, 350, 353, 356, 365*
Vautin, Lieutenant Claude, *90, 94, 95*

Vickers aircraft Bullet, *104*
Vickers guns, *33*
   mounted on aircraft, *18, 100*
Vietnam War, *180, 185, 214*
Vyner, Lieutenant Charles James, *68*

W

Wadi Fara, *140, 141, 142, 145, 151, 156, 216, 367*
Warden, John, *271, 294*
warfare, *180, 296*
Warner, Squadron Leader Luke, *301*
weapons of mass destruction (WMD), *156*
weather, impact of, *314*
Weekes, Flight Sergeant Col, *306*
Weir, Lieutenant, *132*
Weli Sheikh Nuran, *104*
whole-of-government 'Effects-Based Approach', *180*
Williams, Lieutenant Colonel (Sir) Richard, *71, 78, 83, 95, 111, 151, 255, 265, 324*
   Air Marshal, *114*
   Allenby's offensive, *140, 141*
   awards, *114*
   background, *111, 114*
   biography, *49*
   letters to command, *90, 94*
   mapping mission, *121*
   Middle East Service, *105, 108, 114*
   No 40 Wing, command, *130, 132, 140*
   RAAF, establishment of, *114, 126, 197*
World Trade Centre attack, *156*
World War I background,
   modern parallels, *151*
   Ottoman Empire, and,

Y

Yemen Arab Spring, *180*

www.ingramcontent.com/pod-product-compliance
Lightning Source LLC
Chambersburg PA
CBHW010717300426
44114CB00022B/2884